Natural Language Annotation for Machine Learning

James Pustejovsky and Amber Stubbs

O'REILLY®

Beijing · Cambridge · Farnham · Köln · Sebastopol · Tokyo

Natural Language Annotation for Machine Learning

by James Pustejovsky and Amber Stubbs

Published by O'Reilly Media, Inc., 1005 Gravenstein Highway North, Sebastopol, CA 95472.

O'Reilly books may be purchased for educational, business, or sales promotional use. Online editions are also available for most titles (*http://my.safaribooksonline.com*). For more information, contact our corporate/institutional sales department: 800-998-9938 or *corporate@oreilly.com*.

Editors: Julie Steele and Meghan Blanchette	**Indexer:** WordCo Indexing Services
Production Editor: Kristen Borg	**Cover Designer:** Randy Comer
Copyeditor: Audrey Doyle	**Interior Designer:** David Futato
Proofreader: Linley Dolby	**Illustrator:** Rebecca Demarest

October 2012:   First Edition

Revision History for the First Edition:

2012-10-10:   First release

2013-02-22:   Second release

2013-07-12:   Third release

See *http://oreilly.com/catalog/errata.csp?isbn=9781449306663* for release details.

ISBN: 978-1-449-30666-3

[LSI]

Table of Contents

Preface

This book is intended as a resource for people who are interested in using computers to help process natural language. A *natural language* refers to any language spoken by humans, either currently (e.g., English, Chinese, Spanish) or in the past (e.g., Latin, ancient Greek, Sanskrit). *Annotation* refers to the process of adding metadata information to the text in order to augment a computer's capability to perform Natural Language Processing (NLP). In particular, we examine how information can be added to natural language text through annotation in order to increase the performance of *machine learning algorithms*—computer programs designed to extrapolate rules from the information provided over texts in order to apply those rules to unannotated texts later on.

Natural Language Annotation for Machine Learning

This book details the multistage process for building your own annotated natural language dataset (known as a *corpus*) in order to train machine learning (ML) algorithms for language-based data and knowledge discovery. The overall goal of this book is to show readers how to create their own corpus, starting with selecting an annotation task, creating the annotation specification, designing the guidelines, creating a "gold standard" corpus, and then beginning the actual data creation with the annotation process.

Because the annotation process is not linear, multiple iterations can be required for defining the tasks, annotations, and evaluations, in order to achieve the best results for a particular goal. The process can be summed up in terms of the *MATTER Annotation Development Process*: Model, Annotate, Train, Test, Evaluate, Revise. This book guides the reader through the cycle, and provides detailed examples and discussion for different types of annotation tasks throughout. These tasks are examined in depth to provide context for readers and to help provide a foundation for their own ML goals.

Additionally, this book provides access to and usage guidelines for lightweight, user-friendly software that can be used for annotating texts and adjudicating the annotations. While a variety of annotation tools are available to the community, the Multipurpose Annotation Environment (MAE) adopted in this book (and available to readers as a free download) was specifically designed to be easy to set up and get running, so that confusing documentation would not distract readers from their goals. MAE is paired with the Multidocument Adjudication Interface (MAI), a tool that allows for quick comparison of annotated documents.

Audience

This book is written for anyone interested in using computers to explore aspects of the information content conveyed by natural language. It is not necessary to have a programming or linguistics background to use this book, although a basic understanding of a scripting language such as Python can make the MATTER cycle easier to follow, and some sample Python code is provided in the book. If you don't have any Python experience, we highly recommend *Natural Language Processing with Python* by Steven Bird, Ewan Klein, and Edward Loper (O'Reilly), which provides an excellent introduction both to Python and to aspects of NLP that are not addressed in this book.

It is helpful to have a basic understanding of markup languages such as XML (or even HTML) in order to get the most out of this book. While one doesn't need to be an expert in the theory behind an XML schema, most annotation projects use some form of XML to encode the tags, and therefore we use that standard in this book when providing annotation examples. Although you don't need to be a web designer to understand the book, it does help to have a working knowledge of tags and attributes in order to understand how an idea for an annotation gets implemented.

Organization of This Book

Chapter 1 of this book provides a brief overview of the history of annotation and machine learning, as well as short discussions of some of the different ways that annotation tasks have been used to investigate different layers of linguistic research. The rest of the book guides the reader through the MATTER cycle, from tips on creating a reasonable annotation goal in Chapter 2, all the way through evaluating the results of the annotation and ML stages, as well as a discussion of revising your project and reporting on your work in Chapter 9. The last two chapters give a complete walkthrough of a single annotation project and how it was recreated with machine learning and rule-based algorithms. Appendixes at the back of the book provide lists of resources that readers will find useful for their own annotation tasks.

Software Requirements

While it's possible to work through this book without running any of the code examples provided, we do recommend having at least the Natural Language Toolkit (NLTK) installed for easy reference to some of the ML techniques discussed. The NLTK currently runs on Python versions from 2.4 to 2.7. (Python 3.0 is not supported at the time of this writing.) For more information, see *http://www.nltk.org*.

The code examples in this book are written as though they are in the interactive Python shell programming environment. For information on how to use this environment, please see: *http://docs.python.org/tutorial/interpreter.html*. If not specifically stated in the examples, it should be assumed that the command `import nltk` was used prior to all sample code.

Conventions Used in This Book

The following typographical conventions are used in this book:

Italic
> Indicates new terms, URLs, email addresses, filenames, and file extensions.

`Constant width`
> Used for program listings, as well as within paragraphs to refer to program elements such as variable or function names, databases, data types, environment variables, statements, and keywords.

> This icon signifies a tip, suggestion, or general note.

> This icon indicates a warning or caution.

Using Code Examples

This book is here to help you get your job done. In general, you may use the code in this book in your programs and documentation. You do not need to contact us for permission unless you're reproducing a significant portion of the code. For example, writing a program that uses several chunks of code from this book does not require permission. Selling or distributing a CD-ROM of examples from O'Reilly books does require permission. Answering a question by citing this book and quoting example code does not require permission. Incorporating a significant amount of example code from this book into your product's documentation does require permission.

We appreciate, but do not require, attribution. An attribution usually includes the title, author, publisher, and ISBN. For example: "*Natural Language Annotation for Machine Learning* by James Pustejovsky and Amber Stubbs (O'Reilly). Copyright 2013 James Pustejovsky and Amber Stubbs, 978-1-449-30666-3."

If you feel your use of code examples falls outside fair use or the permission given above, feel free to contact us at *permissions@oreilly.com*.

Safari® Books Online

 Safari Books Online (*www.safaribooksonline.com*) is an on-demand digital library that delivers expert content in both book and video form from the world's leading authors in technology and business.

Technology professionals, software developers, web designers, and business and creative professionals use Safari Books Online as their primary resource for research, problem solving, learning, and certification training.

Safari Books Online offers a range of product mixes and pricing programs for organizations, government agencies, and individuals. Subscribers have access to thousands of books, training videos, and prepublication manuscripts in one fully searchable database from publishers like O'Reilly Media, Prentice Hall Professional, Addison-Wesley Professional, Microsoft Press, Sams, Que, Peachpit Press, Focal Press, Cisco Press, John Wiley & Sons, Syngress, Morgan Kaufmann, IBM Redbooks, Packt, Adobe Press, FT Press, Apress, Manning, New Riders, McGraw-Hill, Jones & Bartlett, Course Technology, and dozens more. For more information about Safari Books Online, please visit us online.

How to Contact Us

Please address comments and questions concerning this book to the publisher:

O'Reilly Media, Inc.
1005 Gravenstein Highway North
Sebastopol, CA 95472
800-998-9938 (in the United States or Canada)
707-829-0515 (international or local)
707-829-0104 (fax)

We have a web page for this book, where we list errata, examples, and any additional information. You can access this page at *http://oreil.ly/nat-lang-annotation-ML*.

To comment or ask technical questions about this book, send email to *bookquestions@oreilly.com*.

For more information about our books, courses, conferences, and news, see our website at *http://www.oreilly.com*.

Find us on Facebook: *http://facebook.com/oreilly*

Follow us on Twitter: *http://twitter.com/oreillymedia*

Watch us on YouTube: *http://www.youtube.com/oreillymedia*

Acknowledgments

We would like thank everyone at O'Reilly who helped us create this book, in particular Meghan Blanchette, Julie Steele, Sarah Schneider, Kristen Borg, Audrey Doyle, and everyone else who helped to guide us through the process of producing it. We would also like to thank the students who participated in the Brandeis COSI 216 class during the spring 2011 semester for bearing with us as we worked through the MATTER cycle with them: Karina Baeza Grossmann-Siegert, Elizabeth Baran, Bensiin Borukhov, Nicholas Botchan, Richard Brutti, Olga Cherenina, Russell Entrikin, Livnat Herzig, Sophie Kushkuley, Theodore Margolis, Alexandra Nunes, Lin Pan, Batia Snir, John Vogel, and Yaqin Yang.

We would also like to thank our technical reviewers, who provided us with such excellent feedback: Arvind S. Gautam, Catherine Havasi, Anna Rumshisky, and Ben Wellner, as well as everyone who read the Early Release version of the book and let us know that we were going in the right direction.

We would like to thank members of the ISO community with whom we have discussed portions of the material in this book: Kiyong Lee, Harry Bunt, Nancy Ide, Nicoletta Calzolari, Bran Boguraev, Annie Zaenen, and Laurent Romary.

Additional thanks to the members of the Brandeis Computer Science and Linguistics departments, who listened to us brainstorm, kept us encouraged, and made sure everything kept running while we were writing, especially Marc Verhagen, Lotus Goldberg, Jessica Moszkowicz, and Alex Plotnick.

This book could not exist without everyone in the linguistics and computational linguistics communities who have created corpora and annotations, and, more importantly, shared their experiences with the rest of the research community.

James Adds:

I would like to thank my wife, Cathie, for her patience and support during this project. I would also like to thank my children, Zac and Sophie, for putting up with me while the book was being finished. And thanks, Amber, for taking on this crazy effort with me.

Amber Adds:

I would like to thank my husband, BJ, for encouraging me to undertake this project and for his patience while I worked through it. Thanks also to my family, especially my parents, for their enthusiasm toward this book. And, of course, thanks to my advisor and coauthor, James, for having this crazy idea in the first place.

CHAPTER 1

The Basics

It seems as though every day there are new and exciting problems that people have taught computers to solve, from how to win at chess or *Jeopardy* to determining shortest-path driving directions. But there are still many tasks that computers cannot perform, particularly in the realm of understanding human language. Statistical methods have proven to be an effective way to approach these problems, but machine learning (ML) techniques often work better when the algorithms are provided with pointers to what is relevant about a dataset, rather than just massive amounts of data. When discussing natural language, these pointers often come in the form of annotations—metadata that provides additional information about the text. However, in order to teach a computer effectively, it's important to give it the right data, and for it to have enough data to learn from. The purpose of this book is to provide you with the tools to create good data for your own ML task. In this chapter we will cover:

- Why annotation is an important tool for linguists and computer scientists alike
- How corpus linguistics became the field that it is today
- The different areas of linguistics and how they relate to annotation and ML tasks
- What a corpus is, and what makes a corpus balanced
- How some classic ML problems are represented with annotations
- The basics of the annotation development cycle

The Importance of Language Annotation

Everyone knows that the Internet is an amazing resource for all sorts of information that can teach you just about anything: juggling, programming, playing an instrument, and so on. However, there is another layer of information that the Internet contains, and that is how all those lessons (and blogs, forums, tweets, etc.) are being communicated. The Web contains information in all forms of media—including texts, images, movies, and sounds—and language is the communication medium that allows people to understand the content, and to link the content to other media. However, while computers are excellent at delivering this information to interested users, they are much less adept at understanding language itself.

Theoretical and computational linguistics are focused on unraveling the deeper nature of language and capturing the computational properties of linguistic structures. Human language technologies (HLTs) attempt to adopt these insights and algorithms and turn them into functioning, high-performance programs that can impact the ways we interact with computers using language. With more and more people using the Internet every day, the amount of linguistic data available to researchers has increased significantly, allowing linguistic modeling problems to be viewed as ML tasks, rather than limited to the relatively small amounts of data that humans are able to process on their own.

However, it is not enough to simply provide a computer with a large amount of data and expect it to learn to speak—the data has to be prepared in such a way that the computer can more easily find patterns and inferences. This is usually done by adding relevant metadata to a dataset. Any metadata tag used to mark up elements of the dataset is called an *annotation* over the input. However, in order for the algorithms to learn efficiently and effectively, the annotation done on the data must be accurate, and relevant to the task the machine is being asked to perform. For this reason, the discipline of language annotation is a critical link in developing intelligent human language technologies.

 Giving an ML algorithm too much information can slow it down and lead to inaccurate results, or result in the algorithm being so molded to the training data that it becomes "overfit" and provides less accurate results than it might otherwise on new data. It's important to think carefully about what you are trying to accomplish, and what information is most relevant to that goal. Later in the book we will give examples of how to find that information, and how to determine how well your algorithm is performing at the task you've set for it.

Datasets of natural language are referred to as *corpora*, and a single set of data annotated with the same specification is called an *annotated corpus*. Annotated corpora can be used to train ML algorithms. In this chapter we will define what a corpus is, explain what is meant by an annotation, and describe the methodology used for enriching a linguistic data collection with annotations for machine learning.

The Layers of Linguistic Description

While it is not necessary to have formal linguistic training in order to create an annotated corpus, we will be drawing on examples of many different types of annotation tasks, and you will find this book more helpful if you have a basic understanding of the different aspects of language that are studied and used for annotations. *Grammar* is the name typically given to the mechanisms responsible for creating well-formed structures in language. Most linguists view grammar as itself consisting of distinct modules or systems, either by cognitive design or for descriptive convenience. These areas usually include syntax, semantics, morphology, phonology (and phonetics), and the lexicon. Areas beyond grammar that relate to how language is embedded in human activity include discourse, pragmatics, and text theory. The following list provides more detailed descriptions of these areas:

Syntax

> The study of how words are combined to form sentences. This includes examining parts of speech and how they combine to make larger constructions.

Semantics

> The study of meaning in language. Semantics examines the relations between words and what they are being used to represent.

Morphology

> The study of units of meaning in a language. A *morpheme* is the smallest unit of language that has meaning or function, a definition that includes words, prefixes, affixes, and other word structures that impart meaning.

Phonology

> The study of the sound patterns of a particular language. Aspects of study include determining which phones are significant and have meaning (i.e., the phonemes); how syllables are structured and combined; and what features are needed to describe the discrete units (segments) in the language, and how they are interpreted.

Phonetics

> The study of the sounds of human speech, and how they are made and perceived. A *phoneme* is the term for an individual sound, and is essentially the smallest unit of human speech.

Lexicon

> The study of the words and phrases used in a language, that is, a language's vocabulary.

Discourse analysis

> The study of exchanges of information, usually in the form of conversations, and particularly the flow of information across sentence boundaries.

Pragmatics
> The study of how the context of text affects the meaning of an expression, and what information is necessary to infer a hidden or presupposed meaning.

Text structure analysis
> The study of how narratives and other textual styles are constructed to make larger textual compositions.

Throughout this book we will present examples of annotation projects that make use of various combinations of the different concepts outlined in the preceding list.

What Is Natural Language Processing?

Natural Language Processing (NLP) is a field of computer science and engineering that has developed from the study of language and computational linguistics within the field of Artificial Intelligence. The goals of NLP are to design and build applications that facilitate human interaction with machines and other devices through the use of natural language. Some of the major areas of NLP include:

Question Answering Systems (QAS)
> Imagine being able to actually ask your computer or your phone what time your favorite restaurant in New York stops serving dinner on Friday nights. Rather than typing in the (still) clumsy set of keywords into a search browser window, you could simply ask in plain, natural language—your *own*, whether it's English, Mandarin, or Spanish. (While systems such as Siri for the iPhone are a good start to this process, it's clear that Siri doesn't fully understand all of natural language, just a subset of key phrases.)

Summarization
> This area includes applications that can take a collection of documents or emails and produce a coherent summary of their content. Such programs also aim to provide snap "elevator summaries" of longer documents, and possibly even turn them into slide presentations.

Machine Translation
> The holy grail of NLP applications, this was the first major area of research and engineering in the field. Programs such as Google Translate are getting better and better, but the real killer app will be the BabelFish that translates in real time when you're looking for the right train to catch in Beijing.

Speech Recognition
> This is one of the most difficult problems in NLP. There has been great progress in building models that can be used on your phone or computer to recognize spoken language utterances that are questions and commands. Unfortunately, while these Automatic Speech Recognition (ASR) systems are ubiquitous, they work best in

narrowly defined domains and don't allow the speaker to stray from the expected scripted input (*"Please say or type your card number now"*).

Document classification
This is one of the most successful areas of NLP, wherein the task is to identify in which category (or *bin*) a document should be placed. This has proved to be enormously useful for applications such as spam filtering, news article classification, and movie reviews, among others. One reason this has had such a big impact is the relative simplicity of the learning models needed for training the algorithms that do the classification.

As we mentioned in the Preface, the Natural Language Toolkit (NLTK), described in the O'Reilly book *Natural Language Processing with Python*, is a wonderful introduction to the techniques necessary to build many of the applications described in the preceding list. One of the goals of this book is to give you the knowledge to build specialized language corpora (i.e., training and test datasets) that are necessary for developing such applications.

A Brief History of Corpus Linguistics

In the mid-20th century, linguistics was practiced primarily as a descriptive field, used to study structural properties within a language and typological variations between languages. This work resulted in fairly sophisticated models of the different informational components comprising linguistic utterances. As in the other social sciences, the collection and analysis of data was also being subjected to quantitative techniques from statistics. In the 1940s, linguists such as Bloomfield were starting to think that language could be explained in probabilistic and behaviorist terms. Empirical and statistical methods became popular in the 1950s, and Shannon's information-theoretic view to language analysis appeared to provide a solid quantitative approach for modeling qualitative descriptions of linguistic structure.

Unfortunately, the development of statistical and quantitative methods for linguistic analysis hit a brick wall in the 1950s. This was due primarily to two factors. First, there was the problem of data availability. One of the problems with applying statistical methods to the language data at the time was that the datasets were generally so small that it was not possible to make interesting statistical generalizations over large numbers of linguistic phenomena. Second, and perhaps more important, there was a general shift in the social sciences from data-oriented descriptions of human behavior to introspective modeling of cognitive functions.

As part of this new attitude toward human activity, the linguist Noam Chomsky focused on both a formal methodology and a theory of linguistics that not only ignored quantitative language data, but also claimed that it was misleading for formulating models of language behavior (Chomsky 1957).

This view was very influential throughout the 1960s and 1970s, largely because the formal approach was able to develop extremely sophisticated rule-based language models using mostly introspective (or self-generated) data. This was a very attractive alternative to trying to create statistical language models on the basis of still relatively small datasets of linguistic utterances from the existing corpora in the field. Formal modeling and rule-based generalizations, in fact, have always been an integral step in theory formation, and in this respect, Chomsky's approach on how to do linguistics has yielded rich and elaborate models of language.

Timeline of Corpus Linguistics

Here's a quick overview of some of the milestones in the field, leading up to where we are now.

- **1950s**: Descriptive linguists compile collections of spoken and written utterances of various languages from field research. Literary researchers begin compiling systematic collections of the complete works of different authors. Key Word in Context (KWIC) is invented as a means of indexing documents and creating concordances.

- **1960s**: Kucera and Francis publish *A Standard Corpus of Present-Day American English* (the *Brown Corpus*), the first broadly available large corpus of language texts. Work in Information Retrieval (IR) develops techniques for statistical similarity of document content.

- **1970s**: Stochastic models developed from speech corpora make Speech Recognition systems possible. The vector space model is developed for document indexing. The London-Lund Corpus (LLC) is developed through the work of the *Survey of English Usage*.

- **1980s**: The Lancaster-Oslo-Bergen (LOB) Corpus, designed to match the Brown Corpus in terms of size and genres, is compiled. The COBUILD (Collins Birmingham University International Language Database) dictionary is published, the first based on examining usage from a large English corpus, the Bank of English. The Survey of English Usage Corpus inspires the creation of a comprehensive corpus-based grammar, *Grammar of English*. The Child Language Data Exchange System (CHILDES) Corpus is released as a repository for first language acquisition data.

- **1990s**: The Penn TreeBank is released. This is a corpus of tagged and parsed sentences of naturally occurring English (4.5 million words). The British National Corpus (BNC) is compiled and released as the largest corpus of English to date (100 million words). The Text Encoding Initiative (TEI) is established to develop and maintain a standard for the representation of texts in digital form.

- **2000s**: As the World Wide Web grows, more data is available for statistical models for Machine Translation and other applications. The American National Corpus (ANC) project releases a 22-million-word subcorpus, and the Corpus of Contemporary American English (COCA) is released (400 million words). Google releases its Google N-gram Corpus (*http://books.google.com/ngrams*) of 1 trillion word tokens from public web pages. The corpus holds up to five *n-grams* for each word token, along with their frequencies .

- **2010s**: International standards organizations, such as ISO, begin to recognize and co-develop text encoding formats that are being used for corpus annotation efforts. The Web continues to make enough data available to build models for a whole new range of linguistic phenomena. Entirely new forms of text corpora, such as Twitter, Facebook, and blogs, become available as a resource.

Theory construction, however, also involves testing and evaluating your hypotheses against observed phenomena. As more linguistic data has gradually become available, something significant has changed in the way linguists look at data. The phenomena are now observable in millions of texts and billions of sentences over the Web, and this has left little doubt that quantitative techniques can be meaningfully applied to both test and create the language models correlated with the datasets. This has given rise to the modern age of corpus linguistics. As a result, the corpus is the entry point from which all linguistic analysis will be done in the future.

 You gotta have data! As philosopher of science Thomas Kuhn said: "When measurement departs from theory, it is likely to yield mere numbers, and their very neutrality makes them particularly sterile as a source of remedial suggestions. But numbers register the departure from theory with an authority and finesse that no qualitative technique can duplicate, and that departure is often enough to start a search" (Kuhn 1961).

The assembly and collection of texts into more coherent datasets that we can call *corpora* started in the 1960s.

Some of the most important corpora are listed in Table 1-1.

Table 1-1. A sampling of important corpora

Name of corpus	Year published	Size	Collection contents
British National Corpus (BNC)	1991–1994	100 million words	Cross section of British English, spoken and written
American National Corpus (ANC)	2003	22 million words	Spoken and written texts
Corpus of Contemporary American English (COCA)	2008	425 million words	Spoken, fiction, popular magazine, and academic texts

What Is a Corpus?

A corpus is a collection of machine-readable texts that have been produced in a natural communicative setting. They have been sampled to be *representative* and *balanced* with respect to particular factors; for example, by genre—newspaper articles, literary fiction, spoken speech, blogs and diaries, and legal documents. A corpus is said to be "representative of a language variety" if the content of the corpus can be generalized to that variety (Leech 1991).

This is not as circular as it may sound. Basically, if the content of the corpus, defined by specifications of linguistic phenomena examined or studied, reflects that of the larger population from which it is taken, then we can say that it "represents that language variety."

The notion of a corpus being *balanced* is an idea that has been around since the 1980s, but it is still a rather fuzzy notion and difficult to define strictly. Atkins and Ostler (1992) propose a formulation of attributes that can be used to define the types of text, and thereby contribute to creating a balanced corpus.

Two well-known corpora can be compared for their effort to balance the content of the texts. The Penn TreeBank (Marcus et al. 1993) is a 4.5-million-word corpus that contains texts from four sources: the *Wall Street Journal*, the Brown Corpus, ATIS, and the Switchboard Corpus. By contrast, the BNC is a 100-million-word corpus that contains texts from a broad range of genres, domains, and media.

The most diverse subcorpus within the Penn TreeBank is the Brown Corpus, which is a 1-million-word corpus consisting of 500 English text samples, each one approximately 2,000 words. It was collected and compiled by Henry Kucera and W. Nelson Francis of Brown University (hence its name) from a broad range of contemporary American English in 1961. In 1967, they released a fairly extensive statistical analysis of the word frequencies and behavior within the corpus, the first of its kind in print, as well as the *Brown Corpus Manual* (Francis and Kucera 1964).

There has never been any doubt that all linguistic analysis must be grounded on specific datasets. What has recently emerged is the realization that all linguistics will be bound to corpus-oriented techniques, one way or the other. Corpora are becoming the standard data exchange format for discussing linguistic observations and theoretical generalizations, and certainly for evaluation of systems, both statistical and rule-based.

Table 1-2 shows how the Brown Corpus compares to other corpora that are also still in use.

Table 1-2. Comparing the Brown Corpus to other corpora

Corpus	Size	Use
Brown Corpus	500 English text samples; 1 million words	Part-of-speech tagged data; 80 different tags used
Child Language Data Exchange System (CHILDES)	20 languages represented; thousands of texts	Phonetic transcriptions of conversations with children from around the world
Lancaster-Oslo-Bergen Corpus	500 British English text samples, around 2,000 words each	Part-of-speech tagged data; a British version of the Brown Corpus

Looking at the way the files of the Brown Corpus can be categorized gives us an idea of what sorts of data were used to represent the English language. The top two general data categories are informative, with 374 samples, and imaginative, with 126 samples.

These two domains are further distinguished into the following topic areas:

Informative
> Press: reportage (44), Press: editorial (27), Press: reviews (17), Religion (17), Skills and Hobbies (36), Popular Lore (48), Belles Lettres, Biography, Memoirs (75), Miscellaneous (30), Natural Sciences (12), Medicine (5), Mathematics (4), Social and Behavioral Sciences (14), Political Science, Law, Education (15), Humanities (18), Technology and Engineering (12)

Imaginative
> General Fiction (29), Mystery and Detective Fiction (24), Science Fiction (6), Adventure and Western Fiction (29), Romance and Love Story (29) Humor (9)

Similarly, the BNC can be categorized into *informative* and *imaginative* prose, and further into subdomains such as *educational, public, business,* and so on. A further discussion of how the BNC can be categorized can be found in "Distributions Within Corpora" on page 49.

As you can see from the numbers given for the Brown Corpus, not every category is equally represented, which seems to be a violation of the rule of "representative and balanced" that we discussed before. However, these corpora were not assembled with a specific task in mind; rather, they were meant to represent written and spoken language as a whole. Because of this, they attempt to embody a large cross section of existing texts, though whether they succeed in representing percentages of texts in the world is debatable (but also not terribly important).

For your own corpus, you may find yourself wanting to cover a wide variety of text, but it is likely that you will have a more specific task domain, and so your potential corpus will not need to include the full range of human expression. The Switchboard Corpus (*http://bit.ly/WkBCGG*) is an example of a corpus that was collected for a very specific purpose—Speech Recognition for phone operation—and so was balanced and representative of the different sexes and all different dialects in the United States.

Early Use of Corpora

One of the most common uses of corpora from the early days was the construction of *concordances*. These are alphabetical listings of the words in an article or text collection with references given to the passages in which they occur. Concordances position a word within its context, and thereby make it much easier to study how it is used in a language, both syntactically and semantically. In the 1950s and 1960s, programs were written to automatically create concordances for the contents of a collection, and the results of these automatically created indexes were called "Key Word in Context" indexes, or *KWIC indexes*. A KWIC index is an index created by sorting the words in an article or a larger collection such as a corpus, and aligning them in a format so that they can be searched alphabetically in the index. This was a relatively efficient means for searching a collection before full-text document search became available.

The way a KWIC index works is as follows. The input to a KWIC system is a file or collection structured as a sequence of lines. The output is a sequence of lines, circularly shifted and presented in alphabetical order of the first word. For an example, consider a short article of two sentences, shown in Figure 1-1 with the KWIC index output that is generated.

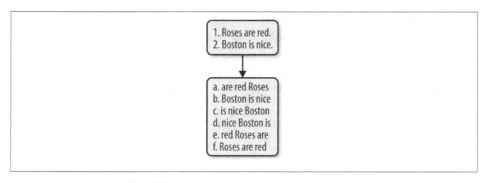

1. Roses are red.
2. Boston is nice.

a. are red Roses
b. Boston is nice
c. is nice Boston
d. nice Boston is
e. red Roses are
f. Roses are red

Figure 1-1. Example of a KWIC index

Another benefit of concordancing is that, by displaying the keyword in its context, you can visually inspect how the word is being used in a given sentence. To take a specific example, consider the different meanings of the English verb *treat*. Specifically, let's look at the first two senses within sense (1) from the dictionary entry shown in Figure 1-2.

treat |trēt|
verb [trans.]
1 behave toward or deal with in a certain way : *she had been brutally treated* | *he **treated her with** grave courtesy.*
• (**treat something as**) regard something as being of a specified nature with implications for one's actions concerning it : *the names are being treated as classified information.*
• give medical care or attention to; try to heal or cure : *the two were **treated for** cuts and bruises.*
• apply a process or a substance to (something) to protect or preserve it or to give it particular properties : *linen creases badly unless it is **treated with** the appropriate finish.*
• present or discuss (a subject) : *the lectures show a striking variation in the level at which subjects are treated.*
2 (**treat someone to**) provide someone with (food, drink, or entertainment) at one's own expense : *the old man had treated him to a drink or two.*
• give someone (something) as a favor : *he treated her to one of his smiles.*
• (**treat oneself**) do or have something that gives one great pleasure : *treat yourself—you can diet tomorrow.*
3 [intrans.] negotiate terms with someone, esp. an opponent : *propagandists claimed that he was **treating with** the enemy.*

Figure 1-2. Senses of the word "treat"

Now let's look at the concordances compiled for this verb from the BNC, as differentiated by these two senses.

These concordances were compiled using the *Word Sketch Engine*, by the lexicographer Patrick Hanks, and are part of a large resource of sentence patterns using a technique called *Corpus Pattern Analysis* (Pustejovsky et al. 2004; Hanks and Pustejovsky 2005).

What is striking when one examines the concordance entries for each of these senses is the fact that the contexts are so distinct. These are presented in Figures 1-3 and 1-4.

```
npr/US    ng to do with the way women should be treated in the workplace,
usacad/US  lored the way the Indians had been treated in the past,
brbooks/UK ost difficult and disruptive, are treated in a humane manner
brbooks/UK o P in 19X0. The situation can be treated in one of two ways.
indy/UK   ear in print, however badly they are treated. In the past, this
indy/UK   s arrival in 1987 had been unfairly treated in the wake of
brmags/UK 's offers. <p> Names/addresses are treated in strictest confidence.
oznews/OZ  e way he, and so manyothers, were treated is being applied again.
usbooks/US nce of Marxism, thus he could only treat it with irony and humor.
guard/UK   in Britain, but not all of them are treated kindly.
guard/UK   have long complained that they are treated less generously
brmags/UK  ug. We find that the applicant was treated less favourably
times/UK   randon's official complaint, an act treated lightly.
```

Figure 1-3. Sense (1a) for the verb "treat"

```
bbc/UK    nsiderable damage. A teenage girl was treated for shock.
bbc/UK    three nights in hospital where he was treated for a broken right
newsci/UK ecies." <p> The tips of shoots are treated for up to 48 hours
newsci/UK cient adults most of whom had been treated for tumours
sunnow/UK n at their usual haunts. Patsy was treated for depression
sunnow/UK had been suffering depression, was treated for 30 minutes
sunnow/UK rned red." Two women cleaners were treated for smoke inhalation.
sunnow/UK sed after pulling up and had to be treated for dehydration.
npr/US    and more than 90,000 people have been treated for secondary
indy/UK   e the hospital in which he was being treated for his first heart attack,
sunnow/UK into hospital to get his addiciton treated. He saw a psychiatrist
newsci/UK t by that time, the doctor who had treated her mother
today/UK  tion by Professor John Browett, who treated his knee injury.
today/UK  hospital when they should have been treated in a surgery."
oznews/OZ irth defect which was unable to be treated in her home country.
bbc/UK    a model of multiple sclerosis, can be treated in animals using the
sunnow/UK  in Bath, Somerset. Jane had to be treated in hospital for serious cuts
sunnow/UK atives in their hired minibus were treated in hospital after the crash
sunnow/UK o short of beds patients are being treated in an ambulance outside.
```

Figure 1-4. Sense (1b) for the verb "treat"

The NLTK provides functionality for creating concordances. The easiest way to make a concordance is to simply load the preprocessed texts into the NLTK and then use the concordance function, like this:

```
>>> import NLTK
>>> from nltk.book import *
>>> text6.concordance("Ni")
```

If you have your own set of data for which you would like to create a concordance, then the process is a little more involved: you will need to read in your files and use the NLTK functions to process them before you can create your own concordance. Here is some sample code for a corpus of text files (replace the directory location with your own folder of text files):

```
>>> corpus_loc = '/home/me/corpus/'
>>> docs = nltk.corpus.PlaintextCorpusReader(corpus_loc,'.*\.txt')
```

You can see if the files were read by checking what file IDs are present:

```
>>> print docs.fileids()
```

Next, process the words in the files and then use the concordance function to examine the data:

```
>>> docs_processed = nltk.Text(docs.words())
>>> docs_processed.concordance("treat")
```

Corpora Today

When did researchers start to actually use corpora for modeling language phenomena and training algorithms? Beginning in the 1980s, researchers in Speech Recognition began to compile enough spoken language data to create language models (from transcriptions using n-grams and Hidden Markov Models [HMMS]) that worked well enough to recognize a limited vocabulary of words in a very narrow domain. In the 1990s, work in Machine Translation began to see the influence of larger and larger datasets, and with this, the rise of statistical language modeling for translation.

Eventually, both memory and computer hardware became sophisticated enough to collect and analyze increasingly larger datasets of language fragments. This entailed being able to create statistical language models that actually performed with some reasonable accuracy for different natural language tasks.

As one example of the increasing availability of data, Google has recently released the *Google Ngram Corpus*. The Google Ngram dataset allows users to search for single words (unigrams) or collocations of up to five words (5-grams). The dataset is available for download (*http://bit.ly/WkBKG0*) from the Linguistic Data Consortium, and directly from Google (*http://ngrams.googlelabs.com/datasets*). It is also viewable online through the Google Ngram Viewer (*http://ngrams.googlelabs.com/*). The Ngram dataset consists of more than one trillion tokens (words, numbers, etc.) taken from publicly available websites and sorted by year, making it easy to view trends in language use. In addition to English, Google provides n-grams for Chinese, French, German, Hebrew, Russian, and Spanish, as well as subsets of the English corpus such as American English and English Fiction.

 N-grams are sets of items (often words, but they can be letters, phonemes, etc.) that are part of a sequence. By examining how often the items occur together we can learn about their usage in a language, and predict what would likely follow a given sequence (using n-grams for this purpose is called *n-gram modeling*).

N-grams are applied in a variety of ways every day, such as in websites that provide search suggestions once a few letters are typed in, and for determining likely substitutions for spelling errors. They are also used in speech disambiguation—if a person speaks unclearly but utters a sequence that does not commonly (or ever) occur in the language being spoken, an n-gram model can help recognize that problem and find the words that the speaker probably intended to say.

Another modern corpus is ClueWeb09 (*http://lemurproject.org/clueweb09.php/*), a dataset "created to support research on information retrieval and related human language technologies. It consists of about 1 billion web pages in ten languages that were collected in January and February 2009." This corpus is too large to use for an annotation project (it's about 25 terabytes uncompressed), but some projects have taken parts of the dataset (such as a subset of the English websites) and used them for research (Pomikálek et al. 2012). Data collection from the Internet is an increasingly common way to create corpora, as new and varied content is always being created.

Kinds of Annotation

Consider the different parts of a language's syntax that can be annotated. These include *part of speech (POS)*, *phrase structure*, and *dependency structure*. Table 1-3 shows examples of each of these. There are many different tagsets for the parts of speech of a language that you can choose from.

Table 1-3. Number of POS tags in different corpora

Tagset	Size	Date
Brown	77	1964
LOB	132	1980s
London-Lund Corpus	197	1982
Penn	36	1992

The tagset in Figure 1-5 is taken from the Penn TreeBank, and is the basis for all subsequent annotation over that corpus.

Number	Tag	Description
1.	CC	Coordinating conjunction
2.	CD	Cardinal number
3.	DT	Determiner
4.	EX	Existential there
5.	FW	Foreign word
6.	IN	Preposition or subordinating conjunction
7.	JJ	Adjective
8.	JJR	Adjective, comparative
9.	JJS	Adjective, superlative
10.	LS	List item marker
11.	MD	Modal
12.	NN	Noun, singular or mass
13.	NNS	Noun, plural
14.	NNP	Proper noun, singular
15.	NNPS	Proper noun, plural
16.	PDT	Predeterminer
17.	POS	Possessive ending
18.	PRP	Personal pronoun
19.	PRP$	Possessive pronoun
20.	RB	Adverb
21.	RBR	Adverb, comparative
22.	RBS	Adverb, superlative
23.	RP	Particle
24.	SYM	Symbol
25.	TO	to
26.	UH	Interjection
27.	VB	Verb, base form
28.	VBD	Verb, past tense
29.	VBG	Verb, gerund or present participle
30.	VBN	Verb, past participle
31.	VBP	Verb, non-3rd person singular present
32.	VBZ	Verb, 3rd person singular present
33.	WDT	Wh-determiner
34.	WP	Wh-pronoun
35.	WP$	Possessive wh-pronoun
36.	WRB	Wh-adverb

Figure 1-5. The Penn TreeBank tagset

The POS tagging process involves assigning the right lexical class marker(s) to all the words in a sentence (or corpus). This is illustrated in a simple example, "The waiter cleared the plates from the table." (See Figure 1-6.)

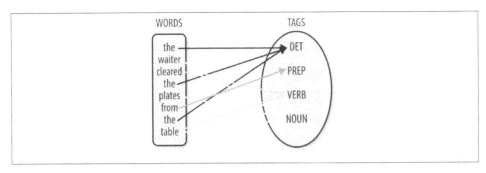

Figure 1-6. POS tagging sample

POS tagging is a critical step in many NLP applications, since it is important to know what category a word is assigned to in order to perform subsequent analysis on it, such as the following:

Speech Synthesis

Is the word a noun or a verb? Examples include *object, overflow, insult*, and *suspect*. Without context, each of these words could be either a noun or a verb.

Parsing

You need POS tags in order to make larger syntactic units. For example, in the following sentences, is "clean dishes" a noun phrase or an imperative verb phrase?

Clean dishes are in the cabinet.
Clean dishes before going to work!

Machine Translation

Getting the POS tags and the subsequent parse right makes all the difference when translating the expressions in the preceding list item into another language, such as French: "Des assiettes propres" (Clean dishes) versus "Fais la vaisselle!" (Clean the dishes!).

Consider how these tags are used in the following sentence, from the Penn TreeBank (Marcus et al. 1993):

"From the beginning, it took a man with extraordinary qualities to succeed in Mexico," says Kimihide Takimura, president of Mitsui group's Kensetsu Engineering Inc. unit.

"/" From/IN the/DT beginning/NN ,/, it/PRP took/VBD a/DT man/NN with/IN extraordinary/JJ qualities/NNS to/TO succeed/VB in/IN Mexico/NNP ,/, "/" says/VBZ Kimihide/NNP Takimura/NNP ,/, president/NN of/IN Mitsui/NNS group/NN 's/POS Kensetsu/NNP Engineering/NNP Inc./NNP unit/NN ./.

Identifying the correct parts of speech in a sentence is a necessary step in building many natural language applications, such as parsers, Named Entity Recognizers, QAS, and

Machine Translation systems. It is also an important step toward identifying larger structural units such as phrase structure.

Use the NLTK tagger to assign POS tags to the example sentence shown here, and then with other sentences that might be more ambiguous:

```
>>> from nltk import pos_tag, word_tokenize
>>> pos_tag(word_tokenize("This is a test."))
```

Look for places where the tagger doesn't work, and think about what rules might be causing these errors. For example, what happens when you try "Clean dishes are in the cabinet." and "Clean dishes before going to work!"?

While words have labels associated with them (the POS tags mentioned earlier), specific sequences of words also have labels that can be associated with them. This is called *syntactic bracketing* (or labeling) and is the structure that organizes all the words we hear into coherent phrases. As mentioned earlier, syntax is the name given to the structure associated with a sentence. The Penn TreeBank is an annotated corpus with syntactic bracketing explicitly marked over the text. An example annotation is shown in Figure 1-7.

John loves Mary.

```
(S (NP (NNP John))
   (VP (VPZ loves)
       (NP (NNP Mary)))
   (..))
```

Figure 1-7. Syntactic bracketing

This is a bracketed representation of the syntactic tree structure, which is shown in Figure 1-8.

Notice that syntactic bracketing introduces two relations between the words in a sentence: order (precedence) and hierarchy (dominance). For example, the tree structure in Figure 1-8 encodes these relations by the very nature of a tree as a directed acyclic graph (DAG). In a very compact form, the tree captures the precedence and dominance relations given in the following list:

{Dom(NNP1,John), Dom(VPZ,loves), Dom(NNP2,Mary), Dom(NP1,NNP1), Dom(NP2,NNP2), Dom(S,NP1), Dom(VP,VPZ), Dom(VP,NP2), Dom(S,VP), Prec(NP1,VP), Prec(VPZ,NP2)}

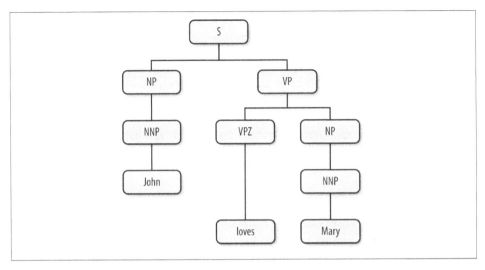

Figure 1-8. Syntactic tree structure

Any sophisticated natural language application requires some level of syntactic analysis, including Machine Translation. If the resources for *full parsing* (such as that shown earlier) are not available, then some sort of *shallow parsing* can be used. This is when partial syntactic bracketing is applied to sequences of words, without worrying about the details of the structure inside a phrase. We will return to this idea in later chapters.

In addition to POS tagging and syntactic bracketing, it is useful to annotate texts in a corpus for their semantic value, that is, what the words mean in the sentence. We can distinguish two kinds of annotation for semantic content within a sentence: what something *is*, and what *role* something plays. Here is a more detailed explanation of each:

Semantic typing
    A word or phrase in the sentence is labeled with a type identifier (from a reserved vocabulary or ontology), indicating what it denotes.

Semantic role labeling
    A word or phrase in the sentence is identified as playing a specific semantic role relative to a role assigner, such as a verb.

Let's consider what annotation using these two strategies would look like, starting with semantic types. Types are commonly defined using an ontology, such as that shown in Figure 1-9.

The word *ontology* has its roots in philosophy, but ontologies also have a place in computational linguistics, where they are used to create categorized hierarchies that group similar concepts and objects. By assigning words semantic types in an ontology, we can create relationships between different branches of the ontology, and determine whether linguistic rules hold true when applied to all the words in a category.

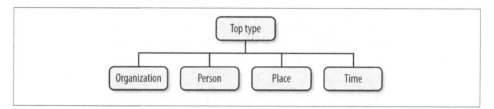

Figure 1-9. A simple ontology

The ontology in Figure 1-9 is rather simple, with a small set of categories. However, even this small ontology can be used to illustrate some interesting features of language. Consider the following example, with semantic types marked:

[Ms. Ramirez]$_{Person}$ of [QBC Productions]$_{Organization}$ visited [Boston]$_{Place}$ on [Saturday]$_{Time}$, where she had lunch with [Mr. Harris]$_{Person}$ of [STU Enterprises]$_{Organization}$ at [1:15 pm]$_{Time}$.

From this small example, we can start to make observations about how these objects interact with one other. People can visit places, people have "of" relationships with organizations, and lunch can happen on Saturday at 1:15 p.m. Given a large enough corpus of similarly labeled sentences, we can start to detect patterns in usage that will tell us more about how these labels do and do not interact.

A corpus of these examples can also tell us where our categories might need to be expanded. There are two "times" in this sentence: Saturday and 1:15 p.m. We can see that events can occur "on" Saturday, but "at" 1:15 p.m. A larger corpus would show that this pattern remains true with other days of the week and hour designations—there is a difference in usage here that cannot be inferred from the semantic types. However, not all ontologies will capture all information—the applications of the ontology will determine whether it is important to capture the difference between Saturday and 1:15 p.m.

The annotation strategy we just described marks up what a linguistic expression refers to. But let's say we want to know the basics for *Question Answering*, namely, the *who*, *what*, *where*, and *when* of a sentence. This involves identifying what are called the *semantic role labels* associated with a verb. What are semantic roles? Although there is no complete agreement on what roles exist in language (there rarely is with linguists), the following list is a fair representation of the kinds of semantic labels associated with different verbs:

Agent
> The event participant that is doing or causing the event to occur

Theme/figure
> The event participant who undergoes a change in position or state

Experiencer
> The event participant who experiences or perceives something

Source
> The location or place from which the motion begins; the person from whom the theme is given

Goal
> The location or place to which the motion is directed or terminates

Recipient
> The person who comes into possession of the theme

Patient
> The event participant who is affected by the event

Instrument
> The event participant used by the agent to do or cause the event

Location/ground
> The location or place associated with the event itself

The annotated data that results explicitly identifies entity extents and the target relations between the entities:

- [The man]$_{agent}$ painted [the wall]$_{patient}$ with [a paint brush]$_{instrument}$.
- [Mary]$_{figure}$ walked to [the cafe]$_{goal}$ from [her house]$_{source}$.
- [John]$_{agent}$ gave [his mother]$_{recipient}$ [a necklace]$_{theme}$.
- [My brother]$_{theme}$ lives in [Milwaukee]$_{location}$.

Language Data and Machine Learning

Now that we have reviewed the methodology of language annotation along with some examples of annotation formats over linguistic data, we will describe the computational framework within which such annotated corpora are used, namely, that of machine learning. Machine learning is the name given to the area of Artificial Intelligence concerned with the development of algorithms that learn or improve their performance from experience or previous encounters with data. They are said to learn (or generate) a function that maps particular input data to the desired output. For our purposes, the "data" that an ML algorithm encounters is natural language, most often in the form of text, and typically annotated with tags that highlight the specific features that are relevant to the learning task. As we will see, the annotation schemas discussed earlier, for example, provide rich starting points as the input data source for the ML process (the training phase).

When working with annotated datasets in NLP, three major types of ML algorithms are typically used:

Supervised learning
> Any technique that generates a function mapping from inputs to a fixed set of labels (the desired output). The labels are typically metadata tags provided by humans who annotate the corpus for training purposes.

Unsupervised learning
> Any technique that tries to find structure from an input set of unlabeled data.

Semi-supervised learning
> Any technique that generates a function mapping from inputs of both labeled data and unlabeled data; a combination of both supervised and unsupervised learning.

Table 1-4 shows a general overview of ML algorithms and some of the annotation tasks they are frequently used to emulate. We'll talk more about why these algorithms are used for these different tasks in Chapter 7.

Table 1-4. Annotation tasks and their accompanying ML algorithms

Algorithms	Tasks
Clustering	Genre classification, spam labeling
Decision trees	Semantic type or ontological class assignment, coreference resolution
Naïve Bayes	Sentiment classification, semantic type or ontological class assignment
Maximum Entropy (MaxEnt)	Sentiment classification, semantic type, or ontological class assignment
Structured pattern induction (HMMs, CRFs, etc.)	POS tagging, sentiment classification, word sense disambiguation

You'll notice that some of the tasks appear with more than one algorithm. That's because different approaches have been tried successfully for different types of annotation tasks, and depending on the most relevant features of your own corpus, different algorithms may prove to be more or less effective. Just to give you an idea of what the algorithms listed in that table mean, the rest of this section gives an overview of the main types of ML algorithms.

Classification

Classification is the task of identifying the labeling for a single entity from a set of data. For example, in order to distinguish *spam* from *not-spam* in your email inbox, an algorithm called a classifier is trained on a set of labeled data, where individual emails have been assigned the label [+spam] or [-spam]. It is the presence of certain (known) words or phrases in an email that helps to identify an email as spam. These words are essentially treated as features that the classifier will use to model the positive instances of spam as compared to not-spam. Another example of a classification problem is patient diagnosis, from the presence of known symptoms and other attributes. Here we would identify a patient as having a particular disease, A, and label the patient record as [+disease-A] or [-disease-A], based on specific features from the record or text. This might include blood pressure, weight, gender, age, existence of symptoms, and so forth. The most common algorithms used in classification tasks are Maximum Entropy (MaxEnt), Naïve Bayes, decision trees, and Support Vector Machines (SVMs).

Clustering

Clustering is the name given to ML algorithms that find natural groupings and patterns from the input data, without any labeling or training at all. The problem is generally viewed as an unsupervised learning task, where either the dataset is unlabeled or the labels are ignored in the process of making clusters. The clusters that are formed are "similar in some respect," and the other clusters formed are "dissimilar to the objects" in other clusters. Some of the more common algorithms used for this task include k-means, hierarchical clustering, Kernel Principle Component Analysis, and Fuzzy C-Means (FCM).

Structured Pattern Induction

Structured pattern induction involves learning not only the label or category of a single entity, but rather learning a sequence of labels, or other structural dependencies between the labeled items. For example, a sequence of labels might be a stream of phonemes in a speech signal (in Speech Recognition); a sequence of POS tags in a sentence corresponding to a syntactic unit (phrase); a sequence of dialog moves in a phone conversation; or steps in a task such as parsing, coreference resolution, or grammar induction. Algorithms used for such problems include Hidden Markov Models (HMMs), Conditional Random Fields (CRFs), and Maximum Entropy Markov Models (MEMMs).

We will return to these approaches in more detail when we discuss machine learning in greater depth in Chapter 7.

The Annotation Development Cycle

The features we use for encoding a specific linguistic phenomenon must be rich enough to capture the desired behavior in the algorithm that we are training. These linguistic descriptions are typically distilled from extensive theoretical modeling of the phenomenon. The descriptions in turn form the basis for the annotation values of the specification language, which are themselves the features used in a development cycle for training and testing an identification or labeling algorithm over text. Finally, based on an analysis and evaluation of the performance of a system, the model of the phenomenon may be revised for retraining and testing.

We call this particular cycle of development the MATTER methodology, as detailed here and shown in Figure 1-10 (Pustejovsky 2006):

Model

Structural descriptions provide theoretically informed attributes derived from empirical observations over the data.

Annotate

An annotation scheme assumes a feature set that encodes specific structural descriptions and properties of the input data.

Train

The algorithm is trained over a corpus annotated with the target feature set.

Test

The algorithm is tested against held-out data.

Evaluate

A standardized evaluation of results is conducted.

Revise

The model and the annotation specification are revisited in order to make the annotation more robust and reliable with use in the algorithm.

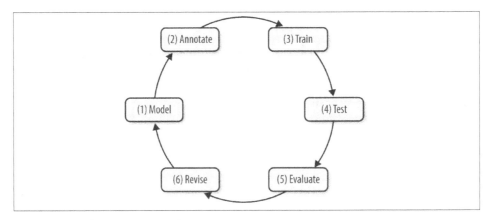

Figure 1-10. The MATTER cycle

We assume some particular problem or phenomenon has sparked your interest, for which you will need to label natural language data for training for machine learning. Consider two kinds of problems. First imagine a direct text classification task. It might be that you are interested in classifying your email according to its content or with a particular interest in filtering out spam. Or perhaps you are interested in rating your incoming mail on a scale of what emotional content is being expressed in the message.

Now let's consider a more involved task, performed over this same email corpus: identifying what are known as *Named Entities (NEs)*. These are references to everyday things in our world that have proper names associated with them; for example, people, countries, products, holidays, companies, sports, religions, and so on.

Finally, imagine an even more complicated task, that of identifying all the different events that have been mentioned in your mail (birthdays, parties, concerts, classes, airline reservations, upcoming meetings, etc.). Once this has been done, you will need to "timestamp" them and order them, that is, identify when they happened, if in fact they did happen. This is called the *temporal awareness problem*, and is one of the most difficult in the field.

We will use these different tasks throughout this section to help us clarify what is involved with the different steps in the annotation development cycle.

Model the Phenomenon

The first step in the MATTER development cycle is "Model the Phenomenon." The steps involved in modeling, however, vary greatly, depending on the nature of the task you have defined for yourself. In this section, we will look at what modeling entails and how you know when you have an adequate first approximation of a model for your task.

The parameters associated with creating a model are quite diverse, and it is difficult to get different communities to agree on just what a model is. In this section we will be pragmatic and discuss a number of approaches to modeling and show how they provide the basis from which to created annotated datasets. Briefly, a model is a characterization of a certain phenomenon in terms that are more abstract than the elements in the domain being modeled. For the following discussion, we will define a model as consisting of a vocabulary of terms, T, the relations between these terms, R, and their interpretation, I. So, a model, M, can be seen as a triple, $M = <T,R,I>$. To better understand this notion of a model, let us consider the scenarios introduced earlier. For spam detection, we can treat it as a binary text classification task, requiring the simplest model with the categories (terms) *spam* and *not-spam* associated with the entire email document. Hence, our model is simply:

- T = {Document_type, Spam, Not-Spam}
- R = {Document_type ::= Spam | Not-Spam}
- I = {Spam = "something we don't want!", Not-Spam = "something we do want!"}

The document itself is labeled as being a member of one of these categories. This is called *document annotation* and is the simplest (and most coarse-grained) annotation possible. Now, when we say that the model contains only the label names for the categories (e.g., sports, finance, news, editorials, fashion, etc.), this means there is no other annotation involved. This does not mean the content of the files is not subject to further scrutiny, however. A document that is labeled as a category, A, for example, is actually analyzed as a large-feature vector containing at least the words in the document. A more fine-grained annotation for the same task would be to identify specific words or phrases in the document and label them as also being associated with the category directly. We'll return to this strategy in Chapter 4. Essentially, the goal of designing a good model of the phenomenon (task) is that this is where you start for designing the features that go into your learning algorithm. The better the features, the better the performance of the ML algorithm!

Preparing a corpus with annotations of NEs, as mentioned earlier, involves a richer model than the spam-filter application just discussed. We introduced a four-category ontology for NEs in the previous section, and this will be the basis for our model to identify NEs in text. The model is illustrated as follows:

- T = {Named_Entity, Organization, Person, Place, Time}
- R = {Named_Entity ::= Organization | Person | Place | Time}
- I = {Organization = "list of organizations in a database", Person = "list of people in a database", Place = "list of countries, geographic locations, etc.", Time = "all possible dates on the calendar"}

This model is necessarily more detailed, because we are actually annotating spans of natural language text, rather than simply labeling documents (e.g., emails) as spam or not-spam. That is, within the document, we are recognizing mentions of companies, actors, countries, and dates.

Finally, what about an even more involved task, that of recognizing all *temporal information* in a document? That is, *questions such as the following*:

- *When* did that meeting take place?
- *How long* was John on vacation?
- Did Jill get promoted *before or after* she went on maternity leave?

We won't go into the full model for this domain, but let's see what is minimally necessary in order to create annotation features to understand such questions. First we need to distinguish between *Time expressions* ("yesterday," "January 27," "Monday"), *Events* ("promoted," "meeting," "vacation"), and *Temporal relations* ("before," "after," "during"). Because our model is so much more detailed, let's divide the descriptive content by domain:

- Time_Expression ::= TIME | DATE | DURATION | SET
  - — TIME: 10:15 a.m., 3 o'clock, etc.
  - — DATE: Monday, April 2011
  - — DURATION: 30 minutes, two years, four days
  - — SET: every hour, every other month
- Event: Meeting, vacation, promotion, maternity leave, etc.
- Temporal_Relations ::= BEFORE | AFTER | DURING | EQUAL | OVERLAP | ...

We will come back to this problem in a later chapter, when we discuss the impact of the initial model on the subsequent performance of the algorithms you are trying to train over your labeled data.

 In later chapters, we'll see that there are actually several models that might be appropriate for describing a phenomenon, each providing a different view of the data. We'll call this *multimodel annotation* of the phenomenon. A common scenario for multimodel annotation involves annotators who have domain expertise in an area (such as biomedical knowledge). They are told to identify specific entities, events, attributes, or facts from documents, given their knowledge and interpretation of a specific area. From this annotation, nonexperts can be used to mark up the structural (syntactic) aspects of these same phenomena, making it possible to gain domain expert understanding without forcing the domain experts to learn linguistic theory as well.

Once you have an initial model for the phenomena associated with the problem task you are trying to solve, you effectively have the first *tag specification*, or *spec*, for the annotation. This is the document from which you will create the blueprint for how to annotate the corpus with the features in the model. This is called the *annotation guideline*, and we talk about this in the next section.

Annotate with the Specification

Now that you have a model of the phenomenon encoded as a specification document, you will need to train human annotators to mark up the dataset according to the tags that are important to you. This is easier said than done, and in fact often requires multiple iterations of modeling and annotating, as shown in Figure 1-11. This process is called the MAMA (Model-Annotate-Model-Annotate) cycle, or the "babeling" phase of MATTER. The *annotation guideline* helps direct the annotators in the task of identifying the elements and then associating the appropriate features with them, when they are identified.

Two kinds of tags will concern us when annotating natural language data: *consuming* tags and *nonconsuming* tags. A consuming tag refers to a metadata tag that has real content from the dataset associated with it (e.g., it "consumes" some text); a nonconsuming tag, on the other hand, is a metadata tag that is inserted into the file but is not associated with any actual part of the text. An example will help make this distinction clear. Say that we want to annotate text for temporal information, as discussed earlier. Namely, we want to annotate for three kinds of tags: times (called Timex tags), temporal relations (TempRels), and Events. In the first sentence in the following example, each tag is expressed directly as real text. That is, they are all consuming tags ("promoted" is marked as an Event, "before" is marked as a TempRel, and "the summer" is marked as a Timex). Notice, however, that in the second sentence, there is no explicit temporal relation in the text, even though we know that it's something like "on". So, we actually insert a TempRel with the value of "on" in our corpus, but the tag is flagged as a "nonconsuming" tag.

- John was [promoted]$_{Event}$ [before]$_{TempRel}$ [the summer]$_{Timex}$.
- John was [promoted]$_{Event}$ [Monday]$_{Timex}$.

An important factor when creating an annotated corpus of your text is, of course, consistency in the way the annotators mark up the text with the different tags. One of the most seemingly trivial problems is the most problematic when comparing annotations: namely, the extent or the *span of the tag*. Compare the three annotations that follow. In the first, the Organization tag spans "QBC Productions," leaving out the company identifier "Inc." and the location "of East Anglia," while these are included in varying spans in the next two annotations.

- [QBC Productions]$_{Organization}$ Inc. of East Anglia
- [QBC Productions Inc.]$_{Organization}$ of East Anglia
- [QBC Productions Inc. of East Anglia]$_{Organization}$

Each of these might look correct to an annotator, but only one actually corresponds to the correct markup in the annotation guideline. How are these compared and resolved?

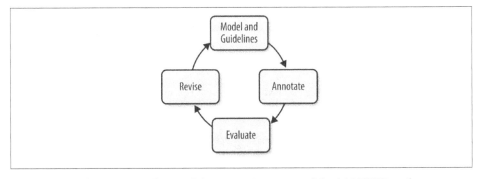

Figure 1-11. The inner workings of the MAMA portion of the MATTER cycle

In order to assess how well an annotation task is defined, we use *Inter-Annotator Agreement* (IAA) scores to show how individual annotators compare to one another. If an IAA score is high, that is an indication that the task is well defined and other annotators will be able to continue the work. This is typically defined using a statistical measure called a *Kappa Statistic*. For comparing two annotations against each other, the *Cohen Kappa* is usually used, while when comparing more than two annotations, a *Fleiss Kappa* measure is used. These will be defined in Chapter 8.

Note that having a high IAA score doesn't necessarily mean the annotations are correct; it simply means the annotators are all interpreting your instructions consistently in the same way. Your task may still need to be revised even if your IAA scores are high. This will be discussed further in Chapter 9.

Once you have your corpus annotated by at least two people (more is preferable, but not always practical), it's time to create the *gold standard corpus*. The gold standard is the final version of your annotated data. It uses the most up-to-date specification that you created during the annotation process, and it has everything tagged correctly according to the most recent guidelines. This is the corpus that you will use for machine learning, and it is created through the process of *adjudication*. At this point in the process, you (or someone equally familiar with all the tasks) will compare the annotations and determine which tags in the annotations are correct and should be included in the gold standard.

Train and Test the Algorithms over the Corpus

Now that you have adjudicated your corpus, you can use your newly created gold standard for machine learning. The most common way to do this is to divide your corpus into two parts: the *development corpus* and the *test corpus*. The development corpus is then further divided into two parts: the *training set* and the *development-test set*. Figure 1-12 shows a standard breakdown of a corpus, though different distributions might be used for different tasks. The files are normally distributed randomly into the different sets.

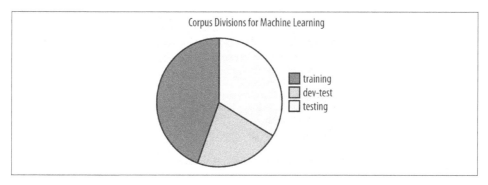

Figure 1-12. Corpus divisions for machine learning

The training set is used to train the algorithm that you will use for your task. The development-test (dev-test) set is used for error analysis. Once the algorithm is trained, it is run on the dev-test set and a list of errors can be generated to find where the algorithm is failing to correctly label the corpus. Once sources of error are found, the algorithm can be adjusted and retrained, then tested against the dev-test set again. This procedure can be repeated until satisfactory results are obtained.

Once the training portion is completed, the algorithm is run against the held-out test corpus, which until this point has not been involved in training or dev-testing. By holding out the data, we can show how well the algorithm will perform on new data, which gives an expectation of how it would perform on data that someone else creates as well. Figure 1-13 shows the "TTER" portion of the MATTER cycle, with the different corpus divisions and steps.

Figure 1-13. The Training–Evaluation cycle

Evaluate the Results

The most common method for evaluating the performance of your algorithm is to calculate how accurately it labels your dataset. This can be done by measuring the fraction of the results from the dataset that are labeled correctly using a standard technique of "relevance judgment" called the *Precision and Recall metric*.

Here's how it works. For each label you are using to identify elements in the data, the dataset is divided into two subsets: one that is labeled "relevant" to the label, and one that is not relevant. *Precision* is a metric that is computed as the fraction of the correct instances from those that the algorithm labeled as being in the relevant subset. *Recall* is computed as the fraction of correct items among those that actually belong to the relevant subset. The following confusion matrix helps illustrate how this works:

		Predicted Labeling	
		positive	negative
Gold	positive	true positive (tp)	false negative (fn)
Labeling	negative	false positive (fp)	true negative (tn)

Given this matrix, we can define both precision and recall as shown in Figure 1-14, along with a conventional definition of *accuracy*.

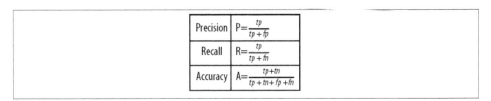

Figure 1-14. Precision and recall equations

The values of P and R are typically combined into a single metric called the *F-measure*, which is the harmonic mean of the two.

$$F = 2 * \frac{P * R}{P + R}$$

This creates an overall score used for evaluation where precision and recall are measured equally, though depending on the purpose of your corpus and algorithm, a variation of this measure, such as one that rates precision higher than recall, may be more useful to you. We will give more detail about how these equations are used for evaluation in Chapter 8.

Revise the Model and Algorithms

Once you have evaluated the results of training and testing your algorithm on the data, you will want to do an error analysis to see where it performed well and where it made mistakes. This can be done with various packages and formulas, which we will discuss in Chapter 8, including the creation of what are called confusion matrices. These will help you go back to the design of the model, in order to create better tags and features that will subsequently improve your gold standard, and consequently result in better performance of your learning algorithm.

A brief example of model revision will help make this point. Recall the model for NE extraction from the previous section, where we distinguished between four types of entities: Organization, Place, Time, and Person. Depending on the corpus you have assembled, it might be the case that you are missing a major category, or that you would be better off making some subclassifications within one of the existing tags. For example, you may find that the annotators are having a hard time knowing what to do with named occurrences or events, such as Easter, 9-11, or Thanksgiving. These denote more than simply Times, and suggest that perhaps a new category should be added to the model: Event. Additionally, it might be the case that there is reason to distinguish geopolitical Places from nongeopolitical Places. As with the "Model-Annotate" and "Train-Test" cycles, once such additions and modifications are made to the model, the MATTER cycle begins all over again, and revisions will typically bring improved performance.

Summary

In this chapter, we have provided an overview of the history of corpus and computational linguistics, and the general methodology for creating an annotated corpus. Specifically, we have covered the following points:

- Natural language annotation is an important step in the process of training computers to understand human speech for tasks such as Question Answering, Machine Translation, and summarization.

- All of the layers of linguistic research, from phonetics to semantics to discourse analysis, are used in different combinations for different ML tasks.

- In order for annotation to provide statistically useful results, it must be done on a sufficiently large dataset, called a *corpus*. The study of language using corpora is *corpus linguistics*.

- Corpus linguistics began in the 1940s, but did not become a feasible way to study language until decades later, when the technology caught up to the demands of the theory.

- A corpus is a collection of machine-readable texts that are representative of natural human language. Good corpora are *representative* and *balanced* with respect to the genre or language that they seek to represent.

- The uses of computers with corpora have developed over the years from simple key-word-in-context (KWIC) indexes and concordances that allowed full-text documents to be searched easily, to modern, statistically based ML techniques.

- Annotation is the process of augmenting a corpus with higher-level information, such as part-of-speech tagging, syntactic bracketing, anaphora resolution, and word senses. Adding this information to a corpus allows the computer to find features that can make a defined task easier and more accurate.

- Once a corpus is annotated, the data can be used in conjunction with ML algorithms that perform classification, clustering, and pattern induction tasks.

- Having a good annotation scheme and accurate annotations is critical for machine learning that relies on data outside of the text itself. The process of developing the annotated corpus is often cyclical, with changes made to the tagsets and tasks as the data is studied further.

- Here we refer to the annotation development cycle as the MATTER cycle—Model, Annotate, Train, Test, Evaluate, Revise.

- Often before reaching the Test step of the process, the annotation scheme has already gone through several revisions of the Model and Annotate stages.

- This book will show you how to create an accurate and effective annotation scheme for a task of your choosing, apply the scheme to your corpus, and then use ML techniques to train a computer to perform the task you designed.

CHAPTER 2

Defining Your Goal and Dataset

Creating a clear definition of your annotation goal is vital for any project aiming to incorporate machine learning. When you are designing your annotation tagsets, writing guidelines, working with annotators, and training algorithms, it can be easy to become sidetracked by details and lose sight of what you want to achieve. Having a clear goal to refer back to can help, and in this chapter we will go over what you need to create a good definition of your goal, and discuss how your goal can influence your dataset. In particular, we will look at:

- What makes a good annotation goal
- Where to find related research
- How your dataset reflects your annotation goals
- Preparing the data for annotators to use
- How much data you will need for your task

What you should be able to take away from this chapter is a clear answer to the questions "What am I trying to do?", "How am I trying to do it?", and "Which resources best fit my needs?". As you progress through the MATTER cycle, the answers to these questions will probably change—corpus creation is an iterative process—but having a stated goal will help keep you from getting off track.

Defining Your Goal

In terms of the MATTER cycle, at this point we're right at the start of "M"—being able to clearly explain what you hope to accomplish with your corpus is the first step in creating your model. While you probably already have a good idea about what you want to do, in this section we'll give you some pointers on how to create a goal definition that is useful and will help keep you focused in the later stages of the MATTER cycle.

We have found it useful to split the goal definition into two steps: first, write a statement of purpose that covers the very basics of your task, and second, use that sentence to expand on the "how"s of your goal. In the rest of this section, we'll give some pointers on how to make sure each of these parts will help you with your corpus task.

The Statement of Purpose

At this point we're assuming that you already have some question pertaining to natural language that you want to explore. (If you don't really have a project in mind yet, check the appendixes for lists of existing corpora, and read the proceedings from related conferences to see if there's anything that catches your eye, or consider participating in Natural Language Process [NLP] challenges, which are discussed later in this chapter.)

But how clearly can you explain what you intend to do? If you can't come up with a one- or two-sentence summary describing your intended line of research, then you're going to have a very hard time with the rest of this task. Keep in mind that we are not talking about a sentence like "Genres are interesting"—that's an opinion, not a starting point for an annotation task. Instead, try to have a statement more like this:

> I want to use keywords to detect the genre of a newspaper article in order to create databases of categorized texts.

This statement is still going to need a lot of refinement before it can be turned into an annotation model, but it answers the basic questions. Specifically, it says:

- What the annotation will be used for (databases)
- What the overall outcome of the annotation will be (genre classification)
- Where the corpus will come from (news articles)
- How the outcome will be achieved (keywords)

Be aware that you may have a task in mind that will require multiple annotation efforts. For example, say you're interested in exploring humor. Even if you have the time, money, and people to do a comprehensive study of all aspects of humor, you will still need to break down the task into manageable segments in order to create annotation tasks for different types of humor. If you want to look at the effects of sarcasm and puns, you will likely need different vocabularies for each task, or be willing to spend the time to create one overarching annotation spec that will encompass all annotations, but we suggest that you start small and then merge annotations later, if possible.

If you do have a broad task that you will need to break down into large subtasks, then make that clear in your summary: "I want to create a program that can generate jokes in text and audio formats, including puns, sarcasm, and exaggeration." Each of the items in that list will require a separate annotation and machine learning (ML) task. Grouping them together, at least at first, would create such a massively complicated task that it would be difficult to complete, let alone learn from.

To provide some more context, Table 2-1 shows a few examples of one-sentence sum-maries, representative of the diverse range of annotation projects and corpora that exist in the field.

Table 2-1. Some corpora and their uses

Corpus	Summary sentence
PropBank	For annotating verbal propositions and their arguments for examining semantic roles
Manually Annotated Sub-Corpus (MASC)	For annotating sentence boundaries, tokens, lemma, and part of speech (POS), noun and verb chunks, and Named Entities (NEs); a subset of the Open American National Corpus (OANC)
Penn Discourse TreeBank	For annotating discourse relations between eventualities and propositions in newswires for learning about discourse in natural language
MPQA Opinion Corpus	For annotating opinions for use in evaluating emotional language
TimeBank	For labeling times, events, and their relationships in news texts for use in temporal reasoning
i2b2 2008 Challenge, Task 1C	For identifying patient smoking status from medical records for use in medical studies
2012 SemEval Task 7—COPA: Choice of Plausible Alternatives	Provides alternative answers to questions; annotation focuses on finding the most likely answer based on reasoning

Naturally, this isn't a complete list of corpora, but it does cover a wide range of different focuses for annotation tasks. These are not high-level descriptions of what these corpora are about, but they answer the basic questions necessary for moving forward with an annotation task. In the next section, we'll look at how to turn this one sentence into an annotation model.

Refining Your Goal: Informativity Versus Correctness

Now that you have a statement of purpose for your corpus, you need to turn it into a task description that can be used to create your model—that is, your corpus, annotation scheme, and guidelines.

When annotating corpora, there is a fine line between having an annotation that will be the most useful for your task (having high informativity) and having an annotation that is not too difficult for annotators to complete accurately (which results in high levels of correctness).

A clear example of where this trade-off comes into play is temporal annotation. Imagine that you want to capture all the relationships between times and events in this simple narrative:

On Tuesday, Pat jogged after work, then went home and made dinner.

Figure 2-1 shows what it would look like to actually create *all* of those relationships, and you can see that a large number of connections are necessary in order to capture all the relationships between events and times. In such tasks, the number of relationships is almost quadratic to the number of times and events [here we have 10, because the links only go in one direction—if we captured both directions, there would be 20 links: $x \cdot (x - 1)$], where x is the number of events/times in the sentence. It wouldn't be very practical to ask an annotator to do all that work by hand; such a task would take an incredibly long time to complete, and an annotation that complex will lead to a lot of errors and omissions—in other words, low correctness. However, asking for a limited set of relations may lead to lower levels of informativity, especially if your annotation guidelines are not very carefully written. We'll discuss annotation guidelines further in Chapter 6.

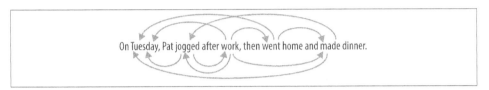

Figure 2-1. All temporal relations over events and times

 You have probably realized that with this particular example it's not necessary to have a human create *all* those links—if A occurs before B and B occurs before C, a computer could use *closure rules* to determine that A occurs before C, and annotators would not have to capture that information themselves. It's always a good idea to consider what parts of your task can be done automatically, especially when it can make your annotator's job easier without necessarily sacrificing accuracy.

The considerations surrounding informativity and correctness are very much intertwined with one of the biggest factors affecting your annotation task: the *scope* of your project. There are two main aspects of project scope that you need to consider: (1) how far-reaching the goal is (the scope of the annotation), and (2) how much of your chosen field you plan to cover (the scope of the corpus). We already touched on (2) a little in the preceding section, and we will have more to say about it later, so for now let's look at (1).

The scope of the annotation task

At this point you have already begun to address the question of your task's scope by answering the four questions from the preceding section—at the very least you've narrowed down what category of features you'll be using (by answering the "means by which the goal will be achieved" question), and what the overall goal of the annotation will be. However, having a general class that your task can be slotted into may still leave you with a lot of variables that you will need to consider.

As always, remember that the MATTER cycle is, in fact, a cycle, and as you go through the steps, you may find new information that causes your scope to widen or shrink.

It's a bit difficult to discuss scope in general terms, so let's look at some specific examples, and then see how the principles can be applied to other projects. In the temporal relation annotation task discussed previously, the scope of the project has to do with exactly what relations are important to the annotation. Are only the main events in each sentence and their relationships important? Do you want to be able to capture only relations inside a sentence, or do you want to capture relations between sentences as well? Maybe you only care about the events that have clear temporal anchors, such as "Jay ran on Sunday." Do you think it's important to differentiate between different types of links?

Similar questions can be asked about the newspaper genre classification example. In that task, the relevant question is "How specific do you want your categories to be?" Is it enough to divide articles into broad categories, such as "news" and "sports," or do you want a more detailed system that specifies "news:global" and "sports:baseball" (or even "sports:baseball:Yankees")?

If this is your first excursion into annotation and corpus building, start with broader categories or simpler tasks—as you learn the ins and outs of your dataset and annotation tags, you'll be able to refine your project in more meaningful and useful ways.

As you can see, the questions being asked about the two examples so far essentially become questions about classification—in the newspaper example this is a much more obvious correlation, but even the temporal relation example touches on this subject. By defining different possible categories of relationships (inter- and intra-sentential, main verbs versus other verbs), it's much easier to identify what parts you feel will be most relevant to your task.

This book is about annotation, and it's necessarily true that if you have an annotation project, classification is some part of your task. This could involve document-level tags, as in the newspaper example; labels that are associated with each word (or a subset of words), as in a POS tagging task; or labeling relationships between existing tags. If you can think of your annotation task in terms of a classification task, then that will provide a stable framework for you to start considering the scope of your task. You most likely already have intuitions about what the relevant features of your data and task are, so use those (at least at first) to determine the scope of your task. This intuition can also help you determine what level of informativity you will need for good classification results, and how accurate you can expect an annotator to be.

Linguistic intuition is an extremely useful way to get started in thinking about a topic, but it can be misleading and even wrong. Once you've started gathering texts and doing some annotation, if you find that the data does not match your expectations, don't hesitate to reevaluate your approach.

Let's go back to our four questions from the previous section and see how informativity and correctness come into effect when elaborating on these aspects of your annotation task. Now that you have a better idea of the scope of your project, it should be fairly easy to see what sorts of things you will want to take into account when answering these questions. (Notice that we didn't say the questions would be *easy* to answer—the trade-off between informativity and correctness is a consideration at all levels, and can make it difficult to decide where to draw the line on a project.)

What will the annotation be used for?

It's likely that the answer to this question hasn't really changed based on the discussion questions we've provided so far—the end product of the annotation, training, and testing is why you're taking on this project in the first place, and is what ultimately informs the answers to the rest of the questions and the project as a whole. However, it's helpful to remind yourself of what you're trying to do before you start expanding your answers to the other questions.

If you have some idea of what ML techniques you'll be using, then that can be a consideration as well at this point, but it's not required, especially if this is your first turn around the MATTER cycle.

What will the overall outcome be?

Thinking about the scope of your project in terms of a classification task, now is the time to start describing the outcome in terms of specific categories. Instead of saying "Classify newspaper articles into genres," try to decide on the number of genres that you think you'll need to encompass all the types of articles you're interested in.

The more categories that your task uses, the harder it will probably be to train an ML algorithm to accurately label your corpus. This doesn't necessarily mean you should limit your project right from the start, but you may find that in later iterations of the MATTER cycle you need to merge some categories.

For the temporal relation annotation, accuracy versus informativity is a huge consideration, for the reasons described earlier (refer back to Figure 2-1 for a refresher on how complicated this task can be). In this case, and in the case of tasks of similar complexity, the specifics of how detailed your task will be will almost certainly have to be worked out through multiple iterations of annotation and evaluation.

For both of these tasks, considering the desired outcome will help you to determine the answer to this question. In the genre case, the use of the database is the main consideration point—who will be using it, and for what? Temporal annotation can be used for a number of things, such as summarization, timeline creation, Question Answering, and so on. The granularity of the task will also inform what needs to be captured in the annotation: if, for example, you are only interested in summarizing the major events in a text, then it might be sufficient to only annotate the relationships of the main event in each sentence.

Where will the corpus come from?

Now that you've thought about the scope of your task, it should be much easier to answer more specific questions about the scope of your corpus. Specifically, it's time to start thinking about the distribution of sources; that is, exactly where all your data will come from and how different aspects of it will be balanced.

Returning to our newspaper classification example, consider whether different news venues have sufficiently different styles that you would need to train an algorithm over all of them, or if a single source is similar enough to the others for the algorithm to be easily generalizable. Are the writing and topics in the *New York Times* similar enough to the *Wall Street Journal* that you don't need examples from each? What about newspapers and magazines that publish exclusively online? Do you consider blogs to be news sources? Will you include only written articles, or will you also include transcripts of broadcasts?

For temporal annotation, our experience has been that different publication styles and genres can have a huge impact on how times are used in text. (Consider a children's story compared to a newspaper article, and how linear [or not] the narration in each tends to be.) If you want your end product to cover all types of sources, this might be another splitting point for your tasks—you may need to have different annotation guidelines for different narrative genres, so consider carefully how far-reaching you want your task to be.

Clearly, these considerations are tied into the scope of your task—the bigger the scope, the more sources you will need to include in your annotation in order to maximize informativity. However, the more disparate sources you include, the more likely it is that you will need to consider having slightly different annotation tasks for each source, which could lower correctness if the tasks are not fully thought out for each genre.

It's also a good idea to check out existing corpora for texts that might be suitable for the task you are working on. Using a preassembled corpus (or a subset of one) has the obvious benefit of lessening the work that you will have to do, but it also means you will have access to any other annotations that have been done on those files. See "Background Research" on page 40 for more information on linguistic resources.

Don't get too caught up in the beginning with creating the perfect corpus—remember that this process is cyclical, and if you find you're missing something, you can always go back and add it later.

How will the result be achieved?

In Chapter 1 we discussed the levels of linguistics—phonology, syntax, semantics, and so on—and gave examples of annotation tasks for each of those levels. Consider at this point, if you haven't already, which of these levels your task fits into. However, don't try to force your task to only deal with a single linguistic level! Annotations and corpora do not always fit neatly into one category or another, and the same is probably true of your own task.

For instance, while the temporal relation task that we have been using as an example so far fits fairly solidly into the discourse and text structure level, it relies on having events and times already annotated. But what is an event? Often events are verbs ("He *ran* down the street.") but they can also be nouns ("The *election* was fiercely contested.") or even adjectives, depending on whether they represent a state that has changed ("The volcano was *dormant* for centuries before the eruption."). But labeling events is not a purely syntactic task, because (1) not all nouns, verbs, and adjectives are events, and (2) the context in which a word is used will determine whether a word is an event or not. Consider "The *party* lasted until 10" versus "The political *party* solicited funds for the campaign." These examples add a semantic component to the event annotation.

It's very likely that your own task will benefit from bringing in information from different levels of linguistics. POS tagging is the most obvious example of additional information that can have a huge impact on how well an algorithm performs an NLP task: knowing the part of speech of a word can help with word sense disambiguation ("call the police" versus "police the neighborhood"), determining how the syllables of a word are pronounced (consider the verb pre*sent* versus the noun *present*—this is a common pattern in American English), and so on.

Of course, there is always a trade-off: the more levels (or partial levels—it might not be necessary to have POS labels for all your data; they might only be used on words that are determined to be interesting in some other way) that your annotation includes, the more informative it's likely to be. But the other side of that is that the more complex your task is, the more likely it is that your annotators will become confused, thereby lowering your accuracy. Again, the important thing to remember is that MATTER is a cycle, so you will need to experiment to determine what works best for your task.

Background Research

Now that you've considered what linguistic levels are appropriate for your task, it's time to do some research into related work. Creating an annotated corpus can take a lot of effort, and while it's possible to create a good annotation task completely on your own, checking the state of the industry can save you a lot of time and effort. Chances are there's some research that's relevant to what you've been doing, and it helps to not have to reinvent the wheel.

For example, if you are interested in temporal annotation, you know by now that ISO-TimeML is the ISO standard for time and event annotation, including temporal relationships. But this fact doesn't require that all temporal annotations use the ISO-TimeML schema as-is. Different domains, such as medical and biomedical text analysis, have found that TimeML is a useful starting place, but in some cases provides too many options for annotators, or in other cases does not cover a particular case relevant to the area being explored. Looking at what other people have done with existing annotation schemes, particularly in fields related to those you are planning to annotate, can make your own annotation task much easier to plan.

While the library and, of course, Google usually provide good starting places, those sources might not have the latest information on annotation projects, particularly because the primary publishing grounds in computational linguistics are conferences and their related workshops. In the following sections we'll give you some pointers to organizations and workshops that may prove useful.

Language Resources

Currently there are a few different resources for locating preassembled corpora. The Linguistic Data Consortium (LDC), for example, has a collection of hundreds of corpora in both text and speech, from a variety of languages. While most of the corpora are available to nonmembers (sometimes for a fee), some of them do require LDC membership. The LDC is run by the University of Pennsylvania, and details about membership and the cost of corpora are available on the LDC website (*http://www.ldc.upenn.edu*).

The European Language Resources Association (ELRA) is another repository of both spoken and written corpora from many different languages. As with the LDC, it is possible to become a member of the ELRA in order to gain access to the entire database, or access to individual corpora can be sought. More information is available at the ELRA website (*http://www.ELRA.info*).

Another useful resource is the LRE (Linguistic Resources and Evaluation) Map (*http://www.languagelibrary.eu/lremap/*), which provides a listing of all the resources used by researchers who submitted papers to the LRE Conference (LREC) for the past few years. However, the list is not curated and so not all the entries are guaranteed to be correct. A shortened version of the corpus and annotation resources in the Map can be found in the appendixes of this book.

With both the LDC and the ELRA, it's possible that while you would need to pay to gain access to the most up-to-date version of a corpus, an older version may be available for download from the group that created the corpus, so it's worth checking around for availability options if you are short of funds. And, of course, check the license on any corpus you plan to use to ensure that it's available for your purposes, no matter where you obtain it from.

Organizations and Conferences

Much of the work on annotation that is available to the public is being done at universities, making conference proceedings the best place to start looking for information about tasks that might be related to your own. Here is a list of some of the bigger conferences that examine annotation and corpora, as well as some organizations that are interested in the same topic:

- Association for Computational Linguistics (ACL)
- Institute of Electrical and Electronics Engineers (IEEE)
- Language Resources and Evaluation Conference (LREC)
- European Language Resources Association (ELRA)
- Conference on Computational Linguistics (COLING)
- American Medical Informatics Association (AMIA)

The LINGUIST List (*http://linguistlist.org*) is not an organization that sponsors conferences and workshops itself, but it does keep an excellent up-to-date list of calls for papers and dates of upcoming conferences. It also provides a list of linguistic organizations that can be sorted by linguistic level.

NLP Challenges

In the past few years, NLP challenges hosted through conference workshops have become increasingly common. These challenges usually present a linguistic problem, a training and testing dataset, and a limited amount of time during which teams or individuals can attempt to create an algorithm or ruleset that can achieve good results on the test data.

The topics of these challenges vary widely, from POS tagging to word sense disambiguation to text analysis over biomedical data, and they are not limited to English. Some workshops that you may want to look into are:

SemEval
This is a workshop held every three years as part of the Association for Computational Linguistics. It involves a variety of challenges including word sense disambiguation, temporal and spatial reasoning, and Machine Translation.

Conference on Natural Language Learning (CoNLL) Shared Task

This is a yearly NLP challenge held as part of the Special Interest Group on Natural Language Learning of the Association for Computational Linguistics. Each year a new NLP task is chosen for the challenge. Past challenges include uncertainty detection, extracting syntactic and semantic dependencies, and multilingual processing.

i2b2 NLP Shared Tasks

The i2b2 group is focused on using NLP in the medical domain, and each year it holds a challenge involving reasoning over patient documents. Past challenges have focused on comorbidity, smoking status, and identification of medication information.

A large number of other shared tasks and challenges are available for participation: the NIST TREC Tracks (*http://trec.nist.gov/tracks.html*) are held every year, the BioNLP workshop (*https://sites.google.com/site/bionlpst/*) frequently hosts a shared task, and each year there are more. If you would like to be involved in an ML task but don't want to necessarily create a dataset and annotation yourself, signing up for one of these challenges is an excellent way to get involved in the NLP community. NLP challenges are also useful in that they are a good reference for tasks that might not have a lot of time or funding. However, it should be noted that the time constraints on NLP challenges often mean the obtained results are not the best possible overall, simply the best possible given the time and data.

Assembling Your Dataset

We've already discussed some aspects that you will need to consider when assembling your dataset: the scope of your task, whether existing corpora contain documents and annotations that would be useful to you, and how varied your sources will be.

If you are planning to make your dataset public, make very sure that you have permission to redistribute the information you are annotating. In some cases it is possible to release only the stand-off annotations and a piece of code that will collect the data from websites, but it's best and easiest to simply ask permission of the content provider, particularly if your corpus and annotation is for business rather than purely educational purposes.

Guidelines for Corpus Creation

Corpus linguist John Sinclair developed guidelines for the creation of linguistic corpora (Sinclair 2005). While these guidelines are primarily directed at corpora designed to study linguistic phenomena, they will be useful for anyone interested in building a corpus. The full paper can be read at *http://www.ahds.ac.uk/creating/guides/linguistic-corpora/chapter1.htm*, but the guidelines are presented here for convenience:

1. The contents of a corpus should be selected without regard for the language they contain, but according to their communicative function in the community in which they arise.

2. Corpus builders should strive to make their corpus as representative as possible of the language from which it is chosen.

3. Only those components of corpora that have been designed to be independently contrastive should be contrasted.

4. Criteria for determining the structure of a corpus should be small in number, clearly separate from each other, and efficient as a group in delineating a corpus that is representative of the language or variety under examination.

5. Any information about a text other than the alphanumeric string of its words and punctuation should be stored separately from the plain text and merged when required in applications.

6. Samples of language for a corpus should, wherever possible, consist of entire documents or transcriptions of complete speech events, or should get as close to this target as possible. This means that samples will differ substantially in size.

7. The design and composition of a corpus should be documented fully with information about the contents and arguments in justification of the decisions taken.

8. The corpus builder should retain, as target notions, representativeness and balance. While these are not precisely definable and attainable goals, they must be used to guide the design of a corpus and the selection of its components.

9. Any control of subject matter in a corpus should be imposed by the use of external, and not internal, criteria.

10. A corpus should aim for homogeneity in its components while maintaining adequate coverage, and rogue texts should be avoided.

The Ideal Corpus: Representative and Balanced

In corpus linguistics, the phrase "representative and balanced" is often used to describe the traits that should be targeted when building a corpus. Because a corpus must always be a selected subset of any chosen language, it cannot contain *all* examples of the language's possible uses. Therefore, a corpus must be created by sampling the existing texts of a language. Since any sampling procedure inherently contains the possibility of skewing the dataset, care should be taken to ensure that the corpus is *representative* of the "full range of variability in a population" (Biber 1993). The "population" being sampled will be determined by the goal and scope of your annotation task. For example, if you want to study movie reviews, you don't need to worry about including other types of reviews or writing in your corpus. You do, however, want to make sure you have examples of different types of reviews in your dataset. McEnery et al. (2006:19–22) provide an excellent discussion of considerations for sampling a language.

The other important concept in corpus creation is that of *balance*. Sinclair (2005) describes a corpus as balanced this way: "the proportions of different kinds of text it contains should correspond with informed and intuitive judgments." This applies predominantly to corpora that are taking samples from different types of text: for example, a corpus that wants to represent "American English" would have to include all types of written and spoken texts, from newspaper articles to chat room discussions to television transcripts, book samples, and so on. A corpus that has been predefined to require a smaller sample will be easier to balance, simply because there will be fewer directions in which the scope of the corpus can be expanded, but the utility of the corpus for general research purposes will be correspondingly decreased.

Admittedly, the concepts of "representativeness and balance" are not easy to define, and whether or not any corpus can be considered truly representative is an issue that corpus linguists have been debating for years. However, considering what aspects of your corpus and the world may impact whether your dataset can be considered "representative and balanced" is an excellent way to gauge how useful it will be for other annotation and ML tasks, and can help ensure that your results are maximally applicable to other datasets as well.

The important thing to look out for is whether or not your corpus matches the goal of your task. If your goal is to be able to process any movie review, then you'll want your corpus to be an accurate representation of how reviews are distributed in the real world. This will help to train your algorithms to more accurately label reviews that you give it later on.

Collecting Data from the Internet

If you are doing textual annotation, you will probably be collecting your corpus from the Internet. There are a number of excellent books that will provide specifics for how to gather URLs and string HTML tags from websites, as well as Twitter streams, forums, and other Internet resources. We will discuss a few of them here.

Natural Language Processing with Python by Steven Bird, Ewan Klein, and Edward Loper (O'Reilly) provides some basic instructions for importing text and web data straight from the Internet. For example, if you are interested in collecting the text from a book in the Project Gutenberg library, the process is quite simple (as the book describes):

```
>>> from urllib import urlopen
>>> url = "http://www.gutenberg.org/files/2554/2554.txt"
>>> raw = urlopen(url).read()
```

However, you should be aware that some websites block such programs from downloading their content, and so you may need to find other ways to download your corpus. If you are interested in taking the raw text from an HTML page, the NLTK includes a package that will clean that input for you:

```
>>> url = "http://www.bbc.co.uk/news/world-us-canada-18963939"
>>> html = urlopen(url).read()
>>> raw = nltk.clean_html(html)
```

Chapter 11 of *Natural Language Processing with Python* provides information and resources for compiling data from other sources, such as from word processor files, databases, and spreadsheets.

In terms of mining information from other web sources, such as Twitter and blogs, *Mining the Social Web* by Matthew A. Russell (O'Reilly) provides detailed information for using the Twitter API, as well as resources for mining information from email, LinkedIn, and blogs.

Eliciting Data from People

So far we have assumed you will be annotating texts or recordings that already exist. But for some tasks, the data just isn't there, or at least it doesn't exist in a form that's going to be of any use.

This applies, we think, more to tasks requiring annotation of spoken or visual phenomena than written work—unless you are looking for something very particular when it comes to text, it's rarely necessary to have people generate writing samples for you. However, it's very common to need spoken samples, or recordings of people performing particular actions for speech or motion recognition projects.

 If you *do* need to elicit data from humans and are affiliated with a university or business, you will probably have to seek permission from lawyers, or even an Internal Review Board (IRB). Even if you are doing your own research project, be very clear with your volunteers about what you're asking them to do and why you're asking them to do it.

When it comes to eliciting data (as opposed to just collecting it), there are a few things you need to consider: in particular, do you want your data to be spontaneous, or read? Do you want each person to say the same thing, or not? Let's take a look at what some of the differences are and how they might affect your data.

Read speech

Read speech means that, while collecting data, you have each person read the same set of sentences or words. If, for example, you wanted to compare different dialects or accents, or train a Speech Recognition program to detect when people are saying the same thing, then this is probably the paradigm you will want to use.

The VoxForge corpus (*http://www.voxforge.org/home*) uses this method—it provides a series of prompts that speakers can record on their own and submit with a user profile describing their language background.

 If you do decide to have people read text from a prompt, be aware that how the text is presented (font, bold, italics) can greatly affect how the text is read. You may need to do some testing to make sure your readers are giving you useful sound bites.

Recordings of news broadcasts can also be considered "read speech," but be careful—the cadence of news anchors is often very different from "standard" speech, so these recordings might not be useful, depending on your goal.

A detailed description of the data collection process for the WSJCAM0 Corpus can be found at *http://www.ldc.upenn.edu/Catalog/readme_files/wsjcam0/wsjcam0.html*.

Spontaneous speech

Naturally, spontaneous speech is collected without telling people what to say. This can be done by asking people open-ended questions and recording their responses, or simply recording conversations (with permission, of course!).

The Size of Your Corpus

Now that you know what kind of data you're looking for and how you're going to present it, you have to decide how much data you're actually going to collect and annotate. If you're planning to use a corpus that already exists, then the overall size of the corpus is decided for you, but you still might have to determine how much of that corpus you want to annotate.

Generally speaking, no matter what your annotation goal is, the more data you collect and annotate, the closer you'll get to achieving that goal. However, most of the time "bigger is better" isn't a very practical mantra when discussing annotation tasks—time, money, limited resources, and attention span are all factors that can limit how much annotation you and your annotators can complete.

 If this is your first pass at data collection, the most important thing is to have a sample corpus that has examples of all the phenomena that you are expecting to be relevant to your task.

That being said, we recommend starting small when it comes to your first attempts at annotating documents—select a handful of documents for your annotators first, and see how well your annotation task and guidelines work (annotation guidelines will be discussed further in Chapter 6). Once you have some of the problems worked out, then you can go back and add to your corpus as needed.

Unfortunately, there's no magic number that we can give you for deciding how big your corpus will need to be in order to get good results. How big your corpus needs to be will depend largely on how complex your annotation task is, but even having a way to quantify "complexity" in an annotation scheme won't solve all the problems. However, corpora that are in use can provide a rule of thumb for how big you can expect your own corpus to be.

Existing Corpora

A rule of thumb for gauging how big your corpus may need to be is to examine existing corpora that are being used for tasks similar to yours. Table 2-2 shows sizes of some of the different corpora that we have been discussing so far. As you can see, they do not all use the same metric for evaluating size. This is largely a function of the purpose of the corpus—corpora designed for evaluation at a document level, such as the movie review corpus included in the Natural Language Toolkit (NLTK), will provide the number of documents as a reference, while annotation tasks that are done at a word or phrase level will report on the number of words or tokens for their metric.

Table 2-2. Existing corpora ranked in terms of estimated size

Corpus	Estimated size
ClueWeb09	1,040,809,705 web pages
British National Corpus	100 million words
American National Corpus	22 million words (as of the time of this writing)
TempEval 2 (part of SemEval 2010)	10,000 to 60,000 tokens per language dataset
Penn Discourse TreeBank	1 million words
i2b2 2008 Challenge—smoking status	502 hospital discharge summaries
TimeBank 1.2	183 documents; 61,000 tokens
Disambiguating Sentiment Ambiguous Adjectives (Chinese language data, part of SemEval 2010)	4,000 sentences

You will notice that the last three corpora are generally smaller in size than the other corpora listed—this is because those three were used in NLP challenges as part of existing workshops, and part of the challenge is to perform an NLP ML task in a limited amount of time. This limit includes the time spent creating the training and testing datasets, and so the corpora have to be much smaller in order to be feasible to annotate, and in some cases the annotation schemes are simplified as well. However, results from these challenges are often not as good as they would be if more time could have been put into creating larger and more thoroughly annotated datasets.

Distributions Within Corpora

Previously we discussed including different types of sources in your corpus in order to increase informativity. Here we will show examples of some of the source distributions in existing corpora.

For example, TimeBank is a selection of 183 news articles that have been annotated with time and event information. However, not all the articles in TimeBank were produced the same way: some are broadcast transcripts, some are articles from a daily newspaper, and some were written for broadcast over the newswire. The breakdown of this distribution is shown in Figure 2-2.

As you can see, while the corpus trends heavily toward daily published newspapers, other sources are also represented. Having those different sources has provided insight into how time and events are reported in similar, but not identical, media.

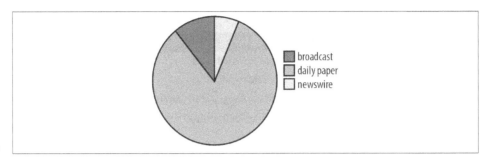

Figure 2-2. Production circumstances in TimeBank

The British National Corpus (BNC) is another example of a corpus that draws from many sources—sources even more disparate than those in TimeBank. Figure 2-3 shows the breakdown of text types in the BNC, as described in the Reference Guide for the BNC (*http://www.natcorp.ox.ac.uk/docs/URG/*).

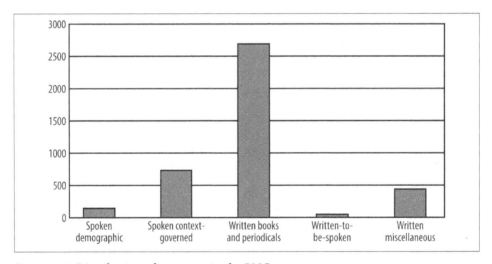

Figure 2-3. Distribution of text types in the BNC

Naturally, other distribution aspects can be considered when evaluating how balanced a corpus is. The BNC also provides analysis of its corpus based on publication dates, domain, medium, and analysis of subgroups, including information about authors and intended audiences (see Figure 2-4).

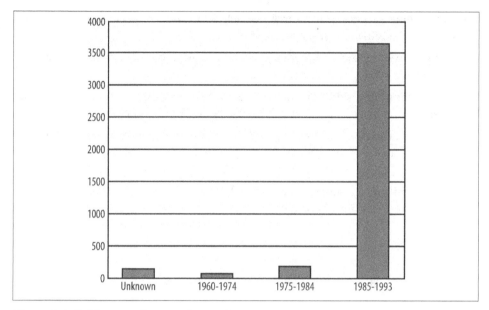

Figure 2-4. Publication dates in the BNC

For your corpus it's unlikely that you will need to be concerned with having representative samples of all of these possible segmentations. That being said, minimizing the number of factors that could potentially make a difference is a good strategy, particularly when you're in the first few rounds of annotations. So, for example, making sure that all of your texts come from the same time period, or checking that all of your speakers are native to the language you are asking them to speak in, is something you may want to take into account even if you ultimately decide to not include that type of diversity in your corpus.

Summary

In this chapter we discussed what you need to create a good definition of your goal, and how your goal can influence your dataset. In particular, we looked at the following points:

- Having a clear definition of your annotation task will help you stay on track when you start creating task definitions and writing annotation guidelines.
- There is often a trade-off in annotation tasks between informativity and accuracy —be careful that you aren't sacrificing too much of one in favor of another.
- Clearly defining the scope of your task will make it much easier to decide on the sources of your corpus—and later, the annotation tags and guidelines.

- Doing some background research can help keep you from reinventing the wheel when it comes to your own annotation task.

- Using an existing corpus for your dataset can make it easier to do other analyses if necessary.

- If an existing corpus doesn't suit your needs, you can build your own, but consider carefully what data you need and what might become a confounding factor.

- There are a variety of existing tools and programming languages that can help you to collect data from the Internet.

- What information you intend to show to your annotators is an important factor that can influence annotation, particularly in tasks that rely on opinion or annotators' interpretations of texts, rather than objective facts.

CHAPTER 3

Corpus Analytics

Now that you have successfully created a corpus for your defined goal, it is important to know what it contains. The goal of this chapter is to equip you with tools for analyzing the linguistic content of this corpus. Hence, we will introduce you to the kinds of techniques and tools you will need in order to perform a variety of statistical analytics over your corpus.

To this end, we will cover the aspects of statistics and probability that you need in order to understand, from a linguistic perspective, just what is in the corpus we are building. This is an area called *corpus analytics*. Topics will include the following:

- How to measure basic frequencies of word occurrence, by lemma and by token
- How to normalize the data you want to analyze
- How to measure the relatedness between words and phrases in a corpus (i.e., distributions)

Knowing what is in your corpus will help you build your model for automatically identifying the tags you will be creating in the next chapter. We will introduce these concepts using linguistic examples whenever possible. Throughout the chapter, we will reference a corpus of movie reviews, assembled from IMDb.com (IMDb). This will prove to be a useful platform from which we can introduce these concepts.

Statistics is important for several reasons, but mostly it gives us two important abilities:

Data analysis
  Discovering latent properties in the dataset

Significance for inferential statistics
  Allowing us to make judgments and derive information regarding the content of our corpus

This chapter does provide an overview of the statistics used to analyze corpora, but it doesn't provide a full course in statistics or probability. If you're interested in reading more about those topics, especially as they relate to corpus linguistics, we recommend the following books/papers:

- *Probability for Linguists*. John Goldsmith. Math. & Sci. hum. / Mathematics and Social Sciences (45e année, no. 180, 2007(4)). *http://hum.uchicago.edu/~jagoldsm/ Papers/probabilityProofs.pdf*.
- *Analyzing Linguistic Data: A Practical Introduction to Statistics using R*. R.H. Baayen. Cambridge University Press; 1st edition, 2008.
- *Statistics for Linguistics with R: A Practical Introduction*. Stefan Th. Gries. De Gruyter Mouton; 1st edition, 2010.

Basic Probability for Corpus Analytics

First let's review some of the basic principles of probability.

State/sample space
> When we perform an experiment or consider the possible values that can be assigned to an attribute, such as an email being identified as *spam* or *not-spam*, we are referring to the state space for that attribute: that is, {spam, not_spam}. Similarly, the possible outcome for a coin toss is *heads* or *tails*, giving rise to the state space of {heads, tails}.

Random variable
> This is a variable that refers not to a fixed value, but to any possible outcome within the defined domain; for example, the *state space* mentioned in the preceding list item.

Probability
> The probability of a specific outcome from the state space, *x*, is expressed as a function, *P(x)*. We say that *P(x)* refers to the "probability of *x*," where *x* is some value of the random variable X, $x \in X$.

Probabilities have two important properties:

- They must have values between 0 and 1, expressed as:

$$\forall x : 0 \leq p(x) \leq 1$$

- The sum of the probabilities of all possible events must add up to 1:

$$\sum_{x \in X} P(x) = 1$$

Let's say you are interested in looking at movie reviews. Perhaps your goal is to collect a corpus in order to train an algorithm to identify the genre of a movie, based on the text from the plot summary, as found on IMDb.com, for example. In order to train an algorithm to classify and label elements of the text, you need to know the nature of the corpus.

Assume that we have 500 movie descriptions involving five genres, evenly balanced over each genre, as follows:

- Action: 100 documents
- Comedy: 100 documents
- Drama: 100 documents
- Sci-fi: 100 documents
- Family: 100 documents

Given this corpus, we can define the random variable G (Genre), where the genre values in the preceding list constitute the state space (sample space) for G. Because this is a balanced corpus, any $g \in G$ will have the same probability: for example, $P(Drama) = .20$, $P(Action) = .20$, and so on.

 If you want to find the probability of a particular variable in a corpus using Python, you can do it quite easily using lists. If you have a list of all the reviews, and a list of the comedies, you can use the length of the respective lists to get the probability of randomly selecting a review with a particular attribute. Let's say that all is a list of the filenames for all the reviews, and comedy is a list of the filenames that are comedies:

```
>>> p_com = float(len(comedy))/float(len(all))
```

Because the len() function returns an int, in order to get a probability, you need to convert the int to a float; otherwise, you get a probability of 0.

Joint Probability Distributions

Usually the kinds of questions we will want to ask about a corpus involve not just one random variable, but multiple random variables at the same time. Returning to our

IMDb corpus, we notice that there are two kinds of plot summaries: short and long. We can define the random variable S (Summary) with the sample space of {short, long}. If each genre has 50 short summaries and 50 long summaries, then $P(short) = .5$ and $P(long) = .5$.

Now we have two random variables, G (Genre) and S (Summary). We denote the *joint probability distribution* of these variables as $P(G,S)$. If G and S are independent variables, then we can define $P(G,S)$ as follows:

$$P(G \cap S) = P(G) \times P(S)$$

So, assuming they are independent, the probability of randomly picking a "short comedy" article is:

$$P(Comedy \cap short) = P(Comedy) \times P(short)$$

$$= 0.20 \times 0.50$$

$$= 0.10$$

But are these two random variables independent of each other? Intuitively, two events are independent if one event occurring does not alter the likelihood of the other event occurring.

So, we can imagine separating out the short articles, and then picking a comedy from those, or vice versa. There are 250 short articles, composed of five genres, each containing 50 articles. Alternatively, the comedy genre is composed of 100 articles, containing 50 short and 50 long articles. Looking at it this way is equivalent to determining the *conditional probability*. This is the probability of outcome A, given that B has occurred (read "the probability of A given B"), and is defined as follows:

$$P(A \mid B) = \frac{P(A \cap B)}{P(B)}$$

This is the fraction of B results that are also A results. For our example, the probability of picking a comedy, given that we have already determined that the article is short, is as follows:

$$P(comedy \mid short) = \frac{P(Comedy \cap short)}{P(short)}$$

We can quickly see that this returns 0.20, which is the same as $P(Comedy)$. The property of independence in fact tells us that, if G and S are independent, then:

$$P(G \mid S) = P(G)$$

Similarly, since $P(S \mid G) = P(S)$, $P(short \mid Comedy) = P(short)$, which is 0.50.

Notice that from the preceding formula we have the following equivalent formula, which is called the *multiplication rule* in probability:

$$P(A \cap B) = P(B)P(A \mid B) = P(A)P(B \mid A)$$

When we need to compute the joint probability distribution for more than two random variables, this equation generalizes to something known as the *chain rule*:

$$P(A_1 \cap A_2 ... \cap A_n) = P(A_1)P(A_2 \mid A_1)P(A_3 \mid A_1 \cap A_2)...P(A_n \mid \cap_{i=1}^{n-1} A_i)$$

This rule will become important when we build some of our first language models over our annotated corpora.

The calculation of the conditional probability is important for the machine learning (ML) algorithms we will encounter in Chapter 7. In particular, the Naïve Bayes Classifier relies on the computation of conditional probabilities from the corpus.

 Understanding how different attributes are connected in your corpus can help you to discover aspects of your dataset that should be included in your annotation task. If it turned out that the probability of a review being short was correlated with one or more movie genres, then including that information in your annotation task (or later on when you are building a feature set for your ML algorithm) could be very helpful.

At the same time, it may turn out that the connection between the length of the review and the genre is purely coincidental, or is a result of your corpus being unbalanced in some way. So checking your corpus for significant joint probability distributions can also ensure that your corpus accurately represents the data you are working with.

Bayes Rule

Once we have the definition for computing a conditional probability, we can recast the rule in terms of an equivalent formula called *Bayes Theorem*, stated as follows:

$$P(A \mid B) = \frac{P(B \mid A)P(A)}{P(B)}$$

This rule allows us to switch the order of dependence between events. This formulates the conditional probability, $P(A \mid B)$, into three other probabilities, that are hopefully easier to find estimates for. This is important because when we want to design an ML algorithm for automatically classifying the different entities in our corpus, we need training data, and this involves being able to easily access statistics for the probabilities associated with the different judgments being used in the algorithm. We return to this in Chapter 7.

Counting Occurrences

When putting together a corpus of linguistic texts, you most likely will not know the probability distribution of a particular phenomenon before you examine the corpus. We could not have known, for example, what the probability of encountering an action film would be in the IMDb corpus, without counting the members associated with each value of the Genre random variable. In reality, no corpus will be so conveniently balanced. Such information constitutes the *statistics* over the corpus by counting occurrences of the relevant objects in the dataset—in this case, movies that are labeled as action films, comedy films, and so on. Similarly, when examining the linguistic content of a corpus, we cannot know what the frequency distribution of the different words in the corpus will be beforehand.

One of the most important things to know about your corpus before you apply any sort of ML algorithm to it is the basic statistical profile of the words contained in it. The corpus is essentially like a textbook that your learning algorithm is going to use as a supply of examples (positive instances) for training. If you don't know the distribution of words (or whatever constitutes the objects of interest), then you don't know what the textbook is supplying for learning. A language corpus typically has an uneven distribution of word types, as illustrated in Figure 3-1. Instructions for how to create this graph for your own corpus can be found in Madnani 2012.

First, a note of clarification. When we say we are counting the "words" in a corpus, we need to be clear about what that means. Word frequencies refer to the number of word *tokens* that are instances of a word *type* (or lemma). So we are correct in saying that the following sentence has 8 words in it, or that it has 11 words in it. It depends on what we mean by "word"!

> "The cat chased the mouse down the street in the dark."

You can perform word counts over corpora directly with the NLTK. Figure 3-2 shows some examples over the IMDb corpus. Determining what words or phrases are most common in your dataset can help you get a grasp of what kind of text you're looking at. Here, we show some sample code that could be used to find the 50 most frequently used words in a corpus of plain text.

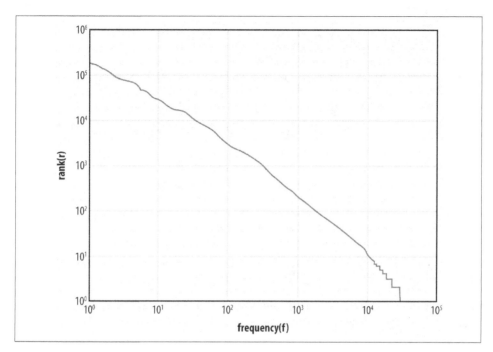

Figure 3-1. Frequency distribution in the NLTK Gutenburg corpus

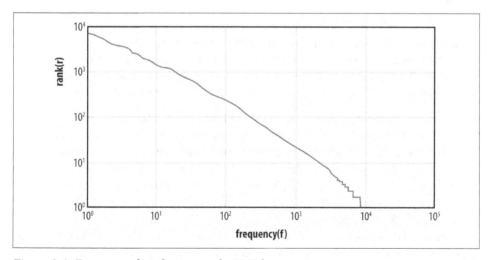

Figure 3-2. Frequency distribution in the IMDb corpus

```
>>> import nltk
>>> from nltk.corpus import PlaintextCorpusReader
>>> imdbcorpus = PlaintextCorpusReader('./training','.*')
>>> from nltk import FreqDist
>>> fd1 = FreqDist(imdbcorpus.words())
>>> fd1.N()  #total number of sample outcomes.  Same as len(imdbcorpus.words())
160035
>>> fd1.B()  #total number of sample values that have counts greater than zero
16715
>>> len(fd1.hapaxes()) #total number of all samples that occur once
7933
>>> frequentwords = fd1.keys() #automatically sorts based on frequency
>>> frequentwords[:50]
[',', 'the', '.', 'and', 'to', 'a', 'of', 'is', 'in', "'", 'his',
's', 'he', 'that', 'with', '-', 'her', '(', 'for', 'by', 'him',
'who', 'on', 'as', 'The', 'has', ')', '"', 'from', 'are', 'they',
'but', 'an', 'she', 'their', 'at', 'it', 'be', 'out', 'up', 'will',
'He', 'when', 'was', 'one', 'this', 'not', 'into', 'them', 'have']
```

Instructions for using the NLTK's collocation functions are availabled at *http://nltk.googlecode.com/svn/trunk/doc/howto/collocations.html*.

Here are two of the basic concepts you need for performing lexical statistics over a corpus:

Corpus size (N)
> The number of tokens in the corpus

Vocabulary size (V)
> The number of types in the corpus

For any tokenized corpus, you can map each token to a type; for example, how many times *the* appears (the number of tokens of the type *the*), and so on. Once we have the word frequency distributions over a corpus, we can calculate two metrics: the *rank/frequency profile* and the *frequency spectrum* of the word frequencies.

To get the rank/frequency profile, you take the type from the frequency list and replace it with its rank, where the most frequent type is given rank 1, and so forth. To build a frequency spectrum, you simply calculate the number of types that have a specific frequency. The first thing one notices with these metrics is that the top few frequency ranks are taken up by function words (i.e., words such as *the*, *a*, and *and*; prepositions; etc.). In the Brown Corpus, the 10 top-ranked words make up 23% of the total corpus size (Baroni 2009). Another observation is that the bottom-ranked words display lots of ties in frequency. For example, in the frequency table for the IMDb corpus, the number of *hapax legomena* (words appearing only once in the corpus) is over 8,000. In the Brown Corpus, about half of the vocabulary size is made up of words that occur only once. The mean or average frequency hides huge deviations. In Brown, the average frequency of a type is 19 tokens, but the mean is increased because of a few very frequent types.

We also notice that most of the words in the corpus have a frequency well below the mean. The mean will therefore be higher than the median, while the mode is usually 1. So, the mean is not a very meaningful indicator of "central tendency," and this is typical of most large corpora.

 Recall the distinctions between the following notions in statistics:

- Mean (or average): The sum of the values divided by the number of values

$$\dot{x} = \frac{1}{n} \sum_{i=4}^{n} x_i$$

- Mode: The most frequent value in the population (or dataset)
- Median: The numerical value that separates the higher half of a population (or sample) from the lower half

Zipf's Law

The uneven distribution of word types shown in the preceding section was first pointed out over a variety of datasets by George Zipf in 1949. He noticed that frequency of a word, $f(w)$, appears as a nonlinearly decreasing function of the rank of the word, $r(w)$, in a corpus, and formulated the following relationship between these two variables:

$$f(w) = \frac{C}{r(w)^a}$$

C is a constant that is determined by the particulars of the corpus, but for now, let's say that it's the frequency of the most frequent word in the corpus. Let's assume that a is 1; then we can quickly see how frequency decreases with rank. Notice that the law is a power law: frequency is a function of the negative power of rank, $-a$. So the first word in the ranking occurs about twice as often as the second word in the ranking, and three times as often as the third word in the ranking, and so on.

N-grams

In this section we introduce the notion of an n-gram. N-grams are important for a wide range of applications in Natural Language Processing (NLP), because fairly straightforward *language models* can be built using them, for speech, Machine Translation, indexing, Information Retrieval (IR), and, as we will see, classification.

Imagine that we have a string of tokens, W, consisting of the elements $w_1, w_2, \ldots, w_n$. Now consider a sliding window over W. If the sliding window consists of one cell (w_i), then the collection of one-cell substrings is called the *unigram* profile of the string; there will be as many unigram profiles as there are elements in the string. Consider now all two-cell substrings, where we look at $w_1\,w_2$, $w_2\,w_3$, and so forth, to the end of the string, $w_{n-1}\,w_n$. These are called *bigram* profiles, and we have $n-1$ bigrams for a string of length n.

Using the definition of conditional probability mentioned earlier, we can define a probability for a token, having seen the previous token, as a *bigram probability*. Thus the conditional probability of an element, w_i, given the previous element, w_{i-1}:

$$P(w_i \mid w_{i-1})$$

Extending this to bigger sliding windows, we can define an n-gram probability as simply the conditional probability of an element given the previous $n-1$ elements. That is:

$$P(w_i \mid w_{i-N-1} \ldots w_{i-1})$$

The most common bigrams in any corpus will most likely not be very interesting to you, however. They involve the most frequent words in word pairs. This happens to usually be boring function word pairs, such as the following:

- of the
- in the
- on the
- in a

If you want to get a more meaningful set of bigrams (and trigrams), you can run the corpus through a part-of-speech (POS) tagger, such as one of those provided by the NLTK. This would filter the bigrams to more content-related pairs involving, for example, adjectives and nouns:

- Star Trek
- Bull Run
- Sidekick Brainiac

This can be a useful way to filter the meaningless n-grams from your results. A better solution, however, is to take advantage of the "natural affinity" that the words in an n-gram have for one another. This includes what are called *collocations*. A collocation is the string created when two or more words co-occur in a language more frequently than by chance. A convenient way to do this over a corpus is through a concept known as *pointwise mutual information (PMI)*. Basically, the intuition behind PMI is as follows. For two words, *X* and *Y*, we would like to know how much one word tells us about the other. For example, given an occurrence of *X*, *x*, and an occurrence of *Y*, *y*, how much does their joint probability differ from the expected value of assuming that they are independent? This can be expressed as follows:

$$pmi(x; y) = \ln \frac{P(x, y)}{P(x)P(y)}$$

In fact, the collocation function provided in the NLTK uses this relation to build bigram collocations. Applying this function to the bigrams from the IMDb corpus, we can see the following results:

```
>>> bigram_measures = nltk.collocations.BigramAssocMeasures()
>>> finder1 = BigramCollocationFinder.from_words(imdbcorpus.words())
>>> finder1.nbest(bigram_measures.pmi, 10)
[('".(', 'Check'), ('10th', 'Sarajevo'), ('16100', 'Patranis'),
('1st', 'Avenue'), ('317', 'Riverside'), ('5000', 'Reward'),
('6310', 'Willoughby'), ('750hp', 'tire'), ('ALEX', 'MILLER'),
('Aasoo', 'Bane')]
>>> finder1.apply_freq_filter(10) #look only at collocations that occur
   10 times or more
>>> finder1.nbest(bigram_measures.pmi, 10)
[('United', 'States'), ('Los', 'Angeles'), ('Bhagwan', 'Shri'),
('martial', 'arts'), ('Lan', 'Yu'), ('Devi', 'Maa'),
('New', 'York'), ('qv', ')),'), ('qv', '))'), ('I', ')'")]
>>> finder1.apply_freq_filter(15)
>>> finder1.nbest(bigram_measures.pmi, 10)
[('Bhagwan', 'Shri'), ('Devi', 'Maa'), ('New', 'York'),
('qv', ')),'), ('qv', '))'), ('I', ')'"), ('no', 'longer'),
('years', 'ago'), ('none', 'other'), ('each', 'other')]
```

One issue with using this simple formula, however, involves the problem of sparse data. That is, the probabilities of observed rare events are overestimated, and the probabilities of unobserved rare events are underestimated. Researchers in computational linguistics have found ways to get around this problem to a certain extent, and we will return to this issue when we discuss ML algorithms in more detail in Chapter 7.

Language Models

So, what good are n-grams? NLP has used n-grams for many years to develop statistical language models that predict sequence behaviors. Sequence behavior is involved in recognizing the next *X* in a sequence of *X*s; for example, Speech Recognition, Machine Translation, and so forth. Language modeling predicts the next element in a sequence, given the previously encountered elements.

Let's see more precisely just how this works, and how it makes use of the tools we discussed in the previous sections. Imagine a sequence of words, $w_1, w_2, \ldots, w_n$. Predicting any "next word" w_i in this sequence is essentially expressed by the following probability function:

$$P(w_i \mid w_1, \ldots, w_{i-1})$$

which is equivalent to:

$$\frac{P(w_1, \ldots, w_i)}{P(w_1, \ldots, w_{i-1})}$$

Notice what's involved with computing these two joint probability distributions. We will assume that the frequency of a word sequence in the corpus will estimate its probability. That is:

$$P(w_1, \ldots, w_{i-1}) = Count(w_1, \ldots, w_{i-1})$$

$$P(w_1, \ldots, w_i) = Count(w_1, \ldots, w_i)$$

giving us the ratio known as the *relative frequency*, shown here:

$$P(w_i \mid w_1, \ldots, w_{i-1}) = \frac{Count(w_1, \ldots, w_i)}{Count(w_1, \ldots, w_{i-1})}$$

 As we just saw, the joint probabilities in the n-gram example can be expressed as conditional probabilities, using the chain rule for sequence behavior, illustrated as follows:

$$P(w_1, w_2 \ldots, w_n) = P(w_1)P(w_2 \mid w_1)P(w_3 \mid w_1, w_2)\ldots P(w_n \mid w_1^{n-1})$$

which can be expressed as:

$$\prod_{k=1}^{n} P(w_k \mid w_1^{k-1})$$

Even though we can, in principle, estimate the probabilities that we need for making our predictive model, there is little chance that we are going to have a lot of data to work with, if we take the joint probability of the entire sequence of words. That is, there are sequences of words that may never have occurred in our corpus, but we still want to be able to predict the behavior associated with the elements contained in them. To solve this problem, we can make some simplifying assumptions regarding the contribution of the elements in the sequence. That is, if we approximate the behavior of a word in a sequence as being dependent on only the word before it, then we have reduced the n-gram probability of:

$$P\left(w_i \mid w_1^{i-1}\right)$$

to this *bigram* probability:

$$P\left(w_i \mid w_{i-1}\right)$$

This is known as the *Markov assumption*, and using it, we can actually get some reasonable statistics for the bigrams in a corpus. These can be used to estimate the bigram probabilities by using the concept of relative frequency mentioned earlier. That is, as before, we take the ratio of the occurrences of the bigram in the corpus to the number of occurrences of the prefix (the single word, in this case) in the corpus, as shown here:

$$P\left(w_i \mid w_{i-1}\right) = \frac{Count\left(w_{i-1},\ w_i\right)}{Count\left(w_i - 1\right)}$$

This procedure is known as a *maximum likelihood estimation (MLE)*, and it provides a fairly direct way to collect statistics that can be used for creating a language model. We will return to these themes in Chapter 7.

Summary

In this chapter we introduced you to the tools you need to analyze the linguistic content of a corpus as well as the kinds of techniques and tools you will need to perform a variety of statistical analytics. In particular, we discussed the following:

- Corpus analytics comprises statistical and probabilistic tools that provide data analysis over your corpus and information for performing inferential statistics. This will be necessary information when you take your annotated corpus and train an ML algorithm on it.
- It is necessary to distinguish between the occurrence of a word in a corpus (the token) and the word itself (the type).
- The total number of tokens in a corpus gives us the corpus size.
- The total number of types in a corpus gives us the vocabulary size.
- The rank/frequency profile of the words in a corpus assigns a ranking to the words, according to how many tokens there are of that word.

- The frequency spectrum of the word gives the number of word types that have a given frequency.

- Zipf's law is a power law stating that the frequency of any word is inversely proportional to its rank.

- Constructing n-grams over the tokens in a corpus is the first step in building language models for many NLP applications.

- Pointwise mutual information is a measure of how dependent one word is on another in a text. This can be used to identify bigrams that are true collocations in a corpus.

- Language models for predicting sequence behavior can be simplified by making the Markov assumption, namely, when predicting a word, only pay attention to the word before it.

CHAPTER 4

Building Your Model and Specification

Now that you've defined your goal and collected a relevant dataset, you need to create the model for your task. But what do we mean by "model"? Basically, the model is the practical representation of your goal: a description of your task that defines the classifications and terms that are relevant to your project. You can also think of it as the aspects of your task that you want to capture within your dataset. These classifications can be represented by metadata, labels that are applied to the text of your corpus, and/or relationships between labels or metadata. In this chapter, we will address the following questions:

- The model is captured by a specification, or spec. But what does a spec look like?

- You have the goals for your annotation project. Where do you start? How do you turn a goal into a model?

- What form should your model take? Are there standardized ways to structure the phenomena?

- How do you take someone else's standard and use it to create a specification?

- What do you do if there are no existing specifications, definitions, or standards for the kinds of phenomena you are trying to identify and model?

- How do you determine when a feature in your description is an element in the spec versus an attribute on an element?

The spec is the concrete representation of your model. So, whereas the model is an abstract idea of what information you want your annotation to capture, and the interpretation of that information, the spec turns those abstract ideas into tags and attributes that will be applied to your corpus.

Some Example Models and Specs

Recall from Chapter 1 that the first part in the MATTER cycle involves creating a model for the task at hand. We introduced a model as a triple, $M = <T,R,I>$, consisting of a vocabulary of terms, T, the relations between these terms, R, and their interpretation, I. However, this is a pretty high-level description of what a model is. So, before we discuss more theoretical aspects of models, let's look at some examples of annotation tasks and see what the models for those look like.

For the most part, we'll be using XML DTD (Document Type Definition) representations. XML is becoming the standard for representing annotation data, and DTDs are the simplest way to show an overview of the type of information that will be marked up in a document. The next few sections will go through what the DTDs for different models will look like, so you can see how the different elements of an annotation task can be translated into XML-compliant forms.

What Is a DTD?

A DTD is a set of declarations containing the basic building blocks that allow an XML document to be validated. DTDs have been covered in depth in other books (O'Reilly's *Learning XML* and *XML in a Nutshell*) and websites (W3schools.com), so we'll give a short overview here.

Essentially, the DTD defines what the structure of an XML document will be by defining what tags will be used inside the document and what attributes those tags will have. By having a DTD, the XML in a file can be validated to ensure that the formatting is correct.

So what do we mean by tags and attributes? Let's take a really basic example: web pages and HTML. If you've ever made a website and edited some code by hand, you're familiar with elements such as <b> and <br />. These are tags that tell a program reading the HTML that the text in between <b> and </b> should be **bold**, and that <br /> indicates a newline should be included when the text is displayed. Annotation tasks use similar formatting, but they define their own tags based on what information is considered important for the goal being pursued. So an annotation task that is based on marking the parts of speech in a text might have tags such as <noun>, <verb>, <adj>, and so on. In a DTD, these tags would be defined like this:

```
<!ELEMENT noun ( #PCDATA ) >
<!ELEMENT verb ( #PCDATA ) >
<!ELEMENT adj ( #PCDATA ) >
```

The string !ELEMENT indicates that the information contained between the < and > is about an element (also known as a "tag"), and the word following it is the name of that tag (noun, verb, adj). The (#PCDATA) indicates that the information between the <noun> and </noun> tags will be parsable character data (other flags instead of #PCDA

TA can be used to provide other information about a tag, but for this book, we're not going to worry about them).

By declaring the three tags in a DTD, we can have a valid XML document that has nouns, verbs, and adjectives all marked up. However, annotation tasks often require more information about a piece of text than just its type. This is where *attributes* come in. For example, knowing that a word is a verb is useful, but it's even more useful to know the tense of the verb—past, present, or future. This can be done by adding an attribute to a tag, which looks like this:

```
<!ELEMENT verb ( #PCDATA ) >
<!ATTLIST verb tense ( past | present | future | none ) #IMPLIED >
```

The !ATTLIST line declares that an attribute called tense is being added to the verb element, and that it has four possible values: past, present, future, and none. The #IMPLIED shows that the information in the attribute isn't required for the XML to be valid (again, don't worry too much about this for now). Now you can have a verb tag that looks like this:

```
<verb tense="present">
```

You can also create attributes that allow annotators to put in their own information, by declaring the attribute's type to be CDATA instead of a list of options, like this:

```
<!ELEMENT verb ( #PCDATA ) >
<!ATTLIST verb tense CDATA #IMPLIED >
```

One last type of element that is commonly used in annotation is a *linking element*, or a *link tag*. These tags are used to show relationships between other parts of the data that have been marked up with tags. For instance, if the part-of-speech (POS) task also wanted to show the relationship between a verb and the noun that performed the action described by the verb, the annotation model might include a link tag called performs, like so:

```
<!ELEMENT performs EMPTY >
<!ATTLIST performs fromID IDREF >
<!ATTLIST performs toID IDREF >
```

The EMPTY in this element tag indicates that the tag will not be applied to any of the text itself, but rather is being used to provide other information about the text. Normally in HTML an empty tag would be something like the <br /> tag, or another tag that stands on its own. In annotation tasks, an empty tag is used to create paths between other, contentful tags.

In a model, it is almost always important to keep track of the order (or *arity*) of the elements involved in the linking relationship. We do this here by using two elements that have the type IDREF, meaning they will refer to other annotated extents or elements in the text by identifiable elements.

We'll talk more about the IDs and the relationship between DTDs and annotated data in Chapter 5, but for now, this should give you enough information to understand the examples provided in this chapter.

 There are other formats that can be used to specify specs for a model. XML schema are sometimes used to create a more complex representation of the tags being used, as is the Backus–Naur Form. However, these formats are more complex than DTDs, and aren't generally necessary to use unless you are using a particular piece of annotation software, or want to have a more restrictive spec. For the sake of simplicity, we will use only DTD examples in this book.

Film Genre Classification

A common task in Natural Language Processing (NLP) and machine learning is classifying documents into categories; for example, using film reviews or summaries to determine the genre of the film being described. If you have a goal of being able to use machine learning to identify the genre of a movie from the movie summary or review, then a corresponding model could be that you want to label the summary with all the genres that the movie applies to, in order to feed those labels into a classifier and train it to identify relevant parts of the document. To turn that model into a spec, you need to think about what that sort of label would look like, presumably in a DTD format.

The easiest way to create a spec for a classification task is to simply create a tag that captures the information you need for your goal and model. In this case, you could create a tag called genre that has an attribute called label, where label holds the values that can be assigned to the movie summary. The simplest incarnation of this spec would be this:

```
<!ELEMENT genre ( #PCDATA ) >
<!ATTLIST genre label CDATA #IMPLIED >
```

This DTD has the required tag and attribute, and allows for any information to be added to the label attribute. Functionally for annotation purposes, this means the annotator would be responsible for filling in the genres that she thinks apply to the text. Of course, a large number of genre terms have been used, and not everyone will agree on what a "standard" list of genres should be—for example, are "fantasy" and "sci-fi" different genres, or should they be grouped into the same category? Are "mystery" films different from "noir"? Because the list of genres will vary from person to person, it might be better if your DTD specified a list of genres that annotators could choose from, like this:

```
<!ELEMENT genre ( #PCDATA ) >
<!ATTLIST genre label ( Action | Adventure | Animation | Biography | Comedy |
    Crime | Documentary | Drama | Family | Fantasy | Film-Noir | Game-Show |
```

History | Horror | Music | Musical | Mystery | News | Reality-TV | Romance |
Sci-Fi | Sport | Talk-Show | Thriller | War | Western) >

The list in the `label` attribute is taken from IMDb's list of genres (*http://www.imdb.com/genre*). Naturally, since other genre lists exist (e.g., Netflix also has a list of genres (*http://www2.netflix.com/AllGenresList*)), you would want to choose the one that best matches your task, or create your own list. As you go through the process of annotation and the rest of the MATTER cycle, you'll find places where your model/spec needs to be revised in order to get the results you want. This is perfectly normal, even for tasks that seem as straightforward as putting genre labels on movie summaries—annotator opinions can vary, even when the task is as clearly defined as you can make it. And computer algorithms don't really think and interpret the way that people do, so even when you get past the annotation phase, you may still find places where, in order to maximize the correctness of the algorithm, you would have to change your model.

For example, looking at the genre list from IMDb we see that "romance" and "comedy" are two separate genres, and so the summary of a romantic comedy would have to have two labels: `romance` and `comedy`. But if, in a significant portion of reviews, those two tags appear together, an algorithm may learn to *always* associate the two, even when the summary being classified is really a romantic drama or musical comedy. So, you might find it necessary to create a `rom-com` label to keep your classifier from creating false associations.

In the other direction, there are many historical action movies that take place over very different periods in history, and a machine learning (ML) algorithm may have trouble finding enough common ground between a summary of *300*, *Braveheart*, and *Pearl Harbor* to create an accurate association with the history genre. In that case, you might find it necessary to add different levels of historical genres, ones that reflect different periods in history, to train a classifier in the most accurate way possible.

 If you're unclear on how the different components of the ML algorithm can be affected by the spec, or why you might need to adapt a model to get better results, don't worry! For now, just focus on turning your goal into a set of tags, and the rest will come later. But if you really want to know how this works, Chapter 7 has an overview of all the different ways that ML algorithms "learn," and what it means to train each one.

Adding Named Entities

Of course, reworking the list of genres isn't the only way to change a model to better fit a task. Another way is to add tags and attributes that will more closely reflect the information that's relevant to your goal. In the case of the movie summaries, it might be useful to keep track of some of the Named Entities (NEs) that appear in the summaries that may give insight into the genre of the film. An NE is an entity (an object in the world) that has a name which uniquely identifies it by name, nickname, abbreviation, and so on. "O'Reilly," "Brandeis University," "Mount Hood," "IBM," and "Vice President" are all examples of NEs. In the movie genre task, it might be helpful to keep track of NEs such as film titles, directors, writers, actors, and characters that are mentioned in the summaries.

You can see from the list in the preceding paragraph that there are many different NEs in the model that we would like to capture. Because the model is abstract, the practical application of these NEs to a spec or DTD has to be decided upon. There are often many ways in which a model can be represented in a DTD, due to the categorical nature of annotation tasks and of XML itself. In this case there are two primary ways in which the spec could be created. We could have a single tag called named_entity with an attribute that would have each of the items from the previous list, like this:

```
<!ELEMENT named_entity ( #PCDATA ) >
<!ATTLIST named_entity role (film_title | director |
  writer | actor | character ) >
```

Or each role could be given its own tag, like this:

```
<!ELEMENT film_title ( #PCDATA ) >
<!ELEMENT director ( #PCDATA ) >
<!ELEMENT writer ( #PCDATA ) >
<!ELEMENT actor ( #PCDATA ) >
<!ELEMENT character ( #PCDATA ) >
```

While these two specs seem to be very different, in many ways they are interchangeable. It would not be difficult to take an XML file with the first DTD and change it to one that is compliant with the second. Often the choices that you'll make about how your spec will represent your model will be influenced by other factors, such as what format is easier for your annotators, or what works better with the annotation software you are using. We'll talk more about the considerations that go into which formats to use in Chapter 5 and Chapter 6.

By giving ML algorithms more information about the words in the document that are being classified, such as by annotating the NEs, it's possible to create more accurate representations of what's going on in the text, and to help the classifier pick out markers that might make the classifications better.

Semantic Roles

Another layer of information that might be useful in examining movie summaries is to annotate the relationships between the NEs that are marked up in the text. These relationships are called *semantic roles*, and they are used to explicitly show the connections between the elements in a sentence. In this case, it could be helpful to annotate the relationships between actors and characters, and the staff of the movie and which movie they worked on. Consider the following example summary/review:

> In *Love, Actually*, writer/director Richard Curtis weaves a convoluted tale about characters and their relationships. Of particular note is Liam Neeson *(Schindler's List, Star Wars)* as Daniel, a man struggling to deal with the death of his wife and the relationship with his young stepson, Sam (Thomas Sangster). Emma Thompson *(Sense and Sensibility, Henry V)* shines as a middle-aged housewife whose marriage with her husband (played by Alan Rickman) is under siege by a beautiful secretary. While this movie does have its purely comedic moments (primarily presented by Bill Nighy as out-of-date rock star Billy Mack), this movie avoids the more in-your-face comedy that Curtis has presented before as a writer for *Blackadder* and *Mr. Bean*, presenting instead a remarkable, gently humorous insight into what love, actually, is.

Using one of the NE DTDs from the preceding section would lead to a number of annotated extents, but due to the density, an algorithm may have difficulty determining who goes with what. By adding semantic role labels such as `acts_in`, `acts_as`, `directs`, `writes`, and `character_in`, the relationships between all the NEs will become much clearer.

As with the DTD for the NEs, we are faced with a choice between using a single tag with multiple attribute options:

```
<!ELEMENT sem_role ( EMPTY ) >
<!ATTLIST sem_role from IDREF >
<!ATTLIST sem_role to IDREF >
<!ATTLIST sem_role label (acts_in |
  acts_as | directs | writes | character_in ) >
```

or a tag for each semantic role we wish to capture:

```
<!ELEMENT acts_in ( EMPTY ) >
<!ATTLIST acts_in from IDREF >
<!ATTLIST acts_in to IDREF >

<!ELEMENT acts_as ( EMPTY ) >
<!ATTLIST acts_as from IDREF >
<!ATTLIST acts_as to IDREF >

<!ELEMENT directs ( EMPTY ) >
<!ATTLIST directs from IDREF >
<!ATTLIST directs to IDREF >

<!ELEMENT writes ( EMPTY ) >
<!ATTLIST writes from IDREF >
<!ATTLIST writes to IDREF >

<!ELEMENT character_in ( EMPTY ) >
<!ATTLIST character_in from IDREF >
<!ATTLIST character_in to IDREF >
```

You'll notice that this time, the DTD specifies that each of these elements is EMPTY, meaning that no character data is associated directly with the tag. Remember that linking tags in annotation are usually defined by EMPTY tags specifically because links between elements do not generally have text associated with them in particular, but rather clarify a relationship between two or more other extents. We'll discuss the application of linking and other types of tags in Chapter 5.

Multimodel Annotations

It may be the case that your annotation task requires more than one model to fully capture the data you need. This happens most frequently when a task requires information from two or more very different levels of linguistics, or if information from two different domains needs to be captured. For example, an annotation over a corpus that's made up of documents that require training to understand, such as clinical notes, scientific papers, or legal documents, may require that annotators have training in those fields, and that the annotation task be tailored to the domain.

In general, employing different annotation models in the same task simply means that more than one MATTER cycle is being worked through at the same time, and that the different models will likely be focused on different aspects of the corpus or language being explored. In these cases, it is important that all the models be coordinated, however, and that changes made to one model during the MATTER cycle don't cause conflict with the others.

If your corpus is made up of domain-specific documents (such as the clinical notes that we mentioned before), and your annotation task requires that your annotators be able to interpret these documents (e.g., if you are trying to determine which patients have a particular disease), then one of your models may need to be a *light annotation task* (Stubbs 2012).

A light annotation task is essentially a way to formulate an annotation model that allows a domain expert (such as a doctor) to provide her insight into a text without being required to link her knowledge to one of the layers of linguistic understanding. Such an annotation task might be as simple as having the domain expert indicate whether a file has a particular property (such as whether or not a patient is at risk for diabetes), or it may involve annotating the parts of the text associated with a disease state. However, the domain expert won't be asked to mark POS tags or map every noun in the text to a semantic interpretation: those aspects of the text would be handled in a different model altogether, and merged at the end.

There is a slightly different philosophy behind the creation of light annotation tasks than that of more "traditional" annotations: light annotations focus on encoding an answer to a particular question about a text, rather than creating a complete record of a particular linguistic phenomenon, with the purpose of later merging all the different models into a single annotation. However, aside from the difference in goal, light annotation tasks still follow the MATTER and MAMA cycles. Because of this, we aren't going to use them as examples in this book, and instead will stick to more traditional linguistic annotations.

If you are interested in performing an annotation task that requires domain-specific knowledge, and therefore would benefit from using a light annotation task, a methodology for creating a light annotation and incorporating it into the MATTER cycle is developed and presented in Stubbs 2012.

Adopting (or Not Adopting) Existing Models

Now that you have an idea of how specs can represent a model, let's look a little more closely at some of the details we just presented. You might recall from Chapter 1 that when we discussed semantic roles we presented a very different list from `acts_in`, `acts_as`, `directs`, `writes`, and `character_in`. Here's what the list looked like:

Agent
> The event participant that is doing or causing the event to occur

Theme/figure
> The event participant who undergoes a change in position or state

Experiencer
> The event participant who experiences or perceives something

Source
> The location or place from which the motion begins; the person from whom the theme is given

Goal
> The location or place to which the motion is directed or terminates

Recipient
> The person who comes into possession of the theme

Patient
> The event participant who is affected by the event

Instrument
> The event participant used by the agent to do or cause the event

Location/ground
> The location or place associated with the event itself

Similarly, we also presented an ontology that defined the categories Organization, Person, Place, and Time. This set of labels can be viewed as a simple model of NE types that are commonly used in other annotation tasks.

So, if these models exist, why didn't we just use them for our film genre annotation task? Why did we create our own sets of labels for our spec? Just as when defining the goal of your annotation you need to think about the trade-off between informativity and correctness, when creating the model and spec for your annotation task, you need to consider the trade-off between *generality* and *specificity*.

Creating Your Own Model and Specification: Generality Versus Specificity

The ontology consisting of Organization, Person, Place, and Time is clearly a very general model for entities in a text, but for the film genre annotation task, it is much too general to be useful for the kinds of distinctions we want to be able to make. Of the NE labels that we identified earlier, four of them ("director," "writer," "actor," and "character") would fall under the label "Person," and "film title" doesn't clearly fit under any of them. Using these labels would lead to unhelpful annotations in two respects: first, the labels used would be so generic as to be useless for the task (labeling everyone as "Person" won't help distinguish one movie review from another); and second, it would be difficult to explain to the annotators that, while you've given them a set of labels, you don't want every instance of those types of entities labeled, but rather only those that are relevant to the film (so, for example, a mention of another reviewer would not be labeled as a "Person"). Clearly, overly general tags in a spec can lead to confusion during annotation.

On the other hand, we could have made the tags in the spec even more specific, such as `actor_star`, `actor_minor_character`, `character_main`, `character_minor`, `writer_film`, `writer_book`, `writer_book_and_film`, and so on. But what would be gained from such a complicated spec? While it's possible to think of an annotation task where it might be necessary to label all that information (perhaps one that was looking at how these different people are described in movie reviews), remember that the task we defined was, first, simply labeling the genres of films as they are described in summaries and reviews, and then expanding it to include some other information that might be relevant to making that determination. Using overly specific tags in this case would decrease how useful the annotations would be, and also increase the amount of work done by the annotators for no obvious benefit. Figure 4-1 shows the different levels of the hierarchy we are discussing. The top two levels are too vague, while the bottom is too specific to be useful. The third level is just right for this task.

We face the same dichotomy when examining the list of semantic roles. The list given in linguistic textbooks is a very general list of roles that can be applied to the nouns in a sentence, but any annotation task trying to use them for film-related roles would have to have a way to limit which nouns were assigned roles by the annotator, and most of the roles related to the NEs we're interested in would simply be "agent"—a label that is neither helpful nor interesting for this task. So, in order to create a task that was in the right place regarding generality and specificity, we developed our own list of roles that were particular to this task.

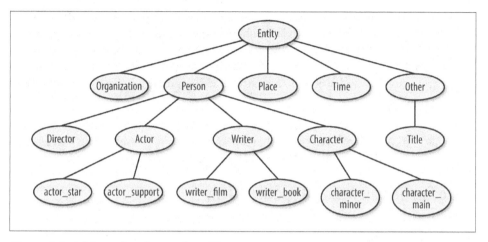

Figure 4-1. A hierarchy of named entities

 We haven't really gotten into the details of NE and semantic role annotation using existing models, but these are not trivial annotation tasks. If you're interested in learning more about annotation efforts that use these models, check out FrameNet (*https://framenet.icsi.berke ley.edu/fndrupal/*) for semantic roles, and the Message Understanding Conferences (MUCs) for examples of NE and coreference annotation.

Overall, there are a few things that you want to make sure your model and specification have in order to proceed with your task. They should:

- Contain a representation of all the tags and links relevant to completing your goal.
- Be relevant to the implementation stated in your goal (if your purpose is to classify documents by genre, spending a lot of time annotating temporal information is probably not going to be of immediate help).
- Be grounded in existing research as much as possible. Even if there's no existing annotation spec that meets your goal completely, you can still take advantage of research that's been done on related topics, which will make your own research much easier.

Specifically to the last point on the list, even though the specs we've described for the film genre annotation task use sets of tags that we created for this purpose, it's difficult to say that they weren't based on an existing model to some extent. Obviously some knowledge about NEs and semantic roles helped to inform how we described the annotation task, and helped us to decide whether annotating those parts of the document would be useful. But you don't need to be a linguist to know that nouns can be assigned to different groups, and that the relationships between different nouns and verbs can be important to keep track of. Ultimately, while it's entirely possible that your annotation task is completely innovative and new, it's still worth taking a look at some related research and resources and seeing if any of them are helpful for getting your model and spec put together.

The best way to find out if a spec exists for your task is to do a search for existing annotated datasets. If you aren't sure where to start, or Google results seem overwhelming, check Appendix A for the list of corpora and their annotations.

Using Existing Models and Specifications

While the examples we discussed thus far had fairly clear-cut reasons for us to create our own tags for the spec, there are some advantages to basing your annotation task on existing models. Interoperability is a big concern in the computer world, and it's actually a pretty big concern in linguistics as well—if you have an annotation that you want to share with other people, there are a few things that make it easier to share, such as using existing annotation standards (e.g., standardized formats for your annotation files), using software to create the annotation that other people can also use, making your annotation guidelines available to other people, and using models or specifications that have already been vetted in similar tasks. We'll talk more about standards and formats later in this chapter and in the next one; for now, we'll focus just on models and specs.

Using models or specs that other people have used can benefit your project in a few ways. First of all, if you use the specification from an annotation project that's already been done, you have the advantage of using a system that's already been vetted, and one that may also come with an annotated corpus, which you can use to train your own algorithms or use to augment your own dataset (assuming that the usage restrictions on the corpus allow for that, of course).

In "Background Research" on page 40, we mentioned some places to start looking for information that would be useful with defining your goal, so presumably you've already done some research into the topics you're interested in (if you haven't, now is a good time to go back and do so). Even if there's no existing spec for your topic, you might find a descriptive model similar to the one we provided for semantic roles.

Not all annotation and linguistic models live in semantic textbooks! The list of film genres that we used was taken from IMDb.com, and there are many other places where you can get insight into how to frame your model and specification. A recent paper on annotating bias used the Wikipedia standards for editing pages as the standard for developing a spec and annotation guidelines for an annotation project (Herzig et al. 2011). Having a solid linguistic basis for your task can certainly help, but don't limit yourself to only linguistic resources!

If you are lucky enough to find both a model and a specification that are suitable for your task, you still might need to make some changes for them to fit your goal. For example, if you are doing temporal annotation, you can start with the TimeML specification, but you may find that the TIMEX3 tag is simply too much information for your purposes, or too overwhelming for your annotators. The TIMEX3 DTD description is as follows:

```
<!ELEMENT TIMEX3 ( #PCDATA ) >
<!ATTLIST TIMEX3 start #IMPLIED >
<!ATTLIST TIMEX3 tid ID #REQUIRED >
<!ATTLIST TIMEX3 type ( DATE | DURATION | SET | TIME ) #REQUIRED >
<!ATTLIST TIMEX3 value NMTOKEN #REQUIRED >
<!ATTLIST TIMEX3 anchorTimeID IDREF #IMPLIED >
<!ATTLIST TIMEX3 beginPoint IDREF #IMPLIED >
<!ATTLIST TIMEX3 endPoint IDREF #IMPLIED >
<!ATTLIST TIMEX3 freq NMTOKEN #IMPLIED >
<!ATTLIST TIMEX3 functionInDocument ( CREATION_TIME | EXPIRATION_TIME |
  MODIFICATION_TIME | PUBLICATION_TIME | RELEASE_TIME | RECEPTION_TIME |
  NONE ) #IMPLIED >
<!ATTLIST TIMEX3 mod ( BEFORE | AFTER | ON_OR_BEFORE | ON_OR_AFTER | LESS_THAN |
  MORE_THAN | EQUAL_OR_LESS | EQUAL_OR_MORE | START | MID | END |
  APPROX )  #IMPLIED >
<!ATTLIST TIMEX3 quant CDATA #IMPLIED >
<!ATTLIST TIMEX3 temporalFunction ( false | true ) #IMPLIED >
<!ATTLIST TIMEX3 valueFromFunction IDREF #IMPLIED >
<!ATTLIST TIMEX3 comment CDATA #IMPLIED >
```

A lot of information is encoded in a TIMEX3 tag. While the information is there for a reason—years of debate and modification took place to create this description of a temporal reference—there are certainly annotation tasks where this level of detail will be unhelpful, or even detrimental. If this is the case, other temporal annotation tasks have been done over the years that have specs that you may find more suitable for your goal and model.

Using Models Without Specifications

It's entirely possible—even likely—that your annotation task may be based on a linguistic (or psychological or sociological) phenomenon that has been clearly explained in the literature, but has not yet been turned into a specification. In that case, you will have to decide the form the specification will take, in much the same way that we discussed in the first section of this chapter. Depending on how fleshed out the model is, you may have to make decisions about what parts of the model become tags, what become attributes, and what become links. In some ways this can be harder than simply creating your own model and spec, because you will be somewhat constrained by someone else's description of the phenomenon. However, having a specification that is grounded in an established theory will make your own work easier to explain and distribute, so there are advantages to this approach as well.

Many (if not all) of the annotation specifications that are currently in wide use are based on theories of language that were created prior to the annotation task being created. For example, the TLINK tag in ISO-TimeML is based largely on James Allen's work in temporal reasoning (Allen 1984; Pustejovsky et al. 2003), and ISO-Space has been influenced by the qualitative spatial reasoning work of Randell et al. (1992) and others. Similarly, syntactic bracketing and POS labeling work, as well as existing semantic role labeling, are all based on models developed over years of linguistic research and then applied through the creation of syntactic specifications.

Different Kinds of Standards

Previously we mentioned that one of the aspects of having an interoperable annotation project is using a standardized format for your annotation files, as well as using existing models and specs. However, file specifications are not the only kind of standards that exist in annotation: there are also annotation specifications that have been accepted by the community as go-to (or de facto) standards for certain tasks. While there are no mandated (a.k.a. de jure) standards in the annotation community, there are varying levels and types of de facto standards that we will discuss here.

ISO Standards

The International Organization for Standardization (ISO) is the body responsible for creating standards that are used around the world for ensuring compatibility of systems between businesses and government, and across borders. ISO is the organization that helps determine what the consensus will be for many different aspects of daily life, such as the size of DVDs, representation of dates and times, and so on. There are even ISO standards for representing linguistic annotations in general and for certain types of specifications, in particular ISO-TimeML and ISO-Space. Of course, you aren't *required* to use ISO standards (there's no Annotation Committee that enforces use of these standards), but they do represent a good starting point for most annotation tasks, particularly those standards related to representation.

ISO standards are created with the intent of interoperability, which sets them apart from other de facto standards, as those often become the go-to representation simply because they were there first, or were used by a large community at the outset and gradually became ingrained in the literature. While this doesn't mean that non-ISO standards are inherently problematic, it does mean that they may not have been created with interoperability in mind.

Annotation format standards

Linguistic annotation projects are being done all over the world for many different, but often complementary, reasons. Because of this, in the past few years ISO has been developing the Linguistic Annotation Framework (LAF), a model for annotation projects that is abstract enough to apply to any level of linguistic annotation.

How can a model be flexible enough to encompass all of the different types of annotation tasks? LAF takes a two-pronged approach to standardization. First, it focuses on the structure of the data, rather than the content. Specifically, the LAF standard allows for annotations to be represented in any format that the task organizers like, so long as it can be transmuted into LAF's XML-based "dump format," which acts as an interface for all manner of annotations. The dump format has the following qualities (Ide and Romary 2006):

- The annotation is kept separate from the text it is based on, and annotations are associated with character or element offsets derived from the text.

- Each level of annotation is stored in a separate document.

- Annotations that represent hierarchical information (e.g., syntax trees) must be either represented with embedding in the XML dump format, or use a flat structure that symbolically represents relationships.

- When different annotations are merged, the dump format must be able to integrate overlapping annotations in a way that is compatible with XML.

The first bullet point—keeping annotation separate from the text—now usually takes the form of stand-off annotation (as opposed to inline annotation, where the tags and text are intermingled). We'll go through all the forms that annotation can take and the pros and cons in Chapter 5.

The other side of the approach that LAF takes toward standardization is encouraging researchers to use established labels for linguistic annotation. This means that instead of just creating your own set of POS or NE tags, you can go to the Data Category Registry (DCR) for definitions of existing tags, and use those to model your own annotation task. Alternatively, you can name your tag whatever you want, but when transmuting to the dump format, you would provide information about what tags in the DCR your own tags are equivalent to. This will help other people merge existing annotations, because it will be known whether two annotations are equivalent despite naming differences. The DCR is currently under development (it's not an easy task to create a repository of all annotation tags and levels, and so progress has been made very carefully). You can see the information as it currently exists at *www.isocat.org*.

Timeline of Standardization

LAF didn't emerge as an ISO standard from out of nowhere. Here's a quick rundown of where the standards composing the LAF model originated:

- 1987: The Text Encoding Initiative (TEI) is founded "to develop guidelines for encoding machine-readable texts in the humanities and social sciences." The TEI is still an active organization today. See *http://www.tei-c.org*.

- 1990: The TEI releases its first set of *Guidelines for the Encoding and Interchange of Machine Readable Texts*. It recommends that encoding be done using SGML (Standard Generalized Markup Language), the precursor to XML and HTML.

- 1993: The Expert Advisory Group on Language Engineering Standards (EAGLES) is formed to provide standards for large-scale language resources (ex, corpora), as well as standards for manipulating and evaluating those resources. See *http://www.ilc.cnr.it/EAGLES/home.html*.

- 1998: The Corpus Encoding Standard (CES), also based on SGML, is released. The CES is a corpus-specific application of the standards laid out in the TEI's *Guidelines* and was developed by the EAGLES group. See *http://www.cs.vassar.edu/CES/*.

- 2000: The Corpus Encoding Standard for XML (XCES) is released, again under the EAGLES group. See *http://www.xces.org/*.

- 2002: The TEI releases version P4 of its *Guidelines*, the first version to implement XML. See *http://www.tei-c.org/Guidelines/P4/*.

- 2004: The first document describing the Linguistic Annotation Framework is released (Ide and Romary 2004).

- 2007: The most recent version (P5) of the TEI *Guidelines* is released. See *http://www.tei-c.org/Guidelines/P5/*.

- 2012: LAF and the TEI *Guidelines* are still being updated and improved to reflect progress made in corpus and computational linguistics.

Annotation specification standards

In addition to helping create standards for annotation formats, ISO is working on developing standards for specific annotation tasks. We mentioned ISO-TimeML already, which is the standard for representing temporal information in a document. There is also ISO-Space, the standard for representing locations, spatial configurations, and movement in natural language. The area of ISO that is charged with looking at annotation standards for all areas of natural language is called TC 37/SC 4. Other projects involve the development of standards for how to encode syntactic categories and morphological information in different languages, semantic role labeling, dialogue act labeling, discourse relation annotation, and many others. For more information, you can visit the ISO web page or check out Appendix A of this book.

Community-Driven Standards

In addition to the committee-based standards provided by ISO, a number of de facto standards have been developed in the annotation community simply through wide use. These standards are created when an annotated resource is formed and made available for general use. Because corpora and related resources can be very time-consuming to create, once a corpus is made available it will usually quickly become part of the literature. By extension, whatever annotation scheme was used for that corpus will also tend to become a standard.

If there is a spec that is relevant to your project, taking advantage of community-driven standards can provide some very useful benefit. Any existing corpora that are related to your effort will be relevant, since they are developed using the spec you want to adopt. Additionally, because resources such as these are often in wide use, searching the literature for mentions of the corpus will often lead you to papers that are relevant to your own research goals, and will help you identify any problems that might be associated with the dataset or specification. Finally, datasets that have been around long enough often have tools and interfaces built around them that will make the datasets easier for you to use.

 Community-driven standards don't necessarily follow LAF guidelines, or make use of other ISO standards. This doesn't mean they should be disregarded, but if interoperability is important to you, you may have to do a little extra work to make your corpus fit the LAF guidelines.

We have a list of existing corpora in Appendix C to help you get started in finding resources that are related to your own annotation task. While the list is as complete as we could make it, it is not exhaustive, and you should still check online for resources that would be useful to you. The list that we have was compiled from the LRE Map (*http://www.resourcebook.eu/LreMap/faces/views/resourceMap.xhtml*), a database of NLP resources maintained by the European Language Resources Association (ELRA).

Other Standards Affecting Annotation

While the ISO and community-driven standards are generally the only standards *directly* related to annotation and NLP, there are many standards in day-to-day life that can affect your annotation project. For example, the format that you choose to store your data in (Unicode, UTF-8, UTF-16, ASCII, etc.) will affect how easily other people will be able to use your texts on their own computers. This becomes especially tricky if you are annotating in a language other than English, where the alphabet uses different sets of characters. Even languages with characters that overlap with English (French, Spanish, Italian, etc.) can be problematic when accented vowels are used. We recommend using UTF-8 for encoding most languages, as it is an encoding that captures most characters that you will encounter, and it is available for nearly all computing platforms.

Other standards that can affect a project are those that vary by region, such as the representation of dates and times. If you have a project in which it is relevant to know when the document was created, or how to interpret the dates in the text, it's often necessary to know where the document originated. In the United States, dates are often represented as MM-DD-YYYY, whereas in other countries dates are written in the format DD-MM-YYYY. So if you see the date 01-03-1999 in a text, knowing where it's from might help you determine whether the date is January 3 or March 1. Adding to the confusion, most computers will store dates as YYYY-MM-DD so that the dates can be easily sorted.

Similarly, naming conventions can also cause confusion. When annotating NEs, if you're making a distinction between given names and family names, again the origin of the text can be a factor in how the names should be annotated. This can be especially confusing, because while it might be a convention in a country for people to be referred to by their family name first (as in Hungary, South Korea, or Japan), if the text you are annotating has been translated, the names may have been (or may not have been) swapped by the translator to follow the convention of the language being translated to.

None of the issues we've mentioned should be deal breakers for your project, but they are definitely things to be aware of. Depending on your task, you may also run into regional variations in language or pronunciation, which can be factors that you should take into account when creating your corpus. Additionally, you may need to modify your model or specification to allow for annotating different formats of things such as dates and names if you find that your corpus has more diversity in it than you initially thought.

Summary

In this chapter we defined what models and specifications are, and looked at some of the factors that should be taken into account when creating a model and spec for your own annotation task. Specifically, we discussed the following:

- The model of your annotation project is the abstract representation of your goal, and the specification is the concrete representation of it.

- XML DTDs are a handy way to represent a specification; they can be applied directly to an annotation task.

- Most models and specifications can be represented using three types of tags: document-level labels, extent tags, and link tags.

- When creating your specification, you will need to consider the trade-off between generality and specificity. Going too far in either direction can make your task confusing and unmanageable.

- Searching existing datasets, annotation guidelines, and related publications and conferences is a good way to find existing models and specifications for your task.

- Even if no existing task is a perfect fit for your goal, modifying an existing specification can be a good way to keep your project grounded in linguistic theories.

- Interoperability and standardization are concerns if you want to be able to share your projects with other people. In particular, text encoding and annotation format can have a big impact on how easily other people can use your corpus and annotations.

- Both ISO standards and community-driven standards are useful bases for creating your model and specification.

- Regional differences in standards of writing, text representation, and other natural language conventions can have an effect on your task, and may need to be represented in your specification.

CHAPTER 5

Applying and Adopting Annotation Standards

Now that you've created the spec for your annotation goal, you're almost ready to actually start annotating your corpus. However, before you get to annotating you need to consider what form your annotated data will take—that is to say, you know *what* you want your annotators to do, but you have to decide *how* you want them to do it. In this chapter we'll examine the different formats annotation can take, and discuss the pros and cons of each one by answering the following questions:

- What does annotation look like?
- Are different types of tasks represented differently? If so, how?
- How can you ensure that your annotation can be used by other people and in conjunction with other tasks?
- What considerations go into deciding on an annotation environment and data format, both for the annotators and for machine learning?

Before getting into the details of how to apply your spec to your corpus, you need to understand what annotation actually looks like when it has been applied to a document or text. So now let's look at the spec examples from Chapter 4 and see how they can be applied to an actual corpus.

There are many different ways to represent information about a corpus. The examples we show you won't be exhaustive, but they will give you an overview of some of the different formats that annotated data can take.

Keep your data accessible. Your annotation project will be much easier to manage if you choose a format for your data that's easy for you to modify and access. Using intricate database systems or complicated XML schemas to define your data is fine if you're used to them, but if you aren't you'll be better off keeping things simple.

Annotation tasks range from simple document labeling to text extent tagging and tag linking. As specs and tasks grow in complexity, more information needs to be contained within the annotation. In the following sections we'll discuss the most common ways that these tasks are represented in data, and the pros and cons of each style.

Metadata Annotation: Document Classification

In Chapter 4 we discussed one example of a document classification task, that of labeling the genres of a movie based on a summary or review by using nonexclusive category labels (a movie can be both a comedy and a Western, for example). However, before we get to multiple category labels for a document, let's look at a slightly simpler example: labeling movie reviews as positive, negative, or neutral toward the movie they are reviewing. This is a simpler categorization exercise because the labels will not overlap; each document will have only a single classification.

Unique Labels: Movie Reviews

Let's say you have a corpus of 100 movie reviews, with roughly equal amounts of positive, negative, and neutral documents. By reading each document, you (or your annotators) can determine which category each document should be labeled as, but how are you going to represent that information? Here are a few suggestions for what you can do:

- Have a text file or other simple file format (e.g., comma-separated) containing a list of filenames, and its associated label.
- Create a database file and have your annotators enter SQL commands to add files to the appropriate table.
- Create a folder for each label on your computer, and as each review is classified, move the file into the appropriate folder.
- Have the annotators change the filename to add the word *positive*, *negative*, or *neutral*, as in *review0056-positive.txt*.
- Add the classification inside the file containing the review.

Notice that these options run the gamut from completely external representations of the annotation data, where the information is stored in completely different files, to entirely internal, where the information is kept inside the same document. They also cover the middle ground, where the information is kept in the filesystem—near the corpus but not completely part of it.

So which of these systems is best? In Chapter 4, we discussed the importance of the LAF standard, and explained why stand-off annotation is preferable to making changes to the actual text of the corpus. So the last option on the list isn't one that's preferable.

But how do you choose between the other four options? They are all recording the annotation information while still preserving the format of the data; is one really better than the other? In terms of applying the model to the data, we would argue that no, there's no real difference between any of the remaining options. Each representation could be turned into any of the others without loss of data or too much effort (assuming that you or someone you know can do some basic programming, or is willing to do some reformatting by hand).

So the actual decision here is going to be based on other factors, such as what will be easiest for your annotators and what will result in the most accurate annotations. Asking your annotators to learn SQL commands in order to create tables might be the best option from your perspective, but unless your annotators are already familiar with that language and an accompanying interface, chances are that using such a system will greatly slow the annotation process, and possibly result in inaccurate annotations or even loss of data if someone manages to delete your database.

 Be aware of sources of error! Annotation tasks are often labor-intensive and require attention to detail, so any source of confusion or mistakes will probably crop up at least a few times.

Having your annotators type information can also be problematic, even with a simple labeling task such as this one. Consider giving your annotators a folder of text files and a spreadsheet containing a list of all the filenames. If you ask your annotators to fill in the spreadsheet slots next to each filename with the label, what if they are using a program that will "helpfully" suggest options for autofilling each box? If you are using the labels *positive*, *negative*, or *neutral*, the last two both start with "ne", and if an annotator gets tired or doesn't pay attention, she may find herself accidentally filling in the wrong label. Figure 5-1 shows how easily this could happen in a standard spreadsheet editor. In a situation like that, you might want to consider using a different set of words, such as *likes*, *dislikes*, and *indifferent*.

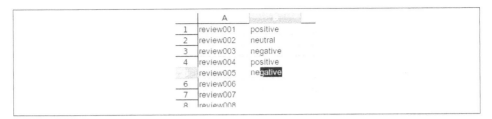

Figure 5-1. A possible source of error in annotation

Of course, this doesn't mean it's impossible to complete a task by using a spreadsheet and classifications that are a bit similar. In some cases, such circumstances are impossible to avoid. However, it's never a bad idea to keep an eye out for places where mistakes can easily slip in.

 While we didn't discuss the movie review annotation scenario in Chapter 4, we have assumed here that we have a schema that contains three categories. However, that is by no means the only way to frame this task and to categorize movie reviews. In the Movie Review Corpus that comes with the Natural Language Toolkit (NLTK), reviews are divided into only positive and negative (based on the scores provided in the reviews themselves), and RottenTomatoes.com also uses a binary classification. On the other hand, Metacritic.com rates everything on a scale from 0 to 100.

Both of these websites provide annotation guidelines for reviews that don't give preassigned numeric ratings, and each of those websites has its editors assign ratings based on their own systems (Metacritic.com; RottenTomatoes.com).

Multiple Labels: Film Genres

As your tasks grow in complexity, there are more limiting factors for how to structure your annotations. For example, there are a number of ways to approach the task of labeling movie reviews that only allow one label per document, but what happens if it's possible for a document to have more than one label? In Chapter 4 we started discussing a spec for a task involving labeling movie summaries with their associated genres. Let's expand on that example now, to see how we can handle more complex annotation tasks.

While it might be tempting to simply say, "Well, we'll only give a single label to each movie," attempting to follow that guideline becomes difficult quickly. Are romantic comedies considered romances, or comedies? You could add "romantic comedy" as a genre label, but will you create a new label for every movie that crosses over a genre line? Such a task quickly becomes ridiculous, simply due to the number of possible combinations. So, define your genres and allow annotators to put as many labels as necessary on each movie (in Chapter 6 we'll discuss in more detail possible approaches to guidelines for such a task).

So how should this information be captured? Of the options listed for the movie review task, some of them can be immediately discarded. Having your annotators change the names of the files to contain the labels is likely to be cumbersome for both the annotators and you: *Casablanca-drama.txt* is easy enough, but *Spaceballs-sciencefiction_comedy_action_parody.txt* would be annoying for an annotator to create, and equally annoying for you to parse into a more usable form (especially if spelling errors start to sneak in).

Moving files into appropriately labeled folders is also more difficult with this task; a copy of the file would have to be created for each label, and it would be much harder to gather basic information such as how many labels, on average, each movie was given. It would also be much, much harder for annotators to determine if they missed a label.

In Figure 5-1 we showed a sample spreadsheet with filenames and positive/negative/neutral labels in different columns, with a different row for each review. While it would certainly be possible to create a spreadsheet set up the same way to give to your annotators, it's not hard to imagine how error-prone that sort of input would be for a task with even more category options and more potential columns per movie.

So where does that leave us? If none of the simpler ways of labeling data are available, then it's probably time to look at annotation tools and XML representations of annotation data.

In this case, since the information you want to capture is metadata that's relevant to the entire document, you probably don't need to worry about character offsets, so you can have tags that look like this:

```
<GenreXML>
  <FILM fid = "f1" title = "Cowboys and Aliens" file_name = "film01.txt" />
  <GENRE gid = "g1" filmid = "f01" label = "western" />
  <GENRE gid = "g2" filmid = = "f01" label = "sci-fi" />
  <GENRE gid = "g3" filmid= "f01" label = "action" />
</GENREXML>
```

This is a very simple annotation, with an equally simple DTD or Document Type Definition [if you aren't sure how to read this DTD, refer back to the sidebar "What Is a DTD?" on page 68]:

```
<!ENTITY name "GenreXML">

<!ELEMENT FILM (#PCDATA) >
<!ATTLIST FILM id ID >
<!ATTLIST FILM title CDATA >
<!ATTLIST FILM file_name CDATA >

<!ELEMENT GENRE (#PCDATA) >
```

```
<!ATTLIST GENRE id ID >
<!ATTLIST GENRE filmid CDATA >
<!ATTLIST GENRE label ( action | adventure | classic | ... ) >
```

This representation of the genre labeling task is not the only way to approach the problem (in Chapter 4 we showed you a slightly different spec for the same task). Here, we have two elements, film and genre, each with an ID number and relevant attributes; the genre element is linked to the film it represents by the filmid attribute.

 Don't fall into the trap of thinking there is One True Spec for your task. If you find that it's easier to structure your data in a certain way, or to add or remove elements or attributes, do it! Don't let your spec get in the way of your goal.

By having the filename stored in the XML for the genre listing, it's possible to keep the annotation completely separate from the text of the file being annotated. However, clearly the file_name attribute is not one that is required, and probably not one that you would want an annotator to fill in by hand. But it is useful, and would be easy to generate automatically during pre- or postprocessing of the annotation data.

Giving each tag an ID number (rather than only the FILM tags) may not seem very important right now, but it's a good habit to get into because it makes discussing and modifying the data much easier, and can also make it easier to expand your annotation task later if you need to.

At this point you may be wondering how all this extra information is going to help with your task. There are a few reasons why you should be willing to take on this extra overhead:

- Having an element that contains the film information allows the annotation to be kept either in the same file as the movie summary, or elsewhere without losing track of the data.

- Keeping data in a structured format allows you to more easily manipulate it later. Having annotation take the form of well-formated XML can make it much easier to analyze later.

- Being able to create a structured representation of your spec helps cement your task, and can show you where problems are in how you are thinking about your goal.

- Representing your spec as a DTD (or other format) means you can use annotation tools to create your annotations. This can help cut down on spelling and other user-input errors.

Figure 5-2 shows what the film genre annotation task looks like in the Multipurpose Annotation Environment (MAE), an annotation tool that requires only a DTD-like document to set up and get running. As you can see, by having the genre options supplied in the DTD, an annotator has only to create a new instance of the GENRE element and select the attribute he wants from the list.

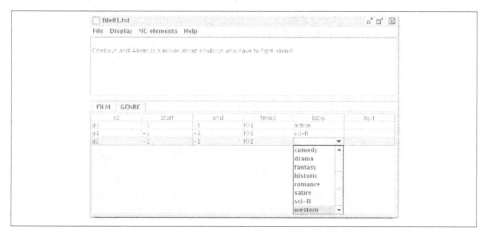

Figure 5-2. Genre annotation in MAE

The output from this annotation process would look like this:

```
<FILM id="f0" start="-1" end="-1" text="" title="Cowboys and Aliens" />
<GENRE id="g0" start="-1" end="-1" text="" label="action" />
<GENRE id="g1" start="-1" end="-1" text="" label="sci-fi" />
<GENRE id="g2" start="-1" end="-1" text="" label="western" />
```

There are a few more elements here than the ones specified in the DTD shown earlier —most tools will require that certain parameters be met in order to work with a task, but in most cases those changes are superficial. In this case, since MAE is usually used to annotate parts of the text rather than create metatags, the DTD had to be changed to allow MAE to make GENRE and FILM nonconsuming tags. That's why the start and end elements are set to -1, to indicate that the scope of the tag isn't limited to certain characters in the text. You'll notice that here, the filmid attribute in the GENRE tag is not present, and neither is the file_name attribute in the FILM tag. While it wouldn't be unreasonable to ask your annotators to assign that information themselves, it would be easier—as well as both faster and more accurate—to do so with a program.

If you plan to keep the stand-off annotation in the same file as the text that's being annotated, then you might not need to add the file information to each tag. However, annotation data can be a lot easier to analyze/manipulate if it doesn't have to be extracted from the text it's referring to, so keeping your tag information in different files that refer back to the originals is generally a best practice.

Text Extent Annotation: Named Entities

The review classification and genre identification tasks are examples of annotation labels that refer to the entirety of a document. However, many annotation tasks require a finer-grained approach, where tags are applied to specific areas of the text, rather than all of it at once. We already discussed many examples of this type of task: part-of-speech (POS) tagging, Named Entity (NE) recognition, the time and event identification parts of TimeML, and so on. Basically, any annotation project that requires sections of the text to be given distinct labels falls into this category. We will refer to this as *extent annotation*, because it's annotating a text extent in the data that can be associated with character locations.

In Chapter 4 we discussed the differences between stand-off and inline annotation, and text extents are where the differences become important. The metadata-type tags used for the document classification task could contain start and end indicators or could leave them out; their presence in the annotation software was an artifact of the software itself, rather than a statement of best practice. However, with stand-off annotation, it is required that locational indicators are present in each tag. Naturally, there are multiple ways to store this information, such as:

- Inline annotation
- Stand-off annotation by location in a sentence or paragraph
- Stand-off annotation by character location

In the following sections we will discuss the practical applications of each of these methods, using Named Entity annotation as a case study.

As we discussed previously, NE annotation concerns marking up what you probably think of as proper nouns—objects in the real world that have specific designators, not just generic labels. So, "The Empire State Building" is an NE, while "the building over there" is not. For now, we will use the following spec to describe the NE task:

```
<!ENTITY name "NamedEntityXML">

<!ELEMENT NE (#PCDATA) >
<!ATTLIST NE id ID >
<!ATTLIST NE type ( person | title | country | building | business |...) >
<!ATTLIST NE note CDATA >
```

Inline Annotation

While we still strongly recommend not using this form of data storage for your annotation project, the fact remains that it is a common way to store data. The phrase "inline annotation" refers to the annotation XML tags being present in the text that is being annotated, and physically surrounding the extent that the tag refers to, like this:

```
<NE id="i0" type="building">The Massachusetts State House</NE> in <NE id="i1" type="city">Boston, MA</NE>
houses the offices of many important state figures, including <NE id="i2" type="title">Governor</NE> <NE id="i3"
type="person">Deval Patrick</NE> and those of the <NE id="i4" type="organization">Massachusetts General Court</
NE>.
```

If nothing else, this format for annotation is extremely difficult to read. But more important, it changes the formatting of the original text. While in this small example there may not be anything special about the text's format, the physical structure of other documents may well be important for later analysis, and inline annotation makes that difficult to preserve or reconstruct. Additionally, if this annotation were to later be merged with, for example, POS tagging, the headache of getting the two different tagsets to overlap could be enormous.

Not all forms of inline annotation are in XML format. There are other ways to mark up data that is inside the text, such as using parentheses to mark syntactic groups, as was done in the following Penn TreeBank II example, taken from "The Penn TreeBank: Annotating Predicate Argument Structure" (Marcus et al. 1994):

```
(S (NP-SUBJ I
   (VP consider
       (S (NP-SUBJ Kris)
          (NP-PRD a fool)))))
```

There are still many programs that provide output in this or a similar format (the Stanford Dependency Parser is one example), and if you want to use tools that do this, you may have to find a way to convert information in this format to stand-off annotation to make it maximally portable to other applications.

Of course, there are some benefits to inline annotation: it becomes unnecessary to keep special track of the location of the tags or the text that the tags are surrounding, because those things are inseparable. Still, these benefits are fairly shortsighted, and we strongly recommend not using this paradigm for annotation.

Another kind of inline annotation is commonly seen in POS tagging, or other tasks where a label is assigned to only one word (rather than spanning many words). In fact, you already saw an example of it in Chapter 1, in the discussion of the Penn TreeBank.

```
"/" From/IN the/DT beginning/NN ,/, it/PRP took/VBD a/DT man/NN with/IN extraordinary/JJ qualities/NNS to/TO succeed/VB
in/IN Mexico/NNP ,/, "/" says/VBZ Kimihide/NNP Takimura/NNP ,/, president/NN of/IN Mitsui/NNS group/NN 's/POS
Kensetsu/NNP Engineering/NNP Inc./NNP unit/NN ./.
```

Here, each POS tag is appended as a suffix directly to the word it is referring to, without any XML tags separating the extent from its label. Not only does this form of annotation make the data difficult to read, but it also changes the composition of the words themselves. Consider how "group's" becomes "group/NN 's/POS"—the possessive "'s" has been separated from "group", now making it even more difficult to reconstruct the original text. Or imagine trying to reconcile an annotation like this one with the NE example in the previous example! It would not be impossible, but it could certainly cause headaches.

While we don't generally recommend using this format either, many existing POS taggers and other tools were originally written to provide output in this way, so it is something you should be aware of, as you may need to realign the original text with the new POS tags.

 We are not, of course, suggesting that you should never use tools that output information in formats other than some variant stand-off annotation. Many of these tools are extremely useful and provide very accurate output. However, you should be aware of problems that might arise from trying to use them.

Another problem with this annotation format is that if it is applied to the NE task, there is the immediate problem that the NE task requires that a single tag apply to more than one word *at the same time*. There is an important distinction between applying the same tag more than once in a document (as there is more than one NN tag in the Penn TreeBank example), and applying one tag across a span of words. Grouping a set of words together by using a single tag tells the reader something about that group that having the same tag applied to each word individually does not. Consider these two examples:

<NE id="i0" type="building">The Massachusetts State House</NE> in <NE id="i1" type="city">Boston, MA</NE> …	The/NE_building Massachusetts/NE_building State/NE_building House/NE_building in Boston/NE_city ,/NE_city MA/NE_city …

In the example on the left, it is clear that the phrase "The Massachusetts State House" is one unit as far as the annotation is concerned—the NE tag applies to the entire group. On the other hand, in the example on the right, the same tag is applied individually to each token, which makes it much harder to determine if each token is an NE on its own, or if there is a connection between them. In fact, we end up tagging some tokens with the wrong tag! Notice that the state "MA" has to be identified as "/NE_city" for the span to be recognized as a city.

Stand-off Annotation by Tokens

One method that is sometimes used for stand-off annotation is *tokenizing* (i.e., separating) the text input and giving each token a number. The tokenization process is usually based on whitespace and punctuation, though the specific process can vary by program (e.g., some programs will split "'s" or "n't" from "Meg's" and "don't", and others will not). The text in the appended annotation example has been tokenized—each word and punctuation mark has been pulled apart.

Taking the preceding text as an example, there are a few different ways to identify the text by assigning numbers to the tokens. One way is to simply number every token in order, starting at 1 (or 0, if you prefer) and going until there are no more tokens left, as shown in Table 5-1.

Table 5-1. Word labeling by token

TOKEN	TOKEN_ID
"	1
From	2
the	3
beginning	4
,	5
...	...
unit	31
.	32

This data could be stored in a tab-separated file or in a spreadsheet, as it's necessary to keep the IDs associated with each token. Another way is to assign numbers to each sentence, and identify each token by sentence number and its place in that sentence, as shown in Table 5-2.

Table 5-2. Word labeling by sentence and token

TOKEN	SENT_ID	TOKEN_ID
"	1	1
From	1	2
the	1	3
beginning	1	4
,	1	5
...		
unit	1	31
.	1	32
Then	2	1
...		

Naturally, more identifying features could be added, such as paragraph number, document number, and so on. The advantage of having additional information (such as sentence number) to identify tokens is that this information can be used later to help define features for the machine learning (ML) algorithms (while sentence number could be inferred again later, if it's known to be important, then it's easier to have that information up front).

Annotation data using this format could look something like Table 5-3.

Table 5-3. POS annotation in tokenized text

POS_TAG	SENT_ID	TOKEN_ID
"	1	1
IN	1	2
DT	1	3
NN	1	4
...		

There are some advantages to using this format: because the annotation is removed from the text, it's unnecessary to worry about overlapping tags when trying to merge annotations done on the same data. Also, this form of annotation would be relatively easy to set up with a tokenizer program and any text that you want to give it.

However, there are some problems with this form of annotation as well. As you can see, because the text is split on whitespace and punctuation, the original format of the data cannot be recovered, so the maxim of "do no harm" to the data has been violated. If the structure of the document that this text appeared in later became important when creating features for a classifier, it could be difficult to merge this annotation with the original text format.

 It is possible to use token-based annotation without damaging the data, though it would require running the tokenizer each time the annotation needed to be paired with the text, and the same tokenizer would always have to be used. This is the suggested way for dealing with token-based stand-off annotation.

Additionally, this format has a similar problem to the appended annotation, in that it appears to assume that each tag applies to only one token. While it's not impossible to apply a tag to a set of tokens, the overhead does become greater. Consider again our NE example, this time tokenized, as shown in Table 5-4.

Table 5-4. Token-based corpus labels

TOKEN	SENT_ID	TOKEN_ID
The	1	1
Massachusetts	1	2
State	1	3
House	1	4
in	1	5
Boston	1	6
,	1	7
MA	1	8
houses	1	9
...		

Table 5-5 shows how we would apply a tag spanning multiple tokens.

Table 5-5. Sample stand-off annotation using token IDs

TAG	START_SENT_ID	START_TOKEN_ID	END_SENT_ID	END_TOKEN_ID
NE_building	1	1	1	4
NE_city	1	6	1	8

The other flaw in this method is that it doesn't easily allow for annotating parts of a word. Annotation projects focusing on morphemes or verb roots would require annotating partial tokens, which would be difficult with this method. It isn't impossible to do—another set of attributes for each token could be used to indicate which characters of the token are being labeled. However, at that point, one might as well move to character-based stand-off annotation, which we will discuss in the next section.

Stand-off Annotation by Character Location

Using character locations to define what part of the document a tag applies to is a reliable way to generate a stand-off annotation that can be used across different systems. Character-based annotations use the character offset information to place tags in a document, like this:

```
The Massachusetts State House in Boston, MA houses the offices
of many important state figures, including Governor Deval Patrick
and those of the Massachusetts General Court.

<NE id="N0" start="5" end="31" text="Massachussetts State House"
  type="building" />
<NE id="N1" start="35" end="45" text="Boston, MA" type="city" />
<NE id="N2" start="109" end="117" text="Governor" type="title" />
<NE id="N3" start="118" end="131" text="Deval Patrick" type="person" />
```

```
<NE id="N4" start="150" end="177" text="Massachusetts General Court"
   type="organization" />
```

At first glance it is difficult to see the benefits to this format for annotation—the start and end numbers don't mean much to someone just looking at the tags, and the tags are so far from the text as to be almost unrelated. However, this distance is precisely why stand-off annotation is important, even necessary. By separating the tags from the text, it becomes possible to have many different annotations pointing to the same document without interfering with one another, and more important, without changing the original text of the document.

As for the start and end numbers, while it is difficult for a human to determine what they are referring to, it's very easy for computers to count the offsets to accomplish that task. And the easier it is for the computer to find the important parts of text, the easier it is to use that text and annotation for machine learning later.

 Using start and end as attribute names to indicate where the tags should be placed in the text is a convention that we use here, but is not one that is a standard in annotation—different annotation tools and systems will use different terms for this information. Similarly, the text attribute does not have any special meaning either. What the attributes are called is not important; what's important is the information that they hold.

Technically, all that's needed for these tags to work are the start and end offset locations and the tag attributes—here, the tags also contain the text that the tag applies to, because it makes the annotation easier to evaluate. Even if that information was not there, the tag would still be functional. Figure 5-3 shows what it might look like to create this annotation in an annotation tool.

Figure 5-3. NE annotation

Naturally, some preparation is necessary to make stand-off annotation work well. For starters, it's important to decide early in the process what character encoding you will use for your corpus, and to stick with that throughout the annotation process. The character encoding that you choose will determine how different computers and programs count where the characters are in your data, and changing encodings partway through can cause a lot of work to be lost. We recommend using UTF-8 encoding for your data.

 Encoding problems can cause a lot of headaches, especially if your data will be transferred between computers using different operating systems. Using Windows can make this particularly difficult, as it seems that Windows does not default to using UTF-8 encoding, while most other operating systems (Mac and most flavors of Unix/Linux that we're aware of) do. It's not impossible to use UTF-8 on Windows, but it does require a little extra effort.

Linked Extent Annotation: Semantic Roles

Sometimes in annotation tasks, it is necessary to represent the connection between two different tagged extents. For example, in temporal annotation, it is not enough to annotate "Monday" and "ran" in the sentence "John ran on Monday"; to fully represent the information presented in the sentence, we must also indicate that there is a connection between the day and the event. This is done by using relationship tags, also called link tags.

Let's look again at our example sentence about Boston. If we were to want to add locational information to this annotation, we would want a way to indicate that there is a relationship between places. We could do that by adding a tag to our DTD that would look something like this:

```
<!ELEMENT L_LINK EMPTY >
<!ATTLIST L-LINK fromID IDREF >
<!ATTLIST L-LINK toID IDREF >
<!ATTLIST L-LINK relationship ( inside | outside | same | other ) >
```

Obviously, this is a very limited set of location relationships, but it will work for now. How would this be applied to the annotation that we already have?

This is where the tag IDs that we mentioned in "Multiple Labels: Film Genres" on page 90 become very important. Because link tags do not refer directly to extents in the text, they need to represent the connection between two annotated objects. The most common way to represent this information is to use the ID numbers from the extent tags to anchor the links. This new information will look like this:

```
The Massachusetts State House in Boston, MA houses the offices
of many important state figures, including Governor Deval Patrick
and those of the Massachusetts General Court.
```

```
<NE id="N0" start="5" end="31" text="Massachusetts State House"
  type="building" />
<NE id="N1" start="35" end="45" text="Boston, MA" type="city" />
<NE id="N2" start="109" end="117" text="Governor" type="title" />
<NE id="N3" start="118" end="131" text="Deval Patrick" type="person" />
<NE id="N4" start="150" end="177" text="Massachusetts General Court"
  type="organization" />

<L-LINK id="L0" fromID="N0" toID="N1" relationship="inside" />
<L-LINK id="L0" fromID="N4" toID="N0" relationship="inside" />
```

By referring to the IDs of the NE tags, we can easily encode information about the relationships between them. And because the L-LINK tags also have ID numbers, it is possible to create connections between them as well—perhaps a higher level of annotation could indicate that two L-LINKs represent the same location information, which could be useful for a different project.

 Once again, the names of the attributes here are not particularly important. We use fromID and toID as names for the link anchors, because that is what the annotation tool MAE does, but other software uses different conventions. The intent, however, is the same.

ISO Standards and You

In "ISO Standards" on page 80 we discussed the LAF (Linguistic Annotation Framework) standard for representing annotated data. It might have sounded pretty formal, but don't worry! If you're following along with our recommendations in this book and using XML-based stand-off annotation, chances are that your annotation structure is already LAF-compliant, and that you would just need to convert it to the LAF dump format. Also keep in mind that LAF is a great foundation for linguistic researchers who want to share their data, but if your annotation is only meant for you, or is proprietary to a company, this might not be something you will need to worry about at all.

Summary

In this chapter we discussed some of the different methods for representing annotations for a corpus annotation task. In particular, we noted the following:

- Annotations can be stored in many different ways, but it's important to choose a format that will be flexible and easy to change later if you need to. We recommend stand-off, XML-based formats.

- In some cases, such as single-label document classification tasks, there are many ways to store annotation data, but these techniques are essentially isomorphic. In such cases, choose which method to use by considering how you plan to use the data, and what methods work best for your annotators.

- For most annotation tasks, such as those requiring multiple labels on a document, and especially those requiring extent annotation and linking, it will be useful to have annotation software for your annotators to use. See Appendix B for a list of available software.

- Extent annotation can take many forms, but character-based stand-off annotation is the format that will make it easier to make any necessary changes to the annotations later, and also make it easier to merge with other annotations.

- If you do choose to use character-based stand-off annotation, be careful about what encodings you use for your data, especially when you create the corpus in the first place. Different programming languages and operating systems have different default settings for character encoding, and it's vital that you use a format that will work for all your annotators (or at least be willing to dictate what resources your annotators use).

- Using industry standards such as XML and annotation standards such as LAF for your annotations will make it much easier for you to interact with other annotated corpora, and make it easier for you to share your own work.

CHAPTER 6

Annotation and Adjudication

Now that you have a corpus and a model, it's time to start looking at the actual annotation process—the "A" in the MATTER cycle. Here is where you define the method by which your model is applied to your texts, both in theory (how your task is described to annotators) and in practice (what software and other tools are used to create the annotations). A critical part of this stage is adjudication—where you take your annotators' work and use it to create the *gold standard* corpus that you will use for machine learning. In this chapter we will answer the following questions:

- What are the components of an annotation task?
- What is the difference between a model specification and annotation guidelines?
- How do you create guidelines that fit your task?
- What annotation tool should you use for your annotation task?
- What skills do your annotators need to create your annotations?
- How can you tell (qualitatively) if your annotation guidelines are good for your task?
- What is involved in adjudicating the annotations?

The Infrastructure of an Annotation Project

It's much easier to write annotation guidelines when you understand how annotation projects are usually run, so before getting into the details of guideline writing, we're going to go over a few different ways that you can structure your annotation effort.

Currently, what we would call the "traditional" approach goes like this. Once a schema is developed and a corpus is collected, an investigator writes up guidelines, finds annotators, and distributes the guidelines and corpus to the annotators, who go off, annotate, and then come back with a marked-up corpus. The researcher then collects the data from each of the annotators, and calculates Inter-Annotator Agreement (IAA) scores. If these scores are low, the guidelines (and sometimes the model) are revised, and the annotation is redone. If the scores are good, adjudication is performed over the data to create a gold standard, which is then used to train and test a machine learning (ML) algorithm. Figure 6-1 visually depicts the annotation process.

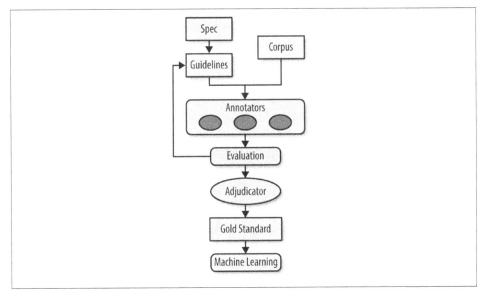

Figure 6-1. The annotation process

So why do researchers use this distributed method of annotation, rather than doing it themselves? There are two main reasons. First, there is a purely practical concern: most annotation tasks now are performed with the end goal of training an ML system, and to do that, there needs to be sufficient data to train the algorithm. Since for most tasks this requires hundreds or even thousands of annotated articles or examples, it would be completely impractical for only one or two people to create the required corpus.

The second reason for distributed annotation is that by having other people do the bulk of the tagging, and then using that data to calculate agreement scores, the researcher gets a sense of whether the task is sufficiently well defined to provide consistent data should a bigger corpus be needed. If there is little agreement among annotators as to how each tag and attribute should be used, it may be a sign that the guidelines are simply not well written, but it may also be a sign that the task itself is flawed, or goes against the way people generally understand language.

Before computers were as fast as they are now, researchers wanting to examine language data did so by hand, and usually by themselves or with the help of a student in the field. However, annotated corpora from before the 1980s tended to be relatively small, simply because of the infeasibility of creating and cataloging a large amount of data. While large corpora were being put together in the 1970s and 1980s (such as the Brown Corpus), it wasn't until later that large, computer-based annotation efforts became common.

However, even with larger datasets becoming more available, it's still sometimes necessary to return to an existing task and create a larger annotated corpus for it. This is why it is important to have well-defined guidelines and good IAA scores; if a task is clear, then it can be reproduced later by other groups of people. In Chapter 4 we discussed interoperability and reproducibility as it applies to data formats, but the concept applies to the annotation task as well.

Crowdsourcing

Crowdsourcing is another approach that is being used more frequently in the annotation community. Essentially, instead of asking a small number of annotators to tag a large number of extents, the task is broken down into a large number of smaller tasks, and a large number of annotators are asked to tag only a few examples each. One popular crowdsourcing platform is Amazon's Mechanical Turk (*https://www.mturk.com/mturk/welcome*)(MTurk), a resource where people who have tasks that require human intelligence to perform can place requests that are then fulfilled by people across the country and around the world. These HITs (human intelligence tasks) are generally formatted to be very quick and relatively easy to perform, so workers are usually paid in cents rather than dollars. Because of the availability of annotators and how inexpensive each HIT is, many researchers have looked into using crowdsourcing as a resource for annotation.

Generally, MTurk will only be useful for tasks that don't require any special linguistic or other domain knowledge. Additionally, due to the restricted nature of the HIT interface, workers can't be given pages and pages of annotation guidelines—aside from the impracticality of the layout, it's generally not worth a worker's time to read that many instructions for only a few cents. So, if you have an annotation task that can be broken down into simple steps and explained easily in a few sentences, then MTurk may be a good resource for you to look into. Because such tasks do have to be given a different format and broken down into smaller pieces, we're not going to go into the details of creating good annotation HITs in this book, but Appendix E has a list of MTurk-related resources that you may find useful if you decide to use MTurk.

Specification Versus Guidelines

In the previous chapters we explored how models are created, and we looked at different ways to define your task in terms of tags and XML. These tags encapsulate what your schema is capable of capturing: they are an abstraction of what you want your data to represent. The *annotation guidelines* represent the application of the schema to the data: they are the guidebook for how the schema is used on your data.

 If it helps, think of the distinction between schema and guidelines as the difference between a list of ingredients and the actual baking instructions. The guidelines determine how the ingredients (the schema: tags, attributes, and data) are mixed together, and what they make when you're done. In baking, the same ingredients can be used to make bread or cake, and in annotation, the same specification can sometimes be used for different annotation projects.

The distinction between schema and guidelines is important, because it's possible for a single schema to be used for different annotation tasks, or for the same basic task but with different data than has been used in the past. If you have decided to use or modify an existing schema for your annotation task, then this distinction is one that you will probably need to pay particular attention to, as existing guidelines for your task may not fit your specific goal or corpus.

For example, the original TimeML annotation guidelines were written to be applied to newspaper articles, which led to specific examples and notes in the guidelines that did not apply to other genres. Specifically, when TimeML was applied to medical data, a few changes were made to the schema, but for the most part, it was the annotation guidelines that needed to be modified to give relevant examples to the annotators. While you might feel that it's reasonable to expect that an annotator could extrapolate the events and relationships from "The president is hopeful that reconciliation can be reached" to "The patient is feverish and may experience nausea," it is better to provide genre-relevant examples than to rely too much on your annotators' intuitions.

Another example of a guideline changing the use of a spec would be having a task that limits the application of the spec. Consider the Named Entity (NE) relations that we discussed in "Adding Named Entities" on page 71. These relation sets were derived from an existing specification relating to *semantic role labels*. However, rather than use the entire set of semantic role relationships defined in that task, we used only a subset of those that relate to movies and the roles that people play in creating them.

Finally, you may be in a situation where you have one spec that defines your task, but you find it necessary to split the task into different steps. Sometimes this is useful if you have a complicated model, and want to maximize accuracy by performing annotations on only a few tags at a time, then adjudicating those tags, then moving on to the next set of tags or relations. You may also find this approach necessary if your task requires both general knowledge of the language and more specific knowledge that would require a domain expert to provide. In those cases, you can have two tasks being performed simultaneously by different groups of people on the same corpus, and then merge the annotations later for ML purposes.

Be Prepared to Revise

While it is true that the entire MATTER process is a cycle, it is important to remember that there is a smaller cycle of revision between the Model and Annotation stages. We discussed in Chapter 4 how you may find it necessary to reformulate the spec as you develop your model, but chances are good that once you start writing your annotation guidelines, you will quickly find places where your data and spec don't quite meet up.

 Revising the spec while working on the guidelines and doing the annotation occurs frequently enough that we refer to it as the MAMA cycle: Model-Annotate-Model-Annotate (the Annotate step includes writing the guidelines). See Figure 6-2.

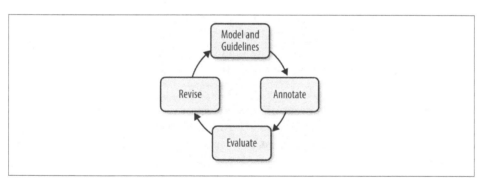

Figure 6-2. The inner workings of the MAMA cycle

Once the guidelines are written and given to your annotators, the annotators themselves will probably have questions about the spec and guidelines that may lead to more revisions. This is completely normal! To have an annotation task that can be reused in the future, it's important to take the time to make sure the spec and guidelines are clear and well written.

Preparing Your Data for Annotation

Data preparation falls into two main tasks: the more theoretical act of deciding how to present your documents to your annotators, and the very practical matter of coercing those documents into a form that will work with the annotation tool that you choose. A discussion of annotation tools will take place later in this chapter, so for now, we'll just focus on deciding what information to present to your annotators.

Metadata

Deciding what information to give to your annotators can be trickier than it seems. You have the text files that you want annotated, but how much do you want your annotators to know about the source of those files? For example, should they know where the files came from and who produced them?

This may seem like a trivial problem, but information about a document can influence annotators in sometimes unexpected ways. Opinion annotation in particular can be susceptible to this problem. An obvious example would be, in examining the polarity of movie reviews, informing the annotators of the star rating that the reviewer gave the movie. If you want an annotator to look for both positive and negative adjectives, informing the annotator that the reviewer gave the movie 10 stars can prime her to look only for positive adjectives.

In the same vein, if annotators are examining newspaper or Wikipedia articles for factuality, informing them of the source of the article, or if the Wikipedia page was flagged for being biased, could influence the annotators, particularly if a source is, to them, associated with biased reporting, or if they tend to believe that Wikipedia flags are accurate.

As another example, say you are working on creating a phonetic transcription of recorded data; informing your annotators of the birthplace of a speaker could potentially bias them to hear pronunciations in a particular way, especially if they are new to phonetic transcription.

 Bias can appear in unexpected ways—it's useful to try a few variations on the data presentation to eliminate different biasing factors.

Preprocessed Data

Another consideration in data presentation is giving your annotators data that already has some information marked up.

There are two things to consider before doing that, however:

- Is this information necessary for a human annotator, or would it be more useful for an algorithm?
- Is this information going to be correct, or is it something that the annotator will have to fix/examine for errors?

Part-of-speech (POS) is a great example of information that would be useful for a machine to have, but that might not be necessary to give to an annotator (especially if the annotator is a native speaker of the language he is evaluating). Presenting an annotator with too much information can make the task confusing, and it could lower accuracy without necessarily increasing informativity.

Whether or not your preprocessed information is correct will have a huge impact on your annotation project. Certainly, it saves time to do part of your annotation automatically if the tools exist, but people in general tend to like simple instructions, and so "Label all the Named Entities/times/events, then create links between them" might be an easier rule to follow (especially since it could be done as two different tasks) than "We have marked up most of the entities/times/events for you, but they might not be correct, so we'd like you to fix any errors while creating links."

If the provided annotations are of poor quality, asking annotators to correct partial annotations can lead to mistakes not being fixed, especially when combined with other instructions at the same time. Splitting the annotation into related tasks, such as correcting the generated labels and then later on adding more tags or creating links between the corrected extents, is probably the best way to deal with this. It is more time-consuming, but it will result in higher-quality annotations.

Splitting Up the Files for Annotation

We already told you about how you'll need to divide your files into training and testing datasets, but you will also want to set aside some documents for testing your annotation guidelines on as well. As you work your way through the MAMA cycle, you'll find that (especially in the beginning) it won't take long for you and your annotators to spot errors and/or gaps in your model or guidelines. Because of this, we suggest having a set of 10–20 files that you can use as a training set on which your annotators can test changes to the guidelines. You can use these files in your gold standard later if you want or need to, but because of how many times your annotators will have gone over those files in particular, you probably won't want to include them in your IAA calculations, because they will be so heavily discussed and dissected.

Also, if you find that your guidelines have gone through many revisions, you'll probably want to switch out the training annotation files. That way, your annotators won't become so familiar with the expected annotations that they stop thinking about the guidelines. As a rule of thumb, switch out your training files every two or three times you revise your guidelines.

Writing the Annotation Guidelines

The annotation guidelines are the instructions for how you want your annotators to apply the model (your schema) to the data (your corpus) for a specific task. Opinions vary on how much information should be included in the annotation guidelines—Dipper et al. (2004), for example, believe that annotation guidelines should include a description of the corpus, linguistic theories underlying the model, and so on. However, we recommend that the annotation guidelines contain only the information needed for the annotators to apply the tagsets to annotate the corpus for your particular annotation task (remember: the same spec can be used for different goals).

 Just because we say the annotation guidelines are only for creating annotations doesn't mean it's not important to keep track of other information and make it available later! It's just that when it comes to creating an annotated corpus, including too much extra information can make it harder for the annotators to figure out what parts of the document are relevant to their task. Information about where the corpus came from and how it was selected, what linguistic theories were used to create your tagset, and how the corpus can be read and accessed should absolutely be monitored and made available as part of the entire annotated corpus package—just don't put it in the guidelines unless it's directly relevant to how you want the text annotated. We'll talk more about what information you should report on in Chapter 9.

So, to make the clearest guidelines you can, there are a few basics that your annotation guidelines should cover. The guidelines should answer, at a minimum, the following questions:

- What is the goal of the project?
- What is each tag called and how is it used? (Be specific: provide examples, and discuss gray areas.)
- What parts of the text do you want annotated, and what should be left alone?
- How will the annotation be created? (For example, explain which tags or documents to annotate first, how to use the annotation tools, etc.)

These bullets points provide a starting place for most tasks, and in the rest of this section we're going to go over what the answers to these questions for a few different tasks might look like, as well as discuss how the questions need to be modified for different types of tasks. Specifically, we're going to look at single label classifications (movie reviews), multiple label classifications (film genres), extent annotations (NEs), and linked annotations (semantic roles). Before you begin writing your own guidelines, you may find it helpful to look at the published guidelines for existing tasks. Check Appendix B for some links to existing annotation tasks.

 Make sure you write down your guidelines! Annotated corpora are most useful when the guidelines used to create them are complete and available for download with the corpus. Having the guidelines around will make it easier for other people to recreate or expand your task later if they need to.

Example 1: Single Labels—Movie Reviews

A classic example of a classification task is sorting movie reviews into positive and negative categories to train a classifier to determine whether someone likes or dislikes a movie based on what she says about it. A Movie Review Corpus (MRC) already exists (it is available for download from *http://www.cs.cornell.edu/people/pabo/movie-review-data/*, and is included in the Natural Language Toolkit [NLTK] dataset), and the creators describe creating the corpus based on reviews from IMDb.com and selecting only those reviews that gave numerical or star ratings in order to automatically categorize whether the reviews were positive or negative (Pang and Lee 2004). So the initial labeling for this task was actually done, in a sense, by the author of the review, and no annotation guidelines were required.

But let's say that you want to create a larger dataset, and to have humans create the labels for the reviews. Let's also say that your goal is to train an algorithm to be able to take any review and label it as being positive or negative, like the creators of the MRC did. However, if you go to IMDb.com right now and look at the reviews of nearly any movie, you'll find that not all reviews make clear good/bad distinctions. What would you do with a review such as the following?

> This movie was all right. The special effects were good, but the plot didn't make a lot of sense. The actors were funny, which helped, but the music was really distracting.

Now, this review doesn't include a star rating, and it's not (to our minds, anyway) clearly positive or negative. It seems to give the movie a resounding "meh." So how does that fit in with your goal, or the goals of the MRC? Well, in the case of the MRC researchers, they were only looking at the differences between positive and negative reviews, and so they specifically collected only those that were clearly one or the other. However, if your goal is to train an algorithm to work on any review selected at random, then you won't want to limit your corpus in that way.

Make sure that your corpus matches your goal! We discussed this in Chapter 2, but now is a good time to check to make sure any changes that the MAMA cycle has made to your task are reflected in your corpus. Otherwise, it will be difficult to train an ML algorithm later on.

So what should an annotator be told to do with the aforementioned review? One way to help make that determination is to look at how other people handle the same problem. The websites RottenTomatoes.com and Metacritic.com both have their editors assign labels to reviews that do not provide specific categories or ratings themselves. Let's take a look at what they say about how these ratings are assigned:

> … Our staffers will go through every publication on our Movies Publications list […] looking for reviews for Iron Chef vs. Godzilla. For each review found, we will take the score given by the critic and convert it to a 0–100 point scale. (For those critics who do not provide a score, we'll assign a score from 0–100 based on the general impression given by the review.) […]
>
> —Metacritic Help and Support

Unfortunately, that doesn't really give guidelines for how to rate a review. Let's look at RottenTomatoes:

> **How do you determine whether a review with no stars is Rotten or Fresh?** Most critics from the Online Film Critics Society (OFCS) enter their own quotes and ratings. For critics who don't enter in their own quotes and ratings, it's basically up to the judgment of the editors. They take into account word choice, rating (if any), tone, and who the critic is in their determination of whether a review is positive or not. If an editor is not certain about a review, it is sent to another editor for a second opinion. "Wishy-washy" reviews, reviews that are really difficult to determine if the critic recommends the film or not, are usually given a Rotten because if the critic is not confident enough to give the movie even an implied recommendation, then we shouldn't either.
>
> —RottenTomatoes Help Center

That's a clear explanation for how to assign a label to a neutral review, with a good reason for how the decision should be made. It also fits in with the stated goal of the corpus, though it may not fit in with your own view of movie reviews. Assuming that you're satisfied with using that line of reasoning, let's see where the project stands with regard to the questions posed earlier.

What is the goal of the project?

To label movie reviews as being positive or negative.

What is each tag called and how is it used?

We have two labels, "positive" and "negative," and each review will be labeled with one of them, based on the tone of the review. Reviews that are not specifically positive or negative will be labeled as "negative."

What parts of the text do you want annotated, and what should be left alone?

Each review will be given a single label, which will be applied to the entire document.

How should the annotation be created?

In Chapter 5 we discussed the different formats that can be used for capturing this type of data. In this situation we would probably use a spreadsheet prepopulated with the names of the files that are being examined, but this decision depends largely on who your annotators are and what works best for them and you.

Keep in mind that we're not going to provide a complete guideline in this chapter for any of the tasks, just a high-level overview of the important points that need to be covered for a good annotation guideline. As we mentioned before, check Appendix A for a list of existing annotation tasks, and see Chapter 10 for a worked-through example of an annotation task.

Example 2: Multiple Labels—Film Genres

A more complicated example of classification is identifying film genres. This type of classification is an excellent example of a task where the annotation guidelines can completely change the outcome of the annotation, and trying to apply the guidelines may lead to changes in the spec.

 Remember that within the MATTER cycle there is also the MAMA (Model-Annotate-Model-Annotate) cycle. Chances are good (especially if you are starting your annotation project from scratch) that you will need to revise your model and guidelines at least a few times before you will be able to annotate your entire corpus. But don't be discouraged; the more you refine your annotation, the easier it will be to define features for your ML algorithms later on.

If you recall from "Film Genre Classification" on page 70, when discussing the spec for a film genre classification task we used IMDb's list of film genres, which included the following 26 genres:

Action	Adventure	Animation	Biography	Comedy
Crime	Documentary	Drama	Family	Fantasy
Film-Noir	Game-Show	History	Horror	Music
Musical	Mystery	News	Reality-TV	Romance
Sci-Fi	Sport	Talk-Show	Thriller	War
Western				

This certainly seems like a reasonable list, and it comes from one of the most (if not the most) popular movie reference websites on the Internet, so at the very least it's a good starting point for your spec. So let's look at the list of questions to be answered for the guidelines.

What is the goal of the project?
> To label film summaries with genre notations.

What is each tag called and how is it used?
> We have 26 tags that can be applied to each summary as needed.

What parts of the text do you want annotated, and what should be left alone?
> Each label will apply to the entire document.

How should the annotation be created?
> Annotation software is probably the best way to apply multiple labels to a document.

Well, that was easy! Except...the answer to the second question, particularly the "how is it used" part, is quite underspecified. When labeling movie reviews as positive or negative it's probably enough to say (as a starting point, at least) that the label will be based on tone, and neutral reviews will be labeled as "negative." However, genre labels are not all mutually exclusive, so annotators are going to need clearer guidelines for how and when to apply each one. One basic question that needs to be answered is: "Is there a maximum number of labels that can be applied to a document?" The answer to this question alone can completely differentiate one annotation task from another, even if each one is using the same spec; guidelines that specify a maximum of, say, two labels per document are likely going to return a vastly different corpus than guidelines that have no such limit. For the imaginary task we are describing here, our guidelines will not specify a limit to the number of tags.

However, while knowing how many labels can be applied partly answers the question of "how" the tags are used, it doesn't address all of the aspects of "how" the tags are used. Another aspect that has to be considered is *when* each tag will be used. In the positive/ negative review task, each document was assigned a single label, and if a document wasn't positive, it was negative: a dichotomy that's fairly straightforward. Since there's no limit to the number of genre tags (or even if there were a limit), annotators will need some clarification about when to apply which tags.

At first, the question of when to use each label seems straightforward. But consider the first two tags in the previous list: action and adventure. What, your annotators will want to know, is the difference? A quick Google search shows that this is hardly the first time this question has been asked, and the general consensus appears to be that action movies tend to be more violent, while adventure movies generally require that the protagonist be going on some sort of journey to a place or situation he has not dealt with previously. However, the same Google search also reveals that other genre lists (such as the one Netflix uses) simply have one genre label called "Action-Adventure," presumably due to a high level of overlap between the two labels.

Let's assume that you're satisfied with the aforementioned distinction between action and adventure, and you put them in your guidelines as definitions for your annotators to refer back to. So now they'll (hopefully) label *Die Hard* as an action movie and *Around the World in 80 Days* as an adventure. But wait a minute, one of the first summaries for *Die Hard* on IMDb.com starts with "New York City Detective John McClane has just arrived in Los Angeles to spend Christmas with his wife. Unfortunately...." So is there a journey involved? The character does go to a different location, but a cop who is used to dealing with criminals going to a different city to deal with criminals doesn't really meet the "new situation" clause of the adventure definition given earlier, so we can probably safely say that *Die Hard* doesn't qualify as an adventure movie.

OK, that's a good start. But what about *Eat, Pray, Love*? The main character clearly goes on a journey to new places and situations, but we suspect that most people wouldn't consider it to be an adventure movie. So, maybe adventure movies also have to have some element of danger? Better amend the definition in your guidelines. Or maybe at this point you feel like trying to differentiate between the two is a bit tedious and/or pointless, and you'd rather amend your spec to have a single action-adventure category.

 Believe it or not, we didn't include the preceding few paragraphs simply because we enjoy nitpicking about movie genres. Rather, we included them because this discussion illustrates the kinds of questions you will need to answer for your annotators when you give them the guidelines for their task. The simplest approach to the task is to just give your annotators a pile of texts and tell them to put on whatever labels seem right to them, but don't forget that an important part of an annotation task is *reproducibility*. If you simply tell annotators to label what they want, it's unlikely that a different set of annotators will be able to give you the same (or even similar) results at a later date.

If you aren't entirely sure what definition to give to each label, now would be a really good time to take another piece of advice that we've repeated a number of times (and will continue to repeat): do some research! One excellent book that we found on the subject is Barry Keith Grant's *Film Genre: From Iconography to Ideology* (Wallflower Press, 2007). While not all of the theory in the book can necessarily be applied to an annotation task, looking at the different genres in terms of themes rather than simply looking at surface details can help clarify what makes a movie fit into a genre. For example, Western movies often are, in part, about exploring new frontiers and the pioneer spirit, a definition that might be more effective and relevant than one that specifies a Western has horses, people wearing cowboy hats, and at least one person who says "pardner" very slowly.

A closer look at the film genres also reveals that not all of the genres in the list are describing the same aspects of the film. While labels such as "Action," "Adventure,"

"Crime," and "Romance" tell the reader something about the events that will take place in the film, the labels "Historical," "Sci-Fi," and "Fantasy" refer to the setting, and "Animation," "Talk-Show," and "Reality-TV" all describe the production circumstances. Therefore, an altogether different approach to this task would be to break up these genres into categories (production, setting, etc.) and ask annotators to assign at least one label from each category. Assuming that the categories and labels are sufficiently well defined (which is not necessarily an easy task), the specific requirement of "at least X number of labels" may greatly improve the IAA and reproducibility of your task. If you were to take this approach, you might create a DTD (Document Type Definition) that looks something like this:

```
<!ELEMENT setting ( EMPTY ) >
<!ATTLIST setting description ( historical | sci-fi | fantasy ) >

<!ELEMENT production ( EMPTY ) >
<!ATTLIST production circumstances ( animation | documentary |
    game-show | musical | news | reality-tv | talk-show | ) >

<!ELEMENT content ( EMPTY ) >
<!ATTLIST content type ( action | adventure | biography |
    crime | drama | mystery | romance ) >
```

Of course, this reorganized DTD is only a start: if you want to mandate that every movie be assigned a setting, then you'll need at least one that can describe a movie set in the present with no particular augmentations to reality. But this is another way to frame the genre task that might prove more useful, depending on the goal you've set.

Overall, it's important to realize that if you have a task with many different labels that you want to use, it's vital that you create clear definitions for each label and to provide examples of when you want your annotators to use each of them (and equally as important, when you *don't* want your annotators to use them). While this might seem more important when you are creating your own labels rather than relying on existing terms, you also want to make sure that your annotators' judgments aren't clouded by their own preconceptions about what a term means.

 Another potential cause of confusion for annotators, aside from their knowledge about a term in the spec, is their knowledge of the material being annotated. If you are asking an annotator to create labels that describe a movie based on a written summary, but the annotator has seen the movie and feels that the summary is inaccurate, you will need to address whether he can use his own world knowledge to augment the information in the document he is labeling. Though for reproducibility and ML purposes, we strongly recommend against using outside knowledge or intuition as a source for annotation data.

Example 3: Extent Annotations—Named Entities

In "Adding Named Entities" on page 71, we gave a sample specification for film-related NEs: film title, director, writer, actor, and character. While the definitions of each of these roles should be a little easier to define than the genres discussed in the preceding section, NE tags are *extent* tags, meaning that they are applied to specific text spans inside a document, rather than to the document as a whole. Extent tags bring with them a new set of considerations, such as the following:

- How should the annotators decide how long each tagged span should be? How many words get included in each tag? For example, should descriptive phrases be included? What about titles, honorifics, or determiners? "A white house" is clearly different from "the White House," but is the determiner really the important part of that phrase?

- What about names that get split up? While it's reasonable to label "The Wachowskis" as a single entity, what if the text says "Lana and Andy Wachowski"? Will that entire phrase be tagged together, or do you want your annotators to do something different in that case?

- Should your annotators annotate every mention of an NE, or only the first time that it's mentioned?

- What if an entity seems to be filling two different roles? In a standard NE annotation, you might see "Boston City Hall"—should "Boston" be marked in the same extent as "City Hall," or are they different? Does one overlap the other?

- What about possessive constructions, such as "John Hughes' *The Breakfast Club*"? And if you do decide that "John Hughes" should be tagged separately from "*The Breakfast Club*," does the annotation include the apostrophe?

The preceding questions will need to be addressed for pretty much any NE task, and more largely, for any task involving extent annotation, and most of them boil down to this: *What is the scope of each tag?* That is, what are the limitations and guidelines for where each tag should be placed, and how many times should it be used?

Fortunately, NEs have been part of natural language annotations for years, so if you're willing to do a little research, you'll find the answers to these questions that other researchers have found useful. One notable NE task took place at the Message Understanding Conference (MUC) 6 in 1995. The guidelines for NE annotation that were formed there have been modified for various other annotations over the years, and the Linguistic Data Consortium (LDC) currently has a few good guidelines for doing NE annotation, which you can find at *http://projects.ldc.upenn.edu/LCTL/Specifications/*. While these guidelines are listed as being for languages other than English, the guidelines themselves are in English and provide English-language examples.

You'll notice that the Simple Named Entity Guidelines V6.5 document from the LDC contains a section called "Difficult cases," which addresses the questions about NE annotation that we posed earlier. This is an excellent way to structure your guidelines—having the first part provide clear examples of how a tag is used, and later on keeping the tricky examples in one place. This will make it much easier for your annotators to find what they need quickly while creating their annotations, and will be much less frustrating for them.

Of course, many of the points that we made about annotations in the other guideline examples also apply (What if someone is both a director and a writer? Does she get two labels? If you're performing a more general NE task, are each of the different types of entities clearly defined so that your annotator knows when to use each one?), but we're not going to go over all of them again here. When it comes to extent tags, it's important for the guidelines to explain the scope of the tag—where the tag should (and shouldn't) be applied, and what to do when a relevant piece of text appears in different contexts. This is particularly important, because, depending on how you calculate IAA, differences in where the annotations start and end can have massive effects on the agreement scores. Low agreement will also make adjudicating more difficult, so save yourself some effort and make the guidelines as clear as you can.

Example 4: Link Tags—Semantic Roles

While the addition of extent tags to an annotation task requires clear guidelines on where those tags should start and end, link tags bring two new questions to the guidelines that need to be answered:

- What are the links connecting?
- When should a link be created?

These questions may seem quite straightforward, but recall our example of a temporal link annotation from the discussion of informativity and correctness in "Refining Your Goal: Informativity Versus Correctness" on page 35. Admittedly, that was a somewhat extreme example of how an annotation task can get out of hand, but it does illustrate the importance of having clear guidelines about when links are needed and when they should be created. Fortunately, most annotation tasks have much clearer boundaries when it comes to linking extents than our sample temporal annotation did. For example, the semantic role task for films that we discussed in "Semantic Roles" on page 72 doesn't have as much potential for getting completely blown out of proportion, although it too has potential for confusion. Remember that the task specified that semantic relationships between actors, characters, writers, directors, and movies would be annotated with the roles `acts_in`, `acts_as`, `directs`, `writes`, and `character_in`. So, for example, in the sentence "James Cameron directed *Avatar*" we would have a link between "James

Cameron" (who would be tagged as a director) and "*Avatar*" (which would be tagged as a `film_title`), and the link would have the semantic role `directs`.

But even this straightforward example has a few places where the task could become more complicated. Let's look at the sample review we saw in the preceiding chapter (here the actors, writers, and directors are in **bold**, film titles are in *italics*, and characters are in `constant width`:

> In *Love, Actually*, writer/director **Richard Curtis** weaves a convoluted tale about characters and their relationships. Of particular note is **Liam Neeson** (*Schindler's List, Star Wars*) as `Daniel`, a man struggling to deal with the death of his `wife` and the relationship with his young stepson, `Sam` (**Thomas Sangster**). **Emma Thompson** (*Sense and Sensibility, Henry V*) shines as a `middle-aged housewife` whose marriage with her `husband` (played by **Alan Rickman**) is under siege by a `beautiful secretary`. While this movie does have its purely comedic moments (primarily presented by **Bill Nighy** as out-of-date rock star `Billy Mack`), this movie avoids the more in-your-face comedy that **Curtis** has presented before as a writer for *Blackadder* and *Mr. Bean*, presenting instead a remarkable, gently humorous insight into what love, actually, is.

While most of the semantic role annotations here are quite straightforward, there are a few pieces that might trip up conscientious annotators. For example, when creating `writes` links for *Black Adder* and *Mr. Bean*, should those film titles be linked to the **Curtis** that appears in the same sentence, or should they be linked back to the **Richard Curtis** in the first sentence, because that's his full name? Similarly, should every `act_in` and `character_in` relationship for the movie being reviewed be linked back to the mention of the title in the first sentence, or should they be linked to (currently unannotated) phrases such as "this movie"? If *Love, Actually* were mentioned more than once in the review, should the annotators link actors and characters to the closest mention of the title, only to the first one, or to all of them?

We aren't going to provide you with the answers to these questions, because there is no One True Answer to them. How you approach the annotation will depend on your goal and model, and simple trial and error with your guidelines and annotators will help determine what the most reasonable and useful answer to these questions is for your task. However, don't forget to check out guidelines for similar tasks for suggestions on what has worked for other people!

Annotators

A key component of any annotation project is, of course, the people who perform the annotation task. Clearly, this means that some thought needs to be put into who you find to create your annotations. To that end, we suggest being able to answer the following questions:

- What language or languages do your annotators need to know to perform your annotation task?

- Does your annotation task require any specialized knowledge to understand or perform?

- What are the practical considerations that need to be taken into account (money, time, size of the dataset, etc.)?

Let's go through these one at a time.

What language or languages do your annotators need to know to perform your annotation task? And furthermore, how well do they need to know them?

Chances are, the answer to this question is pretty obvious, but it's still worth specifying. If your task requires close reading of a text (e.g., anaphoric relationships, word sense disambiguation, or semantic roles), you may want to limit your annotators to native speakers of the language that you are annotating. For some annotations, you may be able to use nonnative speakers, however, and for some tasks they might even be preferred (e.g., if the purpose of the task is to learn about the second-language learner's perceptions of his new language). Regardless of what you decide, be sure to make any language preferences clear in any job postings or descriptions.

Does your annotation task require any specialized knowledge to understand or perform?

Aside from the language(s) the texts are in, is there any other outside knowledge that your annotators need to have to perform well on this task? If your task is one of POS tagging, finding annotators who are familiar with those concepts (perhaps people who have taken a syntax course or two) will probably lessen the time needed to train your annotators and increase IAA.

There are other factors that can affect what your annotators need to know to perform well at your annotation task, such as the actual source material. Biomedical and clinical annotations are areas that more and more Natural Language Processing (NLP) researchers are looking into, but it's much easier for an annotator to identify and label gene expressions in scientific papers if she is already familiar with the concepts and vocabulary. Clinical documents such as hospital notes and discharge summaries can be even trickier, because chances are, you will need someone trained as an RN (if not an MD) to interpret any medical information you might be interested in due to how dense and jargon-filled the text is.

If you do decide that you will be selecting annotators with certain skills or knowledge, be sure to keep track of that information and make it available to other people who use your corpus and guidelines. An annotation task's reproducibility is increased when all the variables are accounted for, just like any other experiment!

What are the practical considerations that need to be taken into account?

One thing you need to consider when planning your annotation project and where to find annotators is that annotation takes time. Obviously, tasks that have a high density of tags, such as POS tagging, are time-consuming simply because there is a one-to-one ratio of tags to words. But more than that, most annotation tasks can only be done for a few hours at a time by most people. Annotation requires a lot of concentration and attention to detail, and if you expect your annotators to do it from 9:00 to 5:00 for days in a row, you will likely get very inconsistent annotations. Annotation will speed up as your workers get used to the task, but make sure you allow enough time in your schedule for your annotators to do good work.

If you are expanding on an annotation task/guideline that already exists, it's worth the time to train your annotators on data from the previous dataset. That way, you have a solid way to evaluate whether your annotators understand the given task, and you can make necessary adjustments to the guidelines without compromising your own dataset.

In theory, if you were on a tight schedule, you could simply hire and train more annotators to all work at the same time. However, as we will discuss further in "Evaluating the Annotations" on page 126, you need to make sure each file gets annotated at least twice (so that you can calculate IAA scores), and these things are generally easier to manage when you aren't overwhelmed with annotators.

Also, even if your annotation guidelines have been repeatedly modified and perfected, the longer that an annotator has to adjust to a task, the better he will be at it, and the more time you allocate to getting the annotation done, the better your annotators will be able to acclimate to the task and thereby generate more accurate annotations.

Choosing an Annotation Environment

Many different annotation environments are available for use, ranging from free, stand-alone tools, such as the Multipurpose Annotation Environment (MAE) and Callisto, to workbenches that provide annotation task management and adjudication options all packaged together (such as SLATE and the Brandeis Annotation Tool [BAT]). A user guide for MAE is provided in Appendix C, and MAE is a good tool to start with if you've never annotated before, but annotation projects are not one-tool-fits-all. We aren't going to go through the entire list of tools here (a list in Appendix B gives an overview of what's available and some of the basic features of each piece of software), but there are a few questions that you should be able to answer about your task, and that will help narrow down what annotation software will be best for you.

Don't forget that you will need to also give your annotators instructions for how you want them to use the annotation tool you choose for the annotation task, and probably provide at least one in-person tutorial as well. Picking an annotation tool with a very steep learning curve for annotators, or one that is easy to make mistakes in, can also cause errors in annotation and lower resultant agreement scores.

There are always basic considerations that you need to think about when it comes to choosing software. For example, is it currently being supported, so if you have questions about it there will be a way to find an answer? Will it work on all the computers and operating systems that you and your annotators will be using? If the software is open source and you want to make a change, do you have someone who can change the code to make the adjustments you want? (This isn't required in order to use open source software, of course, but it can be a good way to get the annotation that you want.) However, these questions are all fairly generic, so here are some annotation-specific questions that will affect your choice of software.

What parts of your task does the annotation software need to support?

If you are annotating extents in a text and want your annotators to be able to easily modify attributes associated with the tags they create, you'll want to make sure the tool you choose makes that functionality easy to access. Not all (or even most) annotation software was built to be completely all-purpose: some software doesn't allow users to create links between annotated extents, and if you want to be able to give your annotators access to ontologies or other existing resources while they work, you'll have to choose software that has that built in.

What are the units of your annotation task?

In "Text Extent Annotation: Named Entities" on page 94, we discussed the different ways that extent annotation can be represented, as token-based or character-based. The current standards favor character-based, stand-off annotations, but not all tools use that system for their annotation representation. This isn't necessarily a problem if you aren't committed to the stand-off paradigm, or if you are able to convert from one format to another later on. However, as we discussed before, some tasks require that partial words be annotated, and tools that only annotate at a token level, so if you have one of those tasks, you will want to avoid software with that restriction.

Do you want your annotators to do all parts of the annotation task at once, or should the task be divided into layers?

Some annotation tools (such as BAT), enforce a layered annotation process, which means that each type of tag is annotated separately, with extent tags being annotated and adjudicated first, and then link tags created on top of the adjudicated extents. This format means that links will inherently have higher adjudication scores, because the annotators will be working from the same set of annotated extents. However, if you are still working out the kinks in your annotation task, this might not be the best format to use, because it requires that large portions of the annotation and adjudication be done before moving on to the rest of the annotation, which means that if there is an error in your guidelines relating to extent tags that affect how links are created, you'll have to redo a lot of work to fix the error. However, layered annotation can be an excellent way to break down a task into manageable pieces, and the paradigm can be used even if you aren't using a tool that enforces that format.

What other features do you want to be able to incorporate?

As we mentioned at the beginning of this section, some tools provide task management features (for managing which annotators get which files, keeping track of accuracy, etc.), while others provide simple annotation interfaces. However, some tools (such as GATE) also integrate POS taggers, tokenizers, and ML algorithms. These features certainly aren't mandatory for annotation tasks, but they can provide some helpful tools for annotators (and for you, of course).

Evaluating the Annotations

Before you actually start creating the gold standard by adjudicating the annotations, you'll want to evaluate the annotation task, especially if you're still working through the MAMA cycle with your test set of annotation files. We've talked a lot so far about IAA scores (sometimes called *inter-coder* or *inter-tagger* agreement scores), and how it's important to have good IAA scores to make sure your task is reproducible. IAA scores provide a way to evaluate how accurately your annotation task can be done by two or more annotators.

Good IAA scores don't necessarily mean that your corpus will produce good results when used to train an ML algorithm. However, the more data that you can get annotated, the better your ML results are likely to be, so it's still worth your time to make a task reproducible—the easier your task is for others to do, the more annotators you can train, so you can have a bigger corpus for testing and training.

At first it might seem that calculating IAA is just a matter of counting up how many tags there are in the dataset and calculating how many times the annotators agree on whether each tag should be there. However, using straight percentages like that doesn't take into account random chance agreements that are likely to occur when people annotate texts. If, for example, you want a set of movie reviews to be labeled as positive or negative, if your annotators simply pick the label for each document without reading the text, there's a 50% chance that they will agree on the label they assign, which means that agreement scores will seem artificially high.

To create numbers that can be compared across studies, various metrics have been developed and used over the years for calculating IAA. The two most commonly used in computational and corpus linguistics are *Cohen's Kappa* (and its variation, *Fleiss's Kappa*) and *Krippendorff's Alpha*. Whether or not these metrics appropriately measure all aspects of agreement in an annotation task is still being debated (for excellent reviews of the topic, see Artstein and Poesio 2008 and Bayerl and Paul 2011), but here we'll just cover the basics of the kappa metrics, as they apply to most annotation tasks.

Cohen's Kappa (κ)

Cohen's Kappa (κ) measures the agreement between two annotators, while taking into account the possibility of chance agreement. The equation is:

$$K = \frac{Pr(a) - Pr(e)}{1 - Pr(e)}$$

In the equation, *Pr(a)* is the relative observed agreement between annotators, and *Pr(e)* is the expected agreement between annotators, if each annotator was to randomly pick a category for each annotation. Let's take a look at a specific example.

Going back to one of the examples we've been discussing, assume that we had an annotation task where two annotators, A and B, were asked to assign the labels "positive," "neutral," and "negative" to a set of 250 movie reviews, and that the resultant annotations looked like this:

		B positive	B neutral	B negative
A	positive	54	28	3
A	neutral	31	18	23
A	negative	0	21	72

The preceding table shows that while the annotators rarely had situations where one labeled a review as "positive" and the other labeled it as "negative," the "neutral" label contributed a lot to the level of disagreement. But how do we turn these numbers into an evaluation metric?

 This table is essentially a *confusion matrix,* which is a table that's used to compare the output of an algorithm to a gold standard. We'll talk more about confusion matrices in Chapter 8.

First, we calculate *Pr(a)*, the actual agreement between the annotators. Out of 250 documents, A and B both said "positive" 54 times, both said "neutral" 18 times, and both said "negative" 72 times. So the percentage of observed agreement is:

$Pr(a)$= (54 + 18 + 72) / 250 = **.576** (57.6%)

Next we calculate $Pr(e)$, the expected chance agreement, for each label. To do that, we determine the percentage of the time that each annotator used each label and multiply those percentages to determine how often the two annotators would use the same label on the same document at the same time, then add each of those together to get $Pr(e)$. If that sounds confusing, just watch:

A used the label "positive" 85 times (54 + 28 + 3), or .34% of the time. B also used the "positive" label 85 times (54 + 31), which is also .34. Multiplied together, .34 × .34 = .116, so A and B have a **.116** chance of both randomly choosing "positive" as a label.

Now we do the same calculations for "neutral" and "negative." A used "neutral" 72 times, or .288%, and B used the tag 67 times, or .268%. Combined, (.268 × .288), there is a **.077** chance of them both using the "neutral" tag. Finally, A used "negative" 93 times (.372) and B used "negative" 98 times (.392), giving a **.146** chance of agreement on the "negative" tag.

Adding those three chance agreement scores together gives us:

$Pr(e)$ = .116 + .077 + .146 = **.339**

Putting $Pr(a)$ and $Pr(e)$ into the equation gives us:

κ = (.576 − .339) / (1 − .339) = .237 / .661 = **.359**

We'll discuss how to interpret the scores in "Interpreting Kappa Coefficients" on page 131; for now, let's move on to another example.

Fleiss's Kappa (κ)

Cohen's Kappa can determine the agreement between two annotators, but what if you have three or more people annotating the same document? In that case, you'll need to use Fleiss's Kappa instead. Fleiss's Kappa isn't actually based on Cohen's Kappa; rather, it's an extension of Scott's pi (π), but for most contexts, they are similar enough that it's OK to compare them.

The base equation for Fleiss's κ is essentially the same as for Cohen's κ, with the actual agreement and expected agreement due to chance being calculated and compared. However, the manner in which these are calculated differs, so we will use slightly different symbols here to avoid confusion:

$$k = \frac{P - P_e}{1 - P_e}$$

The table used to represent annotator values for Fleiss's Kappa, rather than having one axis per annotator, has one axis for the possible values an annotator could assign, and the other axis for each of the items being annotated. The contents of the cells show how many annotators assigned each category to each item. Note that Fleiss's Kappa does not assume that all items are annotated by the *same* annotators, but it does assume that all items are annotated the same number of times. Just so we can look at some bigger numbers, let's assume we redid our movie review annotation task as a crowdsourcing project (see Chapter 12). Instead of having 250 movie reviews annotated by 2 people, let's say that we had 5 movie reviews annotated as positive, neutral, or negative by 250 people each. These annotations would be represented like this:

	positive	neutral	negative
Review 1	85	72	93
Review 2	85	67	98
Review 3	68	99	83
Review 4	88	88	74
Review 5	58	120	72
total	384	446	420

In this table, the categories are across the top, the movie review documents are down the side, and the content of each cell represents how many times that an annotator assigned each category to each review.

First, we need to calculate how many assignments went (proportionally) to each category. This is represented by P_c, where c stands for the category being evaluated. We do this by summing up the contents of each row and dividing by the total number of annotations. In the following equation, A is the number of reviews, a is the number of annotations per review, k is the number of categories, and i represents the current table cell:

$$P_c = \frac{1}{Aa} \sum_{i=1}^{A} a_{ic}, \ 1 = \frac{1}{a} \sum_{c=1}^{k} a_{ic}$$

This looks a bit complicated, but basically all it says is that P_c (in this case, c will stand for positive, neutral, and negative) will equal the sum of the values in its column divided by the number of reviews (5) times the number of annotations per review (250). The second version of the equation simply says that if you add up all the annotations that an annotator made and divide by the number of annotations each annotator made individually, you will get 1, because both numbers should be the same.

So, if we apply the P_c equation to the first annotation category, we get the following equation:

$P(positive) = (85 + 85 + 68 + 88 + 58) / (5 \times 250)$
$= 384 / 1250$
$= .3072$

If we apply this calculation to the rest of the table, we can fill in the bottom row of the table, like so:

	positive	neutral	negative
Review 1	85	72	93
Review 2	85	67	98
Review 3	68	99	83
Review 4	88	88	74
Review 5	58	120	72
total	384	446	420
P_c	.3072	.3568	.336

Next, we need to calculate P_i, which represents the annotator's agreement per review compared to all possible agreement values. As before, a is the number of annotations per review, k is the number of categories, c is the current category, and i is the current review.

$$P_i = \frac{\left(\sum_{c=1}^{k} a_{ic}^2\right) - (a)}{a(a-1)}$$

Again, this isn't as difficult to apply as it seems: for each row, we're just summing up the squares of the values in each column and moderating the output by the number of total annotations for each review. So for Review 1, we would calculate this:

$P(Review\ 1) = ((85^2 + 72^2 + 93^2) - 250) / 250(250-1)$
$= 21058 - 250 / 62250$
$= 20808/62250$
$= .3343$

By performing this calculation for each Review row in the table, we can fill out the last column, like this:

	positive	neutral	negative	Pi
Review 1	85	72	93	.3343
Review 2	85	67	98	.3384

Review 3	68	99	83	.3384
Review 4	88	88	74	.3328
Review 5	58	120	72	.3646
total	384	446	420	
P_c	.3072	.3568	.336	

We're almost done. P in the original Fleiss equation is the average of the P_i values, so we calculate that by summing the P_i column and dividing by the number of reviews:

$$P(= (.3343 + .3384 + .3384 + .3328 + .3646) / 5$$
$$= 1.7085 / 5$$
$$= .3417$$

Then we calculate $P(e)$ by summing the squares of the P_c values, like so:

$$P(e) = .3072^2 + .3568^2 + .336^2 = .335$$

Now we can finally plug these values into Fleiss's Kappa equation and calculate our IAA score:

$$\kappa = (.3417 - .335) / (1 - .335)$$
$$= .0067 / .665$$
$$= .010$$

Interpreting Kappa Coefficients

In the two preceding sections we came up with two different values of κ for two different annotation tasks, .359 and .010.

But how are these scores actually interpreted? In many cases, the interpretation of the kappa depends on the complexity and objectivity of the annotation task, so there's no hard-and-fast rule that can always be used to determine whether scores are good or not. For example, a task such as POS tagging, even though it requires a lot of effort, would be expected to get a κ score close to 1.0, due to how well defined the terms and underlying theories are. On the other hand, tasks that require more interpretation of the text, such as semantic role labeling or temporal annotation (where the text may actually have multiple valid interpretations), are not generally held to such a high standard.

Landis and Koch 1977 provide these guidelines for interpreting κ and other agreement metrics:

κ	Agreement level
< 0	poor
0.01–0.20	slight

κ	Agreement level
0.21–0.40	fair
0.41–0.60	moderate
0.61–0.80	substantial
0.81–1.00	perfect

There has been some debate about how strictly these numbers should be interpreted, but they provide a good place to start. Another way to determine how your IAA scores should be interpreted is to do some research and find out what kind of IAA scores other, similar annotation tasks are getting. Naturally you should always strive to do well, but some tasks are simply harder than others.

So what can we say about the IAA scores from the examples in the previous sections? From our Cohen κ example, we obtained an agreement score of .359, which according to this chart is only "fair." And really, considering how few categories were included in the task (the more categories a task includes, the more room there is for ambiguity between labels), a score of .359 is pretty bad. Looking at the table of annotations, it's clear that there was a lot of confusion over how to spot a neutral review, so that part of the guideline would definitely need to be revised. Also, the fact that Annotator B labeled a few reviews as negative when Annotator A labeled them as positive—a fairly unusual error, considering the presence of the "neutral" tag—could indicate that Annotator B is having some trouble with the software as well as the guidelines.

As for the Fleiss's Kappa score…well, that's definitely one that would have to be revisited. Looking at the chart again, we can see that there's a lot of variation in all of the columns —in fact, none of the reviews seem to have any real sense of agreement. There are a lot of factors that can influence a crowdsourced project, such as not being able to train annotators, not being able to ensure that the annotators meet certain guidelines (such as native language), or just sheer online mischief; see Chapter 12 for discussion of some of the most common platforms and pitfalls. Of course, our example was made up, but agreement scores like these definitely mean that you need to review your annotation guidelines, and probably your dataset as well.

However, don't be discouraged by low agreement scores, especially when you're just starting a new MAMA cycle. Poor initial results are normal, which is why we encourage use of a small test set for annotation, just like you'll do later for training your ML algorithm—it's the best way to work out the kinks in your annotation task.

Calculating κ in Other Contexts

Both of the sample calculations we provided were only about annotators applying a set number of labels to a document, which made determining percent agreements much easier, because the divisor for calculating percentages was the same as the number of documents. However, what happens if you are trying to calculate agreement for tags that are applied to the words/tokens in a document, such as for POS tagging or for the example of annotating actors, characters, directors, and so on in movie reviews that we have been discussing?

For the POS tagging example, assuming that every token receives a tag, then the set of items being annotated is the same as the number of words in each document (or in all the documents at once, if you prefer). So your agreement table for two annotators would still look much the same as it did in our example of positive, negative, and neutral movie reviews, only the numbers in the table would be much bigger because they would reflect the number of words in the document or corpus, rather than just the number of documents.

However, what about annotation tasks where every token *isn't* annotated, particularly if the annotation is rather sparse? Let's say, for example, that you ask two annotators to only annotate the creature names and pronouns in Lewis Carroll's "Jabberwocky". "Jabberwocky" has 216 tokens (with punctuation marks considered individual tokens), but most of them aren't creature names or pronouns. So how should the nonannotated words be counted? If we consider "untagged" to be a tag, then we might end up with a comparison table that looks like this:

		B creature	B pronoun	B untagged
A	creature	5	0	2
A	pronoun	0	10	2
A	untagged	1	7	189

Apparently our imaginary annotators were a bit confused about our guidelines for pronouns, and whether some of the made-up words were creatures or something else. Regardless, if we calculate Cohen's Kappa for this table, we end up with a coefficient of .691, which isn't really bad considering that most of the poem's nouns are made up anyway. However, it's clear that the IAA score is being heavily influenced by the fact that there are so few tags in the text—the majority of the tokens go untagged, so the agreement over the *lack* of tags may be skewing the results.

$Pr(a) = .944$
$a(creature) = .032, b(creature) = .028 \longrightarrow creature = .0009$
$a(pronoun) = .056, b(pronoun) = .079 \longrightarrow pronoun = .0044$
$a(untagged) = .912, b(untagged) = .893 \longrightarrow untagged = .814$
$Pr(e) = .009 + .0044 + .814 = .819$
$k = (.944 - .819) / (1 - .819)$
$= .125 / .181$
$= .691$

It can be argued that in cases of sparse annotation, the set of items being examined should be limited to only the items that were tagged by one or both annotators. In this case, the number of items being investigated for agreement drops to 27.

		B creature	B pronoun	B untagged
A	creature	5	0	2
A	pronoun	0	10	2
A	untagged	1	7	0

$Pr(a) = .556$
$a(creature) = .259, b(creature) = .222 \longrightarrow creature = .057$
$a(pronoun) = .444, b(pronoun) = .629 \longrightarrow pronoun = .279$
$a(untagged) = .296, b(untagged) = .148 \longrightarrow untagged = .044$
$Pr(e) = .057 + .279 + .044 = .38$
$k = (.556 - .38) / (1 - .38)$
$= .176 / .62$
$= .284$

Clearly, the IAA score drops dramatically from "substantial" agreement at .691 to merely "fair" agreement at .284 when the investigation space is limited to only those tokens that were tagged by one or more annotators. You can imagine how much more complicated the discussion of IAA scores can become when evaluating a task that involves character-level rather than token-level annotations, where the length of the word being annotated can also affect IAA scores!

Compelling arguments can be made for both sides of these IAA calculation discussions (some would argue that, since annotation guidelines must also specify what *not* to annotate, discounting agreement on that score is foolish; others would say that using more rigorous agreement metrics increases the value of the calculations). We are not taking a side on which metric is better, but whatever method you use for these calculations, be sure to fully report on how you calculated the agreement. Regardless of how you calculate your IAA score, remember that it indicates relative agreement, and for our "Jabberwocky" example, both sets of scores would indicate that the guidelines will need to be revised and another round of annotation done—back to the MAMA cycle!

If your tags have attributes, don't forget to calculate IAA scores for those too! In those cases, it's fine to only compare attributes for a tag where the annotators agree that a tag should exist (since comparing tags when the annotators don't agree on the existence of a tag won't give you any useful information), but if you only compare the attributes for matching tags (extents that are identical or that at least overlap, links with the same anchors, etc.), make sure you report that information with the scores.

Creating the Gold Standard (Adjudication)

Once you've created a set of annotation guidelines that is getting you IAA scores that you are satisfied with and you've had your annotators apply those guidelines to your entire corpus, it's time to actually adjudicate their annotations and create your gold standard dataset, which is what you will use to train and test your ML algorithm. Generally it's best to have adjudicators who were involved in creating the annotation guidelines, as they will have the best understanding of the purpose of the annotation. Hiring new adjudicators means that you'll have the same problem you did with annotators.

Since you're already familiar with the annotation task, you should find the adjudication process to be fairly straightforward. You'll need software to perform the adjudication in (see Appendix B again for a list of what's available), and after that, it's just a matter of taking the time to do a careful job. There are a few things to think about, however:

- It will take you just as long, possibly longer, to do a careful job of adjudicating your corpus as it took one of your annotators to annotate it. Don't forget to allocate sufficient time to get this done.

- Consider breaking up the adjudication task into layers: first adjudicate each extent tag or label individually, then each link tag. This will make it much easier to pay attention to how each tag is being used, and will make link tags much more accurate (because they'll be connecting accurate extents).

- Just because two (or more) of your annotators agree about the presence of attributes of a tag at a location doesn't mean they're right! Remember that annotators can randomly be in agreement (which is why we spent so much time calculating kappa scores). So don't take for granted that annotators agreeing means they're right, at least until you have a good sense of your annotators' abilities.

- If you do use more than one adjudicator, consider giving them all some of the same documents so that you can also calculate IAA scores for them—that way, you'll be able to make sure they're all on the same page.

Once you have all your files adjudicated, you'll be ready to move on to the ML parts of the MATTER cycle.

Summary

In this chapter we discussed how to apply your model and spec to your corpus through the process of annotation, and how to create a gold standard corpus that can be used to train and test your ML algorithms. Some of the important points are summarized here:

- The "A" in the MATTER cycle is composed of a lot of different parts, including creating annotation guidelines, finding annotators, choosing an annotation tool, training annotators, checking for IAA scores, revising guidelines, and finally, adjudicating. Don't be put off by the number of steps outlined in this chapter; just take your time and take good notes.

- Guidelines and specifications are related, but they are not the same thing. The guidelines will determine how the model is applied to the text—even if you are using the same model, if the guidelines are different, they can result in a very different set of annotations.

- Creating a good set of annotation guidelines and an accurate and useful annotation won't happen on the first try. You will need to revise your guidelines and retrain your annotators, probably more than once. That's fine; just remember to allow yourself time when planning your annotation task. Within the MATTER cycle is the MAMA cycle, and no task is perfect straight off the bat.

- One of the things you will have to consider about the annotation process is what information you want to present to your annotators—giving them preprocessed data could ease the annotation process, but it could also bias your annotators, so consider what information you want to present to your annotators.

- Because you'll need to go through the MAMA cycle multiple times, it's a good idea to set aside a portion of your corpus on which to test your annotation guidelines while you work out the kinks. This set can be used in your gold standard later, but shouldn't be given to your annotators right away once the guidelines are finalized.

- When you're writing your annotation guidelines, there are a few questions that you'll find it necessary to answer for your annotators in the document. But the most important thing is to keep your guidelines clear and to the point, and provide plenty of examples for your annotators to follow.

- When finding annotators for a task, you need to consider what type of knowledge they will need to complete your annotation task accurately (and, if possible, quickly), what language they should speak natively, and how much time you have to annotate. The last consideration may play a role in how many annotators you need to hire to complete your task on schedule.

- The annotation software that you give to your annotators to create the annotations will have an effect on how easily and accurately the annotations are created, so keep that in mind when choosing what tool you will use. Using more than one piece of software for the same task could cause confusion and irregularities in the annotation, so it's better to pick one and stick with it.

- Once your annotators have annotated your sample set of texts, it's time to evaluate the IAA scores. While there are many different ways to determine agreement, the two most common in computational linguistics are Cohen's Kappa and Fleiss's Kappa. Cohen's Kappa is used if you have only two annotators annotating a document, while Fleiss's Kappa is used for situations where more than two annotators are used on a dataset.

- Based on how good your agreement scores are, you can decide whether or not your task is ready to go past the test set and on to the full corpus. You will probably need to revise your task at least once, so don't be discouraged by low IAA scores.

- Interpreting IAA scores isn't an exact science—a number of factors can influence whether a score indicates that an annotation task is well defined, including the number of tags, the subjectivity of the annotation task, and the number of annotators.

- Additionally, the items being annotated can have an effect on how you calculate IAA. While it's easy to calculate agreement when applying a single label to an entire document, there is some debate about how IAA scores should be calculated when applying tags to text extents. Regardless of what method you decide to apply for calculating IAA scores, keep track of the decisions you make so that other people can understand how you came up with your numbers.

- Having high IAA scores mean your task is likely to be reproducible, which is helpful when creating a sufficiently large corpus. However, just because a task is reproducible doesn't necessarily mean it will be suitable for feeding to ML algorithms. Similarly, just because a task doesn't have great agreement scores doesn't mean it will not be good for ML tasks. However, a reproducible task will be easier to create a large corpus for, and the bigger your corpus, the more likely you are to get good ML results, so putting some effort into creating your annotation guidelines will pay off in the end.

- Once you've reached acceptable IAA scores on your annotation test set, you can set your annotators loose on the full corpus. When you have the full corpus, it's time to adjudicate the annotations and create the gold standard corpus that you will use to train your ML algorithms.

- Adjudication is best performed by people who helped create the annotation guidelines. Bringing in new people to perform the adjudication can cause more confusion and noise in your dataset.

- Calculating IAA agreement scores between adjudicators can be a good way to ensure that your adjudicated corpus is consistent. The more consistent your corpus is, the more accurate your ML results will be.

CHAPTER 7

Training: Machine Learning

In this chapter we finally come to the topic of designing machine learning (ML) algorithms that will be run over our annotated text data. That is, we describe the task of taking linguistic data (annotated and unannotated) to train ML algorithms to automatically classify, tag, and mark up the text for specific purposes. We will present the goals and techniques of machine learning, and review the different algorithms that you will want to consider using for your annotated corpus. Here are the questions we will answer in this chapter:

- How do we define the learning problem formally? Learning as distinguishing or classifying objects into different categories? Learning as problem solving or planning?

- How does the design of a specification and annotation improve a learning algorithm?

- What kinds of features are in the dataset that you can exploit with your algorithm?

- What kinds of learning algorithms are there?

- When should you use one algorithm over another?

The purpose of this chapter is to give you an overview of the different types of algorithms and approaches that are used for machine learning, and help you figure out which kind will best suit your own annotation task. It is not meant to provide an in-depth discussion of the math underlying all the different algorithms, or any of the details for using them. There are a number of other books that provide that information in much more depth than we intend to provide here. If you are interested in learning more about ML algorithms, we recommend the following books:

- *Natural Language Processing with Python* by Steven Bird, Ewan Klein, and Edward Loper (O'Reilly, 2009)

- *Foundations of Statistical Natural Language Processing* by Chris Manning and Hinrich Schütze (MIT Press, 1999)
- *Speech and Language Processing* by Daniel Jurafsky and James H. Martin (Prentice Hall, 2008)
- *Machine Learning* by Tom Mitchell (McGraw-Hill/Science/Engineering/Math, 1997)

What Is Learning?

Machine learning refers to the area of computer science focusing on the development and implementation of systems that improve as they encounter more data. To quote the Nobel Prize-winning economist Herbert Simon:

> Learning is any process by which a system improves its performance from experience.

For areas in language technology and computational linguistics, the most important topics for learning include the following:

- Assigning categories to words (part-of-speech [POS] tagging)
- Assigning topics to articles, emails, or web pages
- Mood, affect, or sentiment classification of a text or utterance
- Assigning a semantic type or ontological class to a word or phrase
- Language identification
- Spoken word recognition
- Handwriting recognition
- Syntactic structure (sentence parsing)
- Timestamping of events or articles
- Temporal ordering of historical events
- Semantic roles for participants of events in a sentence
- Named Entity (NE) identification
- Coreference resolution
- Discourse structure identification

Although the preceding list presents a broad range of things to learn, you really only need to study a few strategies to approach these problems computationally. We will discuss three types of ML algorithms in this chapter:

Supervised learning
> Any technique that generates a function mapping from inputs to a fixed set of labels (the desired output). The labels are typically metadata tags provided by humans who annotate the corpus for training purposes.

Unsupervised learning
> Any technique that tries to find structure from an input set of unlabeled data.

Semi-supervised learning
> Any technique that generates a function mapping from inputs of both labeled data and unlabeled data; a combination of both supervised and unsupervised learning.

Because our focus is on how annotated data can improve a system's performance, we will focus our discussion on supervised learning first, and address semi-supervised and unsupervised learning later in the chapter.

As we mentioned in Chapter 1, machine learning involves the development of algorithms that acquire new concepts or generally improve their performance from experience or previous encounters with data. The algorithm learns an approximation of the *target function*, mapping input data to the desired output. The annotation process discussed in this book can be used to provide a richer source of material as the input data for the ML training phase. From this chapter we will see that annotation is relevant to machine learning because it allows us to ask two questions:

- How does the annotation give us a richer idea of what's in the dataset?
- How can we leverage this knowledge as new features for training our algorithms?

When discussing the role of annotation in the application of training ML algorithms, it is important to know what is involved in the process known as *feature selection*. This is the process of finding which features in your dataset are most helpful in solving your learning task. In this chapter we will discuss three types of features in the text that ML algorithms can exploit for learning. They are as follows:

N-gram features
> This is the classic "bag of words" approach to modeling a text document. Each word in the document is treated as a feature for the learning algorithm. If single words are used as features, then we call the resultant approach a *unigram word model*. *Term frequency*—the number of occurrences of a word in a document—is an important component of this model, along with *document frequency*—the frequency of a word throughout the entire corpus. We can also take bigram, trigram, and higher n-gram statistics into account if we want to capture some of the "larger window" around a word.

Structure-dependent features (SD features)
> These are features that can be identified and manipulated by virtue of the properties of the data structure itself. For example, the features associated with a "word" treated

as an ASCII string will include any and all properties that can be derived from examining the string; we can talk about a word's "length," its "first_character" (prefix), its "last_character" (suffix), and so on. Similarly, if a "sentence" is analyzed as a string of tokens (occurring between sentence boundaries, <S> and </S>), then we can refer to the "first_word" and "last_word" features for the structure.

Annotation-dependent features (AD features)
    This includes any features that are associated with an annotation specification that reflects a *model* of the data. For example, labels marking the type of an entity as *Person*, *Organization*, or *Place* within an NE specification (as discussed earlier), are features that reflect the model denoted by the annotations. Annotation-dependent features introduce new dimensions for discrimination, classification, or clustering that are not present in a unigram feature model (although they may be covered by some n-gram models, as we'll see shortly!).

We will learn when to use each of these classes, as well as which algorithms are most appropriate for each feature type. In particular, we will answer the following question: *when does annotation actually help in a learning algorithm?*

Defining Our Learning Task

To develop an algorithm, we need to have a precise representation of what we are trying to learn. We'll start with Tom Mitchell's [1] definition of a learning task:

> Learning involves improving on a task, T, with respect to a performance metric, P, based on experience, E.

Given this statement of the problem (inspired by Simon's concise phrasing shown earlier), Mitchell then discusses the five steps involved in the design of a learning system. Consider what the role of a specification and the associated annotated data will be for each of the following steps for designing a learning system:

1. Choose the "training experience." For our purposes, this is the corpus that you just built. The way we encode the "experience" surrounding our training samples reflects how much we know about the dataset. The model we arrived at in Chapter 4 can be used to mark up the dataset with annotations that might prove fruitful in representing the target function. Hence, we can think of annotation as enriching the *available feature space* for the domain.

2. Identify the target function (what is the system going to learn?). A model and annotation can help to define the class of target functions.

---

1. Mitchell's book, *Machine Learning* (1997), is still a valuable and very relevant introduction to the field of machine learning. Read it today!

3. Choose how to represent the target function. Since annotations provide richer representations of the data than n-gram or structure-dependent features permit, the target function can be formulated in a more general and possibly more broadly applicable form.

4. Choose a learning algorithm to infer the target function from the experience you provide it with.

5. Evaluate the results according to the performance metric you have chosen.

Rule-based Systems

It is important to point out that the design of a model and the creation of a specification can serve as the starting point for many different types of algorithms. In fact, a good way to start off is to take the model for the annotation that you have developed and convert it directly to a rule-based system. This involves converting the features from the model to rules using the basic pattern of a *condition-action pair*. This is a general template that can be used to label a single token or a sequence of tokens, and it is at the core of most programs that parse sentences or programs, as well as verify the content of Web-based applications, from email to Web-based queries and transactions.

The condition-action paradigm is the general term that includes *parsing*, and with that, compiling, and other applications. For our purposes here, we are interested in the more mundane problem of recognizing a token or sequence of tokens (the condition), and then applying some sort of tag or performing some sort of labeling (the action).

In many areas of computational linguistics, in fact, rule-based systems will perform as well as if not better than statistically trained ML algorithms. Rules are connections between the condition and the resultant action. As we discuss in Chapter 11, rule-based systems have been successfully applied to domain-constrained recognition tasks such as the following:

- Finding event expressions across parts of speech (e.g., *wedding, have eaten, hungry*)
- Identifying times, dates, and temporal expressions (e.g., *June 11, 1989*; *yesterday*; *early March*; *three weeks from tomorrow*)
- NEs, such as People, Organizations, and Locations (e.g., *Bill Clinton*; *10 Downing Street*; *Apple Corporation*; *Paris, France*)

Classifier Algorithms

In its most basic form, a classifier is a function that takes input in the form of a bundle of features and outputs class labels associated with these features. The goal in classifier learning is to learn this function from a labeled training set of input-output pairs (the annotated training corpus). Because we are actively engaged in directing the algorithm toward discovery of the function, this is called a *supervised learning technique*.

From the perspective of this book, the goal of supervised learning is to train an algorithm with the most informative and representative examples you can find or create, for the learning task at hand.

The goal of a classification task is to correctly sort a collection of things into the proper category. If there are only two categories, then the task is called a *binary classification task*, and the learner is called a *binary classifier*. We encountered annotations providing this kind of problem in previous chapters. For example, if you are teaching a classifier to recognize spam in your email, then you have two categories: *spam* and *not-spam*. As with other text classification problems, the tag can be assigned to the text at the document level, upon inspection of the contents of the document. In this sense, there is no linguistic annotation at all, but merely document-level annotation. Nevertheless, it still falls within the general characterization of a classification problem: you have a training set, $d_1, \ldots ,d_n$, that has been labeled with the tags associated with annotations from the (rather trivial) model, *M, Spam (S)*, or *Ham (H)*; $\{(d_1,S),(d_2,H), \ldots (d_n,S)\}$.

How the different types of features described in the preceding paragraph contribute to solving such classifications is one of the topics of this chapter. Using n-gram features is the simplest place to start when the label is associated with a document-level tag. Surprisingly, however, as you quickly discover with your own tweaking (feature engineering), unigrams are often the best of all, beating out even bigram and trigram features on certain tasks. This is counterintuitive at first, since it would always seem that "more is better" when it comes to finding features for solving a task such as classification. But the problem immediately emerges that, with too many features, most of the learning algorithms we describe in this chapter get "confused" since the properties associated with these features are distributional values over the corpus. So the challenge is somehow to select which features do the best job.

 When is one algorithm better than another? This depends on the scope of the classification task relative to the data being used to create the features for the classifiers.

When is one set or type of feature better than another? This depends on what the target function is for the learning task.

This is where annotation comes in. The point of linguistic annotation is to identify textual components of your document that can be associated with particular features for the phenomena for which you want to develop learning algorithms. Let's take some examples beyond the spam-ham distinction. Consider sentiment analysis applied to movie reviews or hotel ratings. The most expedient method for classifying movie reviews is to set up the learning problem with n-gram features. The words in the reviews are taken as independent features (lexical clues), and thrown into a description of the target function. While this works remarkably well in general, this approach will fail to capture properties that show up as nonlocal dependencies, such as the ways that negation and modality are often expressed in language. Having an annotation that captures such properties can provide additional features for learning algorithms that would otherwise be unavailable.

Imagine that you're trying to distinguish negative opinions of a product from positive ones, such as for a digital camera. Think about how we express ourselves:

- The Plandex J45 is a terrible camera.
- This is not a good camera.

In these cases, we can readily identify a negative judgment (terrible), but even a simple negation (not) may be difficult to recognize, unless we know how to place the positive judgment (good camera) within the scope of the negation, assuming they're all treated as lexical clues.

Things get harder, however, with other cases. What happens when we have negative judgments such as these?

- I don't think this is a good camera.
- I cannot recommend this as a great camera.

It's not clear whether learners trained with just n-gram features will be able to catch such cases. These won't present a problem if the annotation scheme we've created can identify negation, regardless of where it appears in the sentence.

In the rest of this section, we review the basic learning algorithms used in the field, and the advantages and disadvantages of each approach.

Decision Tree Learning

This is the most intuitive of all classifier algorithms, and is essentially a formal way of asking "20 questions" of a corpus. For any annotation task you have defined, there will be basic categories that are amenable to this approach. A decision tree is an upside-down tree, which classifies instances of the dataset by sorting them "down the tree" from the root question to a leaf node, at which point there is a specific classification of the instance. Along the way, the nodes of the tree each represent a question that is answered by the branches that shoot out of the node, "down the tree."

The questions that are "asked" can pertain to any information available that is from the dataset, but they are typically typed according to one of the three classes mentioned earlier: n-gram features, structure-dependent features, or annotation-dependent features.

Let's take, as an example, our old friend the *spam filter*. We mentioned before what the annotation model for such a simple binary classifier would be, so now let's see how we can build the actual classifier that goes with the model. For example, for classifying texts into spam or not-spam, we can make use of the logical structure of a decision tree by asking about unigram or n-gram properties of the document, that is, lexical features. For spam, this might include words or characters such as *html, !, @*, and *<table>*, which are n-gram features (see Figure 7-1).

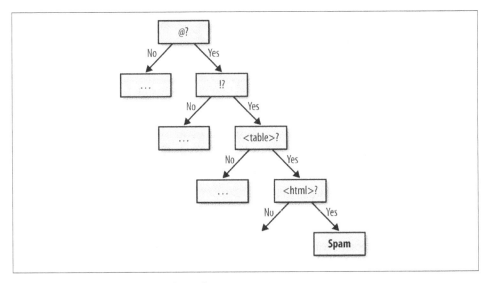

Figure 7-1. Decision tree over lexical triggers

We can, of course, ask questions regarding quantitative values associated with n-gram (or lexical) features, such as the following, which are structure-dependent features:

- What percentage of the document is HTML tags?
- How many tables are there in the document?

These questions are structure-dependent features that exploit the nature of the token (word) and its distribution in the document.

We can also ask questions that assume a more sophisticated model of the data, such as that associated with a specification and annotation schema. For example, our model of spam may have a schema element called neg-content-term, which is a label that identifies stereotypical spam-related vocabulary, be it pornography, physical dysfunction, or unbelievably good financial offers. This type of question exploits an *annotation-dependent feature* that we have made or abstracted over the dataset.

```
<!ELEMENT neg-content-term ( #PCDATA ) >

<!ATTLIST neg-content-term label ( viagra | bank | inheritance | transfer |
    sex | dysfunction | performance | ... ) >
```

Any of these feature types can be combined into the same decision tree structure, as illustrated in Figure 7-2.

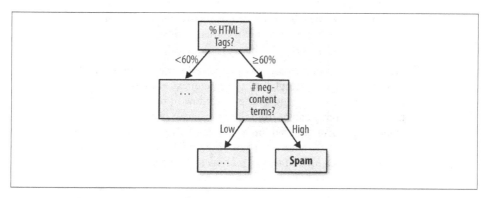

Figure 7-2. Decision tree over mixed feature types

Gender Identification

Now let's get our hands dirty with decision trees. We'll start with the "first name gender" classification problem described in *Natural Language Processing with Python*. This is the problem of automatically recognizing whether a (first) name is male or female, as illustrated in Figure 7-3.

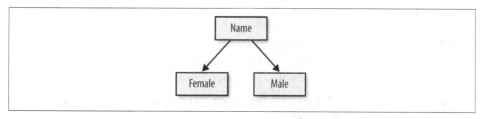

Figure 7-3. Gender target function

The approach the authors of the aforementioned book describe is to look at properties of the name as a token to determine how these properties can contribute to discriminating between male and female. This is a great example of what we have called *structure-dependent* (SD) features for learning. Essentially, the name is analyzed in terms of its structure as a token, that is, a string of characters. That's why the features that will be used for training a gender classifier are structure-dependent, and not n-gram or annotation-dependent features.

 What would n-gram features for the first name gender problem look like? It wouldn't be pretty, since we would have to train on individual full-token first name instances, where the corpus would be token-based. No generalizations would be possible, since there is only one feature associated with the target function values: for example, (female, male). So, the algorithm can only correlate a tag with a known token, which means it can only use this pairing in the future on tokens that it has already identified.

What would an annotation-based feature be for this problem? Well, you might have an annotation of the context around the name; for example, words occurring within a window of the token. This might help in identifying names from the syntactic or semantic context. This would be particularly useful in a language that carried morphological marking for gender on the verb or on modifiers that might accompany the name: *La belle Mary* (Fr.), *Le beau Peter* (Fr.).

Upon examination of the corpus of first names, finding the most relevant structure-dependent features for this problem turns out to be quite straightforward. Gender seems to be reflected in values of two basic properties of the token:

- The value of characters in specific positions; for example, last, first, next to last, and so on
- Other character properties, such as whether it's a vowel, a consonant, and so on

Once we have an inventory of features (in this case, they're all structure-dependent features), then we can get started. Recall the steps in the creation of a learning algorithm:

1. Choose the training experience, E. In this case, the experience is a list of SD features for each name viewed as a token. More specifically, the instances are attribute-value pairs, where the attributes are chosen from a fixed set along with their values.

2. Identify the target function (what is the system going to learn?). We are making a binary choice of whether the token is *male* or *female*. So the target function is a discrete Boolean classification (yes or no) over each example (e.g., Is "Nancy" female? → yes; Is "Peter" female? → no). Formally, we can say that our function, f,

maps from word tokens to the binary classification associated with the gender pair, {female, male}. We will define this as a Boolean value function, and simply refer to the function as *F*, which returns true when the token is a female name and false when the token is a male name.

3. Choose how to represent the target function: this will be some functional combination of the SD features that we identified earlier. Again, using some of the features that are identified in *Natural Language Processing with Python*, we have:[2]

- *F1: last_letter = "a"*
- *F2: last_letter = "k"*
- *F3: last_letter = "f"*
- *F4: last_letter = "r"*
- *F5: last_letter = "y"*
- *F6: last_2_letters = "yn"*

4. Choose a learning algorithm to infer the target function from the experience you provide it with. We will start with the decision tree method.

5. Evaluate the results according to the performance metric you have chosen. We will use accuracy over the resultant classifications as a performance metric.

But, now, where do we start? That is, which feature do we use to start building our tree? When using a decision tree to partition your data, this is one of the most difficult questions to answer. Fortunately, there is a very nice way to assess the impact of choosing one feature over another. It is called *information gain* and is based on the notion of *entropy* from information theory. Here's how it works.

In information theory, entropy measures the average uncertainty involved in choosing an outcome from the set of possible outcomes. In our case, entropy is a measure over a collection of data (the examples to classify) that characterizes how much order exists between the items relative to a particular classification, *C*. Given our corpus, *S*, of training data, the entropy is the sum of probabilities of each class value c_i (p_i), times the log probability for that class value:

---

2. We could also define an approximation to the target function, *F'*, as follows:

$$F' = w_1 F1 + w_2 F2 + w_3 F3 + w_4 F4 + w_5 F5 + w_6 F6$$

Namely, *F'* is a linear combination of the SD features shown in the preceding bulleted list, where w_i refers to the numerical coefficients that are chosen by the learning algorithm to optimize the value returned by *F'*, which approximates *F*.

$$\log_2 \frac{1}{p_i}$$

So, we can state the entropy of the corpus (as the random variable S) as follows:

$$H(S) = \sum_{i=1}^{c} p_i \log_2 \frac{1}{p_i} = -\sum_{i=1}^{c} p_i \log_2 p_i$$

With the concept of entropy given here, we now define the information gain associated with choosing a particular feature to create a partition over the dataset. Assume that through examining the data or through the MATTER cycle, we've come up with a set of features (or attributes) that we want to use for classifying our data. These can be n-gram, structure-dependent, or annotation-dependent features. Let the features that we've come up with for our task be the set, $\{A_1, A_2, \ldots, A_n\}$. To judge the usefulness of a feature as a "separation" between the data points, let's define the information gain, G, associated with an attribute, A_i, as the expected reduction in entropy that results from using this attribute to partition the examples. Here's the formal statement for information gain as just described, where $G(S,A)$ stands for the "information gain" using attribute A relative to the set S:

$$G(S, A) =_{df} H(S) - \sum_{v \in Val(A)} \frac{|S_v|}{|S|} H(S_v)$$

Notice what this says. The measure of how effective an attribute A is in reducing the entropy of a set is computed by taking the difference between the current value before the partitioning, $H(S)$, and the sum of the entropies of each subset S_v, weighted by the fraction belonging to S_v.

Using information gain, let's put the "20 questions" in the most effective order for partitioning the dataset.

One of the problems we have when integrating a lot of features into our learning algorithm, as we saw earlier with decision tree learning, is that features are checked (the questions are asked) in a fixed order in the tree. This ordering is not able to reflect the fact that many features are independent of one another.

Another problem, as pointed out in *Natural Language Processing with Python*, is that decision trees are bad at exploiting "weak predicates" of the correct category value, since they usually show up so far down in the decision tree. The Naïve Bayes method can get around many of these problems, as we will see in the next section.

Naïve Bayes Learning

As described in the preceding section, the classification task is defined as the association of a category or class to an input. The learner tries to approximate this assignment function, as shown here:

$$f{:}X \rightarrow C$$

This function can be equivalently viewed as a conditional probability statement:

$$P(C \mid X)$$

where we are hoping to find the probability of assigning category C, given that we are presented with X (where both are viewed as random variables).

Given that we have been thinking of the input in terms of features (n-gram, structure-dependent, annotation-dependent), we can rephrase this formula using reference to features instead. That is, we want to justify the assignment of a class C, given a set of features associated with the training instance, $F_1, \dots, F_n$. This is stated as:

$$p(C \mid X_{F_1}, \dots, X_{F_n})$$

Essentially, the idea behind a probabilistic Bayesian classifier is a simple one, and one that takes advantage of the correspondence between conditionals from the Bayes Theorem, which we encountered in Chapter 3. There we saw that:

$$P(A \mid B) = \frac{P(B \mid A)P(A)}{P(B)}$$

This is often thought of in terms of the nominal probabilities of *prior*, *likelihood*, and *posterior*, as shown here:

$$\text{posterior} = \frac{\text{likelihood} \times \text{prior}}{\text{evidence}}$$

With this equivalence, our classifier function can now be restated as follows:

$$P(C \mid X_{F_1}, \dots, X_{F_n}) = \frac{P(X_{F_1}, \dots, X_{F_n} \mid C)P(C)}{P(X_{F_1}, \dots, X_{F_n})}$$

A common and reasonable move when training a classifier is to assume that the evidence available to the approximation procedure (i.e., the learner) stays constant. If that's the case, then we can ignore the evidence completely and work with the unnormalized conditional probability:

$$P(C \mid X_{F_1}, ..., X_{F_n}) \propto P(X_{F_1}, ..., X_{F_n} \mid C)P(C)$$

So this is somewhat better, and the assumption here is that we can train the classifier by estimating the two values, $P(X_{F_1}, ..., X_{F_n} \mid C)$ and $P(C)$. Now, this is all well and good, but notice that the number of instances we will need to have at hand to calculate such estimates is exponentially large compared to the number of features! Fortunately, the "naïve" in "Naïve Bayes" learning is not just a value judgment but a functional design choice. If we make the assumption that all of the features, $F_1, ..., F_n$, are conditionally independent of one another, then we have the following:

$$P\left(X_{F_1}, ..., X_{F_n} \mid C\right) = \prod_{i=1}^{n} P\left(X_{F_i} \mid C\right)$$

Plugging this back into the previous equation, we have a much simpler foundation from which to calculate estimates of the probabilities, namely:

$$P\left(C \mid X_{F_1}, ..., X_{F_n}\right) \propto P(C)\prod_{i=1}^{n} P\left(X_{F_i} \mid C\right)$$

Now that we have reformulated the approximation function of the learner in terms that are amenable to realistic calculations over the dataset, we need to institute a policy for how to compare our hypotheses regarding category assignment, given the data. That is, the learning algorithm will need to consider a large number of candidate hypotheses for what category to assign to the data, and we want to choose the most probable one from this set. This hypothesis is called the *maximum a posteriori* (MAP) hypothesis, and it is simply the maximized probability resulting from the application of the Bayes classifier we just built. So now we can identify the learner as the Bayesian classifier from earlier, making the conditional independence assumptions over the feature set, where the result returns the maximum a posteriori probability:

$$\text{Classify}(f_1, ..., f_n) = \text{argmax}_{c \in C} P(C = c)\prod P\left(X_{F_i} = f_i \mid C = c\right)$$

Don't worry about the details of the math; for now, just know that we want the function to return the classification with the highest probability, based on the features provided in the evidence to the learner. Namely, you provide the features; the counts from the corpus create the estimates; and the algorithm provides the probabilities.

We should point out that Naïve Bayes is referred to as a generative classifier, since we can view the distribution $P(X|C)$ as describing how random instances of X can be generated, conditioned on the target C.

Where Do Parameter Estimates Come From?

The estimates for the parameters being used in the model need to come from somewhere. But how do we get them? In Chapter 3 we talked about calculating the prior probability of a given category by using the relative frequencies of the data. Using relative frequencies is a kind of Maximum Likelihood Estimation (MLE). We can do that for Naïve Bayes as well. Namely, divide the number of samples in the category, C, by the total number of samples, X, to estimate the probability distribution $P(X|C)$. The Maximum Likelihood Estimation is so called because it is this selection of the values of the parameters that will give the highest probability for the training corpus.

The problem with this approach for a lot of problems in Natural Language Processing (NLP), however, is that there simply isn't enough data to calculate such values! This is called the *data sparseness problem*. Consider what happens for data that the model hasn't encountered in the training corpus. The MLE will assign a zero probability to any unseen events, which is a very unhelpful value for predicting behavior on a new corpus. To solve this problem, statisticians have developed a number of methods to "discount" the probabilities of known events in order to assign small (but nonzero) values to the events not seen in the corpus. One such technique is *smoothing*. For example, additive smoothing is a common technique that takes the existing MLE for a known event and then discounts by a factor dependent on the size of the corpus and the vocabulary (the set of categories being used to bin the data). For a good review of smoothing techniques as used in NLP, check out Jurafsky and Martin (2008), and Manning and Schuetze (1999).

Movie genre identification

Let's take the classifier we just built out for a test drive. Recall the IMDb movie corpus we discussed in Chapter 3. This corpus consists of 500 movie descriptions, evenly balanced over five genres: Action, Comedy, Drama, Sci-fi, and Family. Let's assume our training corpus to be 400 labeled movie summaries, consisting of 80 reviews from each of the five genres. The learner's task is to choose, from the 400 articles, which genre the summary should belong to. The first question we need to confront is, what are the features we can use as input for this classifier? Recall that, generally, the task of making document-level categorizations is best handled with n-gram features, while annotation of NEs, events, or other text within the summary is not particularly helpful. This is easy to see by simply inspecting a couple of movie summaries. Here are two of the movies from the IMDb corpus, the drama *Blowup*, from 1966; and the family movie *Chitty Chitty Bang Bang*, from 1968.

Blowup (1966): Thomas is a London-based photographer who leads the life of excess typical of late 1960s mod London. He is primarily a highly sought-after studio fashion photographer, although he is somewhat tiring of the vacuousness associated with it. He is also working on a book, a photographic collection of primarily darker images of human life, which is why he spent a night in a flophouse where he secretly took some photos. While he is out one day, Thomas spies a couple being affectionate with each other in a park. From a distance, he clandestinely starts to photograph them, hoping to use the photographs as the final ones for his book. The female eventually sees what he is doing and rushes over wanting him to stop and to give her the roll of film. She states that the photographs will make her already complicated life more complicated. Following him back to his studio, she does whatever she needs to to get the film. He eventually complies, however in reality he has provided her with a different roll. After he develops the photographs, he notices something further in the background of the shots. Blowing them up, he believes he either photographed an attempted murder or an actual murder. The photos begin a quest for Thomas to match his perception to reality.

Chitty Chitty Bang Bang (1968): In the early 20th century England, eccentric Caractacus Potts works as an inventor, a job which barely supports himself, his equally eccentric father, and his two adolescent children, Jeremy and Jemima. But they're all happy. When the children beg their father to buy for them their favorite plaything - a broken down jalopy of a car sitting at a local junk yard - Caractacus does whatever he can to make some money to buy it. One scheme to raise money involves the unexpected assistance of a pretty and wealthy young woman they have just met named Truly Scrumptious, the daughter of a candy factory owner. But Caractacus eventually comes into another one time only windfall of money, enough to buy the car. Using his inventing skills, Caractacus transforms the piece of junk into a beautiful working machine, which they name Chitty Chitty Bang Bang because of the noise the engine makes. At a seaside picnic with his children and Truly, Caractacus spins a fanciful tale of an eccentric inventor, his pretty girlfriend (who is the daughter of a candy factory owner), his two children, and a magical car named Chitty all in the faraway land of Vulgaria. The ruthless Baron Bomburst, the ruler of Vulgaria, will do whatever he can to get his hands on the magical car. But because of Baroness Bomburst's disdain for them, what are outlawed in Vulgaria are children, including the unsuspecting children of a foreign inventor of a magical car.

As you can see, while it might be possible to annotate characters, events, and specific linguistic phrases, their contribution will be covered by the appropriate unigram or bigram feature from the text. Selecting just the right set of features, of course, is still very difficult for any particular learning task. Now let's return to the five-step procedure for creating our learning algorithm, and fill in the specifics for this task.

1. Choose the training experience, *E*. In this case, we start with the movie corpus and take the list of n-gram features for each word in the summary.

2. Identify the target function (what is the system going to learn?). We are making an n-ary choice of whether the summary is Drama, Action, Family, Sci-fi, or Comedy.

3. Choose how to represent the target function. We will assume that target function is represented as the MAP of the Bayesian classifier over the features.

4. Choose a learning algorithm to infer the target function from the experience you provide it with. This is tied to the way we chose to represent the function, namely:

$$\text{Classify}(f_1, ..., f_n) = \text{argmax}_{c \in C} P(C = c) \Pi P(X_{F_i} = f_i \mid C = c)$$

5. Evaluate the results according to the performance metric you have chosen. We will use accuracy over the resultant classifications as a performance metric.

Sentiment classification

Now let's look at some classification tasks where different feature sets resulting from richer annotation have proved to be helpful for improving results. We begin with sentiment or opinion classification of texts. This is really two classification tasks: first, distinguishing fact from opinion in language; and second, if a text is an opinion, determining the sentiment conveyed by the opinion holder, and what object it is directed toward. A simple example of this is the movie-review corpus included in the NLTK corpus package, where movies are judged positively or negatively in a textual review. Here are some examples:

- *Positive:*

  jaws is a rare film that grabs your attention before it shows you a single image on screen . the movie opens with blackness , and only distant , alien-like underwater sounds . then it comes , the first ominous bars of composer john williams' now infamous score . dah-dum . there , director steven spielberg wastes no time , taking us into the water on a midnight swim with a beautiful girl that turns deadly .

- *Positive:*

  ... and while the film , like all romantic comedies , takes a hiatus from laughs towards the end because the plot has to finish up , there are more than enough truly hilarious moments in the first hour that make up for any slumps in progress during the second half . my formal complaints for the wedding singer aren't very important . the film is predicable , but who cares ? the characters are extremely likable , the movie is ridiculously funny , and the experience is simply enjoyable .

- *Negative:*

  synopsis : a mentally unstable man undergoing psychotherapy saves a boy from a potentially fatal accident and then falls in love with the boy's mother , a fledgling restauranteur . unsuccessfully attempting to gain the woman's favor , he takes pictures of her and kills a number of people in his way . comments : stalked is yet another in a seemingly endless string of spurned-psychos-getting-their-revenge type movies which are a stable category in the 1990s film industry , both theatrical and direct-to-video .

- *Negative:*

  sean connery stars as a harvard law professor who heads back into the courtroom , by way of the everglades , to defend a young , educated black man (blair underwood) . the guy is on death row for the murder of a white girl , and says that his confession was coerced from the region's tough , black cop (lawrence fishburne) . watching connery and fishburne bump heads for two hours is amusing enough , but the plot's a joke . there's no logic at work here . tone is also an issue--there is none . director arne glimcher never establishes exactly what his film is trying to say . is it a statement on human rights ? is it a knock-off of silence of the lambs ?

More complicated cases emerge when we look at product reviews, or more nuanced reviews, where the text is conveying a number of different opinions, not all of them negative or positive. Consider the following review, for example:

> I received my Kindle Fire this morning and it is pretty amazing. The size, screen quality, and form factor are excellent. Books and magazines look amazing on the tablet and it checks email and surfs the web quickly. (Kindle Fire review on Amazon.com)

This has been a growing area since around 2002 (Pang et al. 2002), and has also been an area where corpora have been developed, including the MPQA Opinion Corpus (Wiebe et al. 2005), described in Appendix A. There are some early classifiers based entirely on n-gram models (mostly unigram) that perform quite well, so we will not explore those here. Instead, we will look at whether annotation based on model criteria can improve the results seen from n-gram-based models. If we take a model-based approach, as developed in this book, then we are hoping to characterize the text and the learning task with an annotation that reflects a deeper appreciation of the linguistic phenomena being studied (and learned). To handle more nuanced review texts, researchers have proposed model-based schemas that reflect the dependencies between the opinion holder and the product, as well as the type of sentiment. There are a couple of annotation schemas that we can consider for sentiment annotation. For example, following Liu (2012), we can define an opinion as a tuple consisting of the following elements:

Opinion = <h, e, a, so, t>

where h is an opinion holder; e is the target entity of the opinion; a is a feature of the target; so is the sentiment orientation; and t is the time of the opinion event. Using such a description of opinions gives us an annotation language that picks out a much finer-grained set of entities and properties regarding sentiment toward different kinds of objects.

For example, the "orientation of the sentiment" will include values such as negative, positive, neutral, or sarcastic. Furthermore, we may identify the intensity of the opinion as low, medium, or high. Now consider what such an annotation gives us. Rather than creating classifiers based only on n-gram features, we can make references to features that have several advantages. First, they generalize over n-gram values and capture this generalization as an abstraction, captured by the value of an attribute. Second, this attribute can be manipulated as a feature independent of whatever n-grams might be associated with the values. Finally, the elements in the annotation can be associated by relations that are explicitly annotated in the text, or they can be more readily discovered as nonindependent by some algorithms, such as MaxEnt, which we will discuss next.

Maximum Entropy Classifiers

Now we will turn to another important classifer for ML tasks in NLP, called Maximum Entropy (*MaxEnt*, for short). This is known as "logistic regression" in statistics. It is similar in some respects to the Naïve Bayes model we just presented, and the features that we identified and used for defining the target function earlier can be easily adapted for this algorithm as well. The major difference is that the independence assumption made for Naïve Bayes learning is not necessary for MaxEnt. Learning in a Naïve Bayes Classifier involves counting up the number of co-occurrences of features and classes, all in one go. In MaxEnt, on the other hand, the weights are learned using an iterative procedure.

MaxEnt is a way to combine a wide range of pieces of evidence to classify a token or sequence into a category, given some context. Because of data sparseness, a training corpus may not have enough data to determine the probability of a class occurring with all the contextual options. MaxEnt is a strategy for doing just this: namely, it estimates probability distributions from the data. It starts from the assumption (giving it its name) that, when there is no particular information about the data, we should assume that it has a uniform distribution, meaning it has *maximum entropy*.

We use labeled training data to arrive at the constraints that are used for characterizing the "class-specific" expectations for the distribution. These are essentially the features that we encountered earlier with Naïve Bayes. Then, an iterative procedure applies to these features and finds the MaxEnt distribution consistent with these constraints. On this view, the correct distribution of a class a (a label) occurring in a context b (a feature), $p(a,b)$, is that which maximizes the entropy. This is shown in the following equation, where class-context (label-feature) pairs are notated as (a,b):

$$H(p) = - \sum_{(a,b)\in A\times B} p(a, b)\log_2 p(a, b)$$

MaxEnt works by keeping the entropy at a maximum while remaining consistent with the partial information that we have available to us, that is, the evidence. We will define any real-valued function of the context and the class to be a feature, $f_i(b,a)$—these label-feature combinations are often called *joint-features* (as in *Natural Language Processing with Python*).

When using MaxEnt, first we need to identify the set of feature functions that will be most useful in our classification task. For each of these, we measure the expected value over our training data, and this becomes the constraint for the model distribution as seen in the following equation (see Nigam et al. 1999 for a good discussion of this).

When the constraints are estimated in this manner, the distribution will always be of the form shown in the following equation:

$$P(a \mid b) = - \tfrac{1}{Z(b)} \exp(\sum_i \lambda_i f_i(b, a))$$

This states that the probability of a class a given some context b is provided by the exponential of the sum of all the parameterized (λ_i) features, $f_i(b,a)$; Z is a normalizing factor to make sure the probability behaves correctly.

We're not going to work through a whole new example for the MaxEnt model (there are plenty of other books that do that), but put simply, MaxEnt uses the training data available to directly estimate $P(C|X)$, where we are hoping to find the probability of assigning category C, given that we are presented with X, in contrast to Naïve Bayes. Because of this, it is often called a discriminative classifier since the distribution $P(X|C)$ directly discriminates the target value C for any instance X.

Other Classifiers to Know About

In this chapter we have tried to cover the major topics in defining the target function for your ML task. To this end, we have looked at several of the most popular supervised learning algorithms in the field today; decision trees, Naïve Bayes, and MaxEnt. many other algorithms can also be used for corpus annotation tasks, and a few of them are listed here:

- *K-nearest neighbor* is a method for classifying objects based on the closed training example in the feature space, which is dependent on the annotation features you are providing the algorithm. It is a kind of instance-based (memory-based) learning and is the simplest of all ML algorithms. kNN learning does not necessarily require any annotation over the text at all, but rather can take immediate advantage of the features of the text as individual tokens. kNN techniques have been applied to work in Machine Translation and a number of other NLP problems, including semantic relation extraction (Panchenko et al. 2012).

- *Support Vector Machine (SVM)* is a binary classifier that takes a set of input data represented as points in space, and predicts what category each element should be assigned to. SVMs are important because they can handle a very large number of variables (features) and operate with a small number of samples. They have been applied to both simple and quite complex classification tasks (Manning et al. 2008). The main idea behind SVMs is to find the best-fitting decision boundary between two classes, one that is maximally far from any point in the training data. Nonlinearly separable data can be handled elegantly by using a technique called the *kernel trick*, which maps the data into a higher dimension where it behaves in a linear fashion. SVMs have been applied very successfully to sentiment analysis (Pang et al. 2002).

We won't be going into detail about these, however; other books on machine learning (see the list at the start of the chapter) provide excellent guides for how these classifiers work, and the ones we've already discussed are enough to get you started in training algorithms on your annotated data.

Micro Versus Macro

Classifiers are evaluated using the results of a simple table that sums up how often the tags were correctly assigned. From this table we can compute the *accuracy* of the classifier. Recall from "Evaluate the Results" on page 30 that we use four measures:

- Accuracy
- Precision
- Recall
- F-measure

If we have only two categories, then we can choose one of these measures. If we have a problem that involves classifying objects into more than two categories, however, we can focus on the classification accuracy for each category, and then average the evaluation over all the categories to get an overall measure of the accuracy. This is called *macro-averaging*. The other option is called *micro-averaging*, and it involves making one big contingency table for all the data from all the categories. Then, we compute evaluation measures from this table. The advantage of this is that it measures the overall performance of the classification for all the categories, as opposed to what micro-averaging does, which is to focus on the individual category performances rather than the overall averaging.

Sequence Induction Algorithms

So far we have been discussing algorithms that classify a set of objects into distinct (and possibly several) categories, separating emails that are spam from those that are not, movies worth seeing from those that are rotten tomatoes, and so on. These are all examples of simple individual classifiers. An equally important task in machine learning, however, is learning *sequences* of specific categories. This is handled by a class of algorithms called *sequence classifiers*. In this section, we will briefly describe the problem and the major algorithms used for this task.

First let's define the problem. In many areas of language processing, we are presented with data composed of *sequences* of units; for example, letters, morphemes, words, sentences, paragraphs, and so on. In fact, we already encountered sequence prediction briefly in Chapter 3 with n-grams. While language modeling predicts the next element in a sequence, given the previously encountered elements, sequence labeling picks the best label for each element in a sequence. One of the most successful algorithms solving this problem is the *Hidden Markov Model* (HMM). Given a sequence of elements (words, letters, etc.), this algorithm computes a probability distribution over the possible labels associated with them, and then computes the best label sequence.

We can identify two basic methods for sequence classification:

Feature-based classification
> A sequence is tranformed into a feature vector. The vector is then classified according to conventional classifier methods.

Model-based classification
> An inherent model of the probability distribution of the sequence is built. HMMs and other statistical models are examples of this method.

Included in feature-based methods are n-gram models of sequences, where an n-gram is selected as a feature. Given a set of such n-grams, we can represent a sequence as a binary vector of the occurrence of the n-grams, or as a vector containing frequency counts of the n-grams. With this sort of encoding, we can apply conventional methods to model sequences (Manning and Schütze 1999). For example, SVMs have been used for sequence data (Leslie et al. 2002), as have decision trees (Chuzhanova et al. 1998).

One additional measure that can improve feature-based classification is the use of a distance measure, which can be applied to measure the similarity between sequences. This can contribute to the performance of sequence labeling when using conventional methods, such as k-nearest neighbor or SVMs. It should be noted that Euclidean metrics for determining distance will typically not benefit from richer annotation encodings, unless they are captured in the n-gram feature directly.

The most commonly used model-based classifier for sequence labeling is the HMM. This is a technique that assigns a label to each element in a sequence, and computes the score for the most likely label sequence by finding the probability distribution over all possible labels. It has been used successfully in Speech Recognition, handwriting recognition, POS tagging, and many other NLP tasks. Because the number of possible label sequences gets unmanageable with long sequences, the model makes the same assumption that the sequence predictor from Chapter 3 did; namely, look at only the previous *n* labels for calculating the probability (see "Language Models"). The underlying assumption is that the elements transition from state to state via a finite-state automaton behavior, with probabilistic transitions between states. Then, this can be transformed into a new model, with hidden states, where all observation tokens are emitted from each state with a finite probability.

Of particular interest to us is the fact that the richer the encoding of features (e.g., from annotations) the better one can calculate the transition probabilities from state to state in the model. For further information on how HMMs are built, see Jurafsky and Martin 2008.

Finally, there are two other important sequence induction models that we must mention briefly:

Maximum Entropy Markov Models (MEMMs)
This classifier was first proposed by McCallum et al. 2000 as an alternative to HMMs. In this model, the transition and observation probability matrices are replaced by MaxEnt classifiers for each state. This allows the encoding of the probability distribution to make a state-to-state transition, having seen the observed data. Such models have been used for information extraction (McCallum et al. 2000), and identifying semantic role labels (Blunsom 2004).

Conditional Random Field (CRF) models
This classifier is introduced in Lafferty et al. 2001 as a new way to segment sequential data. One advantage over HMMs is that CRFs can relax the strong independence assumptions made in HMMs and stochastic models for sequence labeling. This model overcomes the label bias problem, which MEMMs and other classifiers have. This is a property of the network that causes a bias toward states with fewer outgoing transitions, which can distort the calculation of the probability distribution of a sequence. In a CRF, the weights of different features at different states can be traded off against one another.

The examples for classifier algorithms and the discussions of other types of supervised learning techniques should have given you a good basis for understanding how your own annotation task can fit into the Training part of the MATTER cycle. The next sections of this chapter address other types of learning methodologies: unsupervised and semi-supervised.

Clustering and Unsupervised Learning

In this section we will briefly review ML algorithms that do not require any annotated data to run, a process called *unsupervised learning*. Because there is not an explicit role for annotated data, we will only review these techniques and not explore them in depth.

What kinds of problems are solved by clustering and what sort of algorithm is useful for clustering?

 Be sure to understand the distinction between clustering and classification! *Clustering* takes a body of data that has not been tagged or labeled with any additional information. The goal of clustering is to identify natural groupings (or clusters) that exist in the dataset. These groupings do not correspond to any preconceived categories or labels that you might be looking for, however, since they emerge from the data without any prelabeling over the input.

The goal of *classification*, on the other hand, is to predict what class or category a data element will belong to, after having trained it over a dataset. This requires that the data is labeled with particular classes (the labels you want on the data elements), with positive examples and negative examples for the desired classification.

First, it is important to be clear about what is being learned, and what about the algorithm is unsupervised. The goal of a clustering task is to find natural groupings in the data, based entirely on the properties of the data elements themselves. Hence there is no role for a "teacher," who helps the learning algorithm assign the correct features to the positive instances in the dataset.

It should be pointed out that, even though the dataset is unlabeled, the data being analyzed has intrinsic object properties that might be thought of as "labels," but this is not how we are using the term here. It is these properties that are exploited for making comparisons of similarity and difference to create a cluster over the data elements.

As we just saw, clustering algorithms determine whether one element in a dataset is similar to or different from another element. They can be classified according to the way they treat the data after making this comparison. For example, if a clustering is performed such that, if an item appears in one cluster it cannot appear in any other cluster, then we have what is called an *exclusive clustering*. In exclusive clusterings, we create an *n*-way partition of the dataset (with *n* clusters). *Overlapping clustering*, on the other hand, allows clusters to be nonexclusive, where elements can appear in multiple classes. If the similar elements can form clusters that can themselves combine with similar elements to make new clusters, then we have what is called *hierarchical clustering*. Finally, there is a family of clustering algorithms based entirely on probabilistic methods, and these are called, not surprisingly, *probabilistic clustering* approaches.

Semi-Supervised Learning

Semi-supervised learning (SSL) is a method of learning that employs both labeled data as well as unlabeled data. It is an attractive idea for language-based tasks in particular, because of two reasons: there is an enormous amount of unlabeled data available as input to such an algorithm; and the cost of providing labeled training data can prove to be prohibitively expensive in many cases.

While supervised learning algorithms require enough labeled training data to learn reasonably accurate classifiers, and unsupervised learning methods can be used to discover hidden structures in the unlabeled dataset, semi-supervised learning algorithms combine aspects of both techniques. Figure 7-4 shows how SSL takes both labeled and unlabeled data and puts them in an ML algorithm.

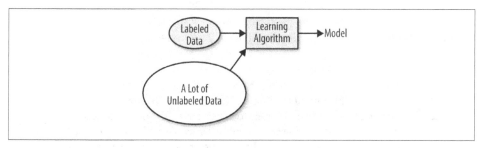

Figure 7-4. Semi-supervised learning

There are reasons why this might be useful to do, independent of the two reasons just mentioned, however. Consider how this might work. In many learning scenarios, we may or may not have a rich and descriptive model with which to create an annotation of the dataset. That is, the phenomena may be quite complex and there may be dimensions that are not well captured, or dependencies among elements in the data that are not identified, simply because you haven't thought about them.

In other words, by first applying an unsupervised learning technique, such as k-means, it might be possible to find clusters in the data that reflect meaningful representations of complex or high dimensional data. The results of this step can then be taken as input for a supervised phase of learning, using these clusters as soft labels. Figure 7-5 shows how the SSL methodology fits into the MATTER cycle.

Statisticians have been using a type of SSL technique since the 1970s, iteratively using the Expectation-Maximization (EM) algorithm to train classifiers by estimating parameters of a generative model.

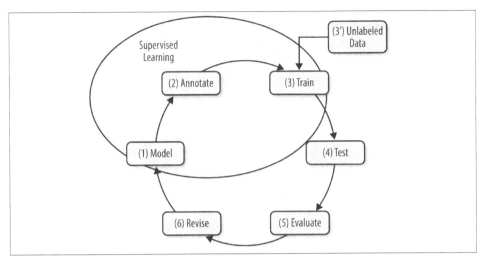

Figure 7-5. Semi-supervised learning in the MATTER cycle

 Expectation-Maximization (EM) is a technique that allows you to find Maximum Likelihood Estimations (MLEs) in circumstances where the data would not normally seem to provide it easily; that is, some of the random variables involved are not observed (see Chapter 3). The basic idea behind EM is to make parameter estimates, given the missing data:

1. Replace missing values with estimates.

2. Estimate the parameters.

3. Repeat (1) using estimated values as correct, and (2) using estimated values as "observed."

For details, see McLachlan and Krishnan 1996.

Several kinds of learning tasks are typically referred to as semi-supervised learning. These include:

Transductive learning
> This is where no general rule for determining a classifier is inferred, only where the labels on the unlabeled data are predicted given the training phase.

Inductive learning
> This is where a general rule for defining the classifier is inferred from the data, and it is this rule (classifier) that is used to label the unlabled data.

Using SSL in a particular task without thinking through the nature of the unlabeled data relative to the labeled training data can bring about a degradation in performance rather than an improvement. However, for many tasks, SSL can actually perform better than using labeled data alone (Singh et al. 2008), depending on the nature of the domain to be explored, as well as the type of labeling task involved.

A particularly interesting kind of SSL is *co-training*. This is a technique that takes advantage of two "views" of the data being examined for learning a concept. That is, each perspective or view has an independent set of features that are used to describe the example instance. Basically, it works when one classifier is able to correctly categorize the instance where the other one could not. The correct assignment of the instance is now added as positive data for the poorly performing classifier, and then is used for iteratively training the classifier to perform better (Blum and Mitchell 1998).

Finally, there is another SSL technique that has recently been used to encouraging effect, namely *coupled training* (Carlson et al. 2010). Given that the limited number of initial labeled examples can be insufficient to reliably constrain the learning process, this method proposes "coupling" the simultaneous training of many extractors over the data. The effect is that more informative constraints can be identified with coupling that are not possible with simple SSL training.

Matching Annotation to Algorithms

One of the difficult tasks when it comes to training an algorithm is actually picking which algorithm matches best with your goal and annotation. Table 7-1 lists some common tasks, as well as recommendations for what algorithms to use if you're not sure where to start. Keep in mind that we're not suggesting these are the *only* algorithms that can be used for these tasks, though! A lot of that decision rests on the corpus that you chose and how you structured your annotation.

Table 7-1. Suggested ML algorithms for sample tasks

Task	Suggested algorithm
Assigning categories to words (POS tagging)	This is a sequence labeling task over annotation-dependent features and is usually seen as a supervised learning task, using labeled training data of token sequences. This suggests one of the following: HMMs, CRFs, or possibly SVMs (e.g., SVM-HMM). Efficient (transformational) rule-based techniques also exist, such as the Brill tagger technique (Brill 1995).
Assigning topics to articles, emails, or web pages	This is a clustering problem usually viewed as an unsupervised learning task. It is a problem best handled as an n-gram feature classification task creating a generative model. Some of the best algorithms are Latent Dirichlet Allocation (LDA), where some number of topics (distributions over words) exist for a document collection; Probabilistic Latent Semantic Analysis (PLSA); and other "bag of words" algorithms.
Mood, affect, or sentiment classification of a text or utterance	This is a classification task using both n-gram and annotation-dependent features. This suggests Naïve Bayes, MaxEnt, and SVM. In any of these approaches, n-grams can be used where appropriate, but as mentioned earlier, unigrams often perform better because of the overfitting problem. Overfitting occurs when you include too many features, causing the learning algorithm to model the training data too precisely, which prevents it from generalizing well.

Task	Suggested algorithm
Assigning a semantic type or ontological class to a word or phrase	This is a classification task using both n-gram and annnotation-dependent features. As above, good choices are Naïve Bayes, MaxEnt, decision trees (e.g., C4.5), and SVMs.
Word sense disambiguation	This is a classification task that can take advantage of a wide variety of feature types. As a purely supervised learning task, both SVMs and memory-based learning (MBL) approaches have been used with both n-gram and annotation features. Viewed as an SSL problem, a classifier is trained and then iteratively bootstrapped over unlabeled data. Pairwise similarity clustering (Rumshisky 2008) can be embedded in an SSL strategy to good effect as well.
Temporal and event recognition	This is a classification task using both n-gram and annotation-dependent features. This suggests Naïve Bayes, decision trees, or MaxEnt. Very good rule-based systems have also been developed, including HeidelTime (Strötgen and Gertz 2010) and Evita (Saurí et al. 2005).
Semantic roles for participants of events in a sentence	This is a classification task that can build either a discriminative model or a generative model, depending on what features are chosen and what dependencies are chosen between them. Models exist using SVMs (Pradhan et al. 2003) and MaxEnt (Lim et al. 2004). SSL techniques have also been used.
NE identification	This is a fairly straightforward classification problem, using both n-gram and annotation-dependent features. Approaches include Naïve Bayes, MaxEnt, SVMs, CRFs, MEMMs, and even MBLs.
Coreference resolution	This can be viewed as a classification task, using mostly annotation-dependent features. Algorithms include decision tree induction (C4.5) (Ng and Cardie 2002), co-training (Goldman and Zhou 2000), CRFs (Wellner et al. 2004), and boosting (Ng and Cardie 2003), and first-order probabilistic models (Culotta et al. 2007).

Summary

In this chapter we looked at how the model and annotation you have been developing are able to feed into the ML algorithm that you will use for approximating the target function you are interested in learning. We discussed the differences between the different feature types: n-gram features, structure-dependent features, and annotation-dependent features. We reviewed how these features are deployed in several important learning algorithms, focusing on decision tree learning and Naïve Bayes learning. Here is a summary of what you learned:

- ML algorithms are programs that get better as they are exposed to more data. ML algorithms have been used in a variety of computational linguistic tasks, from POS tagging to discourse structure recognition.

- There are three main types of ML algorithms: supervised, unsupervised, and semi-supervised.

- Supervised learning uses annotated data to train an algorithm to identify features in the data that are relevant to the intended function of the algorithm.

- N-gram features allow algorithms to take information about the words that are in a document and examine aspects of the data such as term frequency to create associations with different types of classifications.

- Structure-dependent features are defined by the properties of the data, such as strings of characters, HTML or other types of markup tags, or other ways a document can be organized.

- Annotation-dependent features are associated with the annotation and reflect the model of the annotation task.

- A learning task is defined in five steps: choose the corpus that will be trained on, identify the target function of the algorithm, choose how the target function will be represented (the features), select an ML algorithm to train, and evaluate the results.

- Another way to use an annotated corpus in a software system is to design a rule-based system: a program or set of programs that does not rely on an ML algorithm being trained to do a task, but rather has a set of rules that encode the features that an algorithm could be trained to identify.

- Rule-based systems are a good way to identify features that may be useful in a document without having to take the time to train an algorithm. For some tasks (e.g., temporal expression recognition), rule-based systems outperform ML algorithms.

- Classification algorithms are used to apply the most likely label (or classification) to a collection. They can be applied at a document, sentence, phrase, word, or any other level of language that is appropriate for your task.

- Using n-gram features is the simplest way to start with a classification system, but structure-dependent features and annotation-dependent features will help with more complex tasks such as event recognition or sentiment analysis.

- Decision trees are a type of ML algorithm that essentially ask "20 questions" of a corpus to determine what label should be applied to each item. The hierarchy of the tree determines the order in which the classifications are applied.

- The "questions" asked at each branch of a decision tree can be structure-dependent, annotation-dependent, or any other type of feature that can be discovered about the data.

- A Naïve Bayes learning algorithm tries to assign the probability that an item will be assigned a particular classification, based on the association between what features are associated with each item, and how strongly those features are associated with a particular label as determined by the Bayes Theorem.

- The K-nearest neighbor algorithm uses much simpler rules than the Naïve Bayes methods, with simple associations between features and classifications.

- Unsupervised learning is the process of "teaching" an algorithm without giving it any starting information about the classifications that exist in the dataset.

- Classic examples of unsupervised learning are clustering algorithms, which find natural groupings in the data in order to create sets of similar items. Essentially, clustering algorithms find their own features for the datasets.

- Because clustering algorithms don't take features from the users but instead discover their own, the groups that a classifier creates may not be the ones that you have in mind for your task.

- Semi-supervised learning techniques allow you to use a small amount of labeled data to generate labels for larger sets of data, and are an effective way to deal with very large datasets.

- If you aren't sure where to start with your algorithm training, try to find a task or annotation similar to your own and see what algorithms are commonly used for those projects. If there aren't any projects just like yours, try to find ones that have similar features or feature types.

Testing and Evaluation

Once you've selected an algorithm and started picking out your features, then you can actually start testing your algorithm against your *gold standard* corpus and evaluating the results—the "Training through Evaluation" (TE) portion of the MATTER cycle. Like other parts of MATTER, the training, testing, and evaluation phases form their own, smaller cycle. After you train your algorithm on the features you select, then you can start the testing and evaluation processes.

In this chapter we'll answer the following questions:

- When is testing performed?
- Why is there both a dev-test corpus and another test corpus?
- What's being evaluated once the algorithm is run?
- How do you obtain an evaluation score?
- What do the evaluation scores mean?
- What should evaluators be aware of during these phases of the MATTER cycle?
- Which scores get reported at the end of these phases?

Keep in mind that the purpose of evaluating your algorithm is not just to get a good score on your own data! The purpose is to provide testing conditions that convincingly suggest that your algorithm will perform well on *other people's* data, out in the real world. So it's important to keep track of the testing conditions, any modifications you make to your algorithm, and places in your annotation scheme that you think could be changed to improve performance later. Your algorithm getting a good "score" on your test doesn't really matter if no one else can take the same exam!

Testing Your Algorithm

Your algorithm will be tested multiple times during this phase of the MATTER cycle (see Figure 8-1): after being trained on the dev-training set, it is tested on the dev-test set. After evaluating the algorithm's output, either you can go back to the dev-training set and retrain your algorithm with new or modified features, or, if you're satisfied with your algorithm's output, you can run your algorithm on your test corpus and report on the results.

Figure 8-1. The training–evaluation cycle

Remember that the test set (as opposed to the dev-test set) is not used for testing until you are ready to get "official" numbers for your algorithm's performance over your corpus. Think of the test set as a final exam: the best way to determine if your algorithm has learned the material is to give it one last test on material that's similar to what was used for training, but is not exactly the same. The last part is important: test data is kept separate from the development set, and you never train your algorithm on your testing data. You need to have an idea of how your algorithm would perform "in the wild," which you can't do if you use the test data to train on, or run your algorithm multiple times on your final test set—that's why there's a dev-test set that's also separate from both the final test set and the dev-training set.

For the rest of this chapter, we will simply refer to the data being evaluated as the *evaluation set*, because the same evaluations are run on the results from the dev-test set and the final test set. Keep in mind that although evaluations are run on the results of both the dev-test and the final test sets, only the evaluation from the dev-test set is used to tweak the features used for training. We'll talk more about why this is in "Problems That Can Affect Evaluation" on page 178.

Evaluating Your Algorithm

Once you've selected your features, trained your algorithm, and tested it, it's time to evaluate how the output from your algorithm compares to the gold standard annotations on the evaluation set. First you need to calculate and interpret your evaluation scores, after which it can be helpful to create a *confusion matrix* to help determine on what parts of your task the algorithm is failing (or succeeding!).

Confusion Matrices

An extremely useful way to examine the results of your algorithm is to create a *confusion matrix*—you may recall from "Cohen's Kappa (κ)" on page 127 that we created one to compare the annotations of two annotators. A confusion matrix allows us to look at what labels the algorithm is using (and to a certain extent, where it's putting them) compared to the labels in the gold standard.

Because we already saw a similar example when calculating Cohen's Kappa, it's easy to see how a confusion matrix can be used for other tasks where labels are being applied to a document:

		test positive	test neutral	test negative
gold standard	positive	**96**	4	0
gold standard	neutral	13	**87**	0
gold standard	negative	0	0	**100**

Correct annotations are identified by the numbers on the diagonal, shown here in bold. In this example, the algorithm performed very well on identifying negative reviews, but it had a harder time telling positive reviews from neutral ones. Specifically, the algorithm tended to err by labeling entries that are "neutral" in the gold standard as "positive" (though it labeled four as neutral when they should have been positive as well). So we can see here that the algorithm will need to have better features for distinguishing positive reviews from neutral ones.

> The Natural Language Toolkit (NLTK) has a built-in function for creating confusion matrices. Once you have a gold standard loaded and have run your algorithm on an unlabeled test set, just run:
>
> ```
> >>> matrix = nltk.ConfusionMatrix(gs,test)
> ```
>
> where gs is a list of the gold standard annotation of the test set, and test is a list of the output of the algorithm, although the NLTK table displays percents instead of whole numbers. See the NLTK 2.0 metrics documentation (*http://nltk.org/api/nltk.metrics.html*) for more information.

It is also possible to create confusion matrices for tasks where labels are being applied to words in the texts. The setup for the table is essentially the same: the test annotations are on one axis, the gold standard annotations are on the other, and each tag is given a column and a row. Here's a partial example for what a part-of-speech (POS) tagging task might look like:

		test	test	test	test	test	test
		noun	conjunction	determiner	adjective	adverb	...
gold	noun	**12951**	0	0	211	0	
gold	conjunction	0	**2664**	0	0	0	
gold	determiner	0	0	**589**	0	0	
gold	adjective	184	0	0	**4133**	75	
gold	adverb	5	0	0	91	**2166**	
gold	...						

This is very similar to the previous table for the movie review classification, except that each unit in this table is a word rather than an entire document.

So if that is how you create a confusion matrix for a task where every word has a tag, what do you do with an annotation task that results in sparser annotations? We actually showed you the answer to this question before, in the example for calculating Inter-Annotator Agreement (IAA) scores for sparse annotations ["Calculating κ in Other Contexts" on page 132]: just add an "untagged" category to the table, as we did in the table for the "Jabberwocky" annotation task:

		test	test	test
		creature	pronoun	untagged
gold	creature	5	0	2
gold	pronoun	0	19	0
gold	untagged	1	0	189

Creating a confusion matrix isn't mandatory for evaluating an algorithm, but it can help you (and anyone reading about your results) to understand where common sources of error are. Also, they can be useful when calculating evaluation scores for your algorithm, which we will address in the next section.

Calculating Evaluation Scores

Much like IAA scoring, there are a few different methods for evaluating your algorithm's performance. In this section we'll go through how to calculate the most common evaluation metrics, specifically percentage accuracy, precision and recall, and F-measures, and how to apply these to different types of annotation tasks.

Percentage accuracy

The first metric that most people think of as an evaluation score for your algorithm is to grade the output of the algorithm the way that you would grade an exam: simply look at the generated annotations; mark off which ones are wrong and which are right; and figure out what percentage of the total annotations are correct.

If you have a confusion matrix, the percentage accuracy is the sum of the diagonal (top left to bottom right) of the table divided by the sum of all the cells of the table. So in the movie review table from the previous section, we have a total accuracy of:

(96 + 87 + 100) / 300 = **.943**, or 94.3%

Unfortunately, while accuracy is easy to calculate, it can only give us a general idea of how well an algorithm performed at a task: it can't show specifically where the task went wrong, or what aspects of the features need to be fixed. There are other ways to obtain and assign scores to those attributes of a machine learning (ML) task, however, which we will examine next.

Precision and recall

The biggest problem with calculating overall accuracy is that the resultant score doesn't address the two different kinds of mistakes that need to be examined for evaluating an annotation task: places where it put the wrong tag on an item, and places where it failed to put the right tag. These values are calculated by examining the precision and recall for each tag/label in a task, and they help form a clearer picture of what aspects of an algorithm need to be adjusted.

Precision and recall are traditionally associated with Information Retrieval (IR) tasks such as those related to search algorithms. Let's say there was a database of scientific papers, and you wanted the computer to return all of the articles related to string theory. If there are 50 relevant documents in the database and the search returns 75, then it's clear that the search has falsely identified some documents as being related to string theory when they actually weren't. When an item is given a label that it should not have, that is called a *false positive*. On the other hand, if the same database were queried for "string theory" and only 25 documents were returned, there would be multiple cases of *false negatives*, where items were rejected for a label that they should have actually been given. Documents that are returned accurately are called *true positives*, and documents that are correctly ignored when they are irrelevant are *true negatives*.

By applying the idea of false negative and false positive to the results of an ML algorithm, we can compute useful evaluation metrics that will help us to more accurately identify sources of error in the system. However, unlike overall accuracy calculations where all the tags are evaluated together, false positives and false negatives have to be evaluated one tag at a time. If we think about it, this makes sense, particularly in annotation tasks where only one tag (or no tag) is being applied to an item, as a false positive for one tag is a false negative for another.

So how do we calculate the number of false positives and false negatives? With a confusion matrix, it's quite easy. If we look at the matrix for movie review labels again, we see that to evaluate the accuracy of the "positive" label we need to look at the first column, which shows the number of documents the classifier labeled as "positive," and the first row, which shows how many documents in the gold standard were given the "positive" label:

		test positive	test neutral	test negative
gold standard	positive	*96*	*4*	0
gold standard	neutral	*13*	87	0
gold standard	negative	*0*	0	100

In all confusion matrices, the true positives are located at the intersection of the row and column we are examining. In this case, the number of true positives is **96**. False positives are calculated by summing up the column "test—>positive" (minus the number of true positives): here that number is **13** (13 + 0). Similarly, false negatives are calculated by summing across the row for "gold standard—>positive" (again, without counting the true positives), which is **4** (4 + 0). (The number of true negatives is the sum of the rest of the table [187], but we won't be needing that here.)

With the confusion matrix, calculating the true and false positives and negatives is simple enough, but what do we do with them now? The answer is that we calculate *precision* and *recall* values, which provide more nuanced information about our algorithm test.

Precision is the measure of how many items were accurately identified, and is defined as:

$$p = \frac{true\ positive}{true\ positive\ +\ false\ positive}$$

For the "positive" tag, p = 96 / (96 + 13)
= 96 / 109
= **.881**

Recall is the measure of how many relevant items were identified (in other words, how many of the documents that should have been labeled "positive" were actually given that label):

$$r = \frac{true\ positive}{true\ positive\ +\ false\ negative}$$

r = 96 / (96 + 4)
= 96 / 100
= **.96**

We can see from these numbers that for the "positive" label our algorithm has high recall, which means it found most of the documents it should have, but lower precision, which means it's giving too many documents the "positive" label when they should be labeled as something else.

If we perform these calculations with the rest of the matrix, we can make a table that looks like this:

tag	precision	recall
positive	.881	.96
neutral	.95	.87
negative	1	1

In this case, the precision and recall numbers for positive and neutral are very close to being each other's opposite, because here, the "negative" tag isn't influencing the other two. In tables with more variation, such reciprocity is not the norm.

While it's fairly standard to report the precision and recall numbers for each tag (and tag attribute), papers about ML algorithms often mention another number, called the *F-measure*, which we will discuss in the next section.

 You can also se the NLTK to generate accuracy, precision, recall, F-measure, and a number of other analysis metrics for you using the nltk.metrics (*http://nltk.org/api/nltk.metrics.html*) package. Like the confusion matrix, the accuracy metric uses lists to calculate the numbers, while precision, recall, and F-measure use sets of data instead. A good overview of how to create these sets is available at *http:// bit.ly/QViUTB*.

F-measure

The *F-measure* (also called the *F-score* or the *F1 score*) is an accuracy measure calculated by finding the *harmonic mean* of the precision and recall of an algorithm's performance over a tag. The formula for F-measure is as follows (where *p* is precision and *r* is recall):

$$F = 2 \times \left(\frac{p \times r}{p + r} \right)$$

We see that the F-measure for the "positive" tag is 2 * (.881*.96) / (.881 + .96) = 1.692 / 1.841 = **.919.**

While the F-measure won't tell you specifically where your algorithm is producing incorrect results, it does provide a handy way for someone to tell at a glance how your algorithm is performing in general. This is why F-measure is commonly reported in computational linguistics papers: not because it's inherently useful to people trying to find ways to improve their algorithm, but because it's easier on the reader than processing an entire table of precision and recall scores for each tag used.

 You may be wondering why we don't use kappa coefficients for evaluating algorithms. The equations for kappa coefficients are designed to take into account that annotators always bring in some level of random chance, and also that when IAA scores are being calculated, the right answer isn't yet known. While gold standard corpora can certainly have errors in them, they are considered correct for the purpose of training and testing algorithms, and therefore are a mark to be evaluated against, like the answer key on an exam.

Notice that this number is not the same as the overall accuracy from "Percentage accuracy" on page 172, because this is the accuracy measure for only one tag. Again, we can create a table of all the F-scores as shown here:

tag	precision	recall	F-measure
positive	.881	.96	**.919**
neutral	.95	.87	**.908**
negative	1	1	**1**

F-measures, precision and recall, and accuracy are all commonly used metrics for evaluating how an algorithm is performing during development, and are also often discussed in articles and at conferences to report on how well an algorithm does on an annotation task. We will discuss how to interpret these scores in the next section.

Other evaluation metrics

There are many other ways to analyze the various features, distributions, and problems with your dataset, algorithms, and feature selection. Here's an overview of some other methods that you can use to check out how your system is performing:

T-test
Determines whether the means of two distributions are different in a statistically significant way. Useful for comparing the results of two different algorithms over your training and test sets.

Analysis of variance (ANOVA) test
Like a t-test, but allows multiple distributions to be compared at the same time.

X-squared (chi-squared) test
Can be used to test if two variables are independent. Useful for determining if an attribute of a dataset (or a feature in the model) is contributing to part of the data being mislabeled.

Receiver Operator Characteristic (ROC) curves
> Used to compare true positive and false positive rates between classifiers or classifier thresholds.

Also, don't forget about the methods we showed you in Chapter 3. Some of those tests can also be applied here.

For more information on how to apply these tests to your corpus and algorithm, please check a statistics textbook. If you're interested specifically in how statistics can be done in Python, we suggest looking at *Think Stats: Probability and Statistics for Programmers*, Allen B. Downey (O'Reilly, 2011).

Interpreting Evaluation Scores

Unlike IAA scores, there is no table that is used for determining, even roughly, how an evaluation score should be interpreted. Clearly, you want to get your algorithm's results to be as close to 1 as possible, but the accuracy of an algorithm will depend greatly on how difficult the task is, how appropriate the corpus is, and what the state of the art currently is for that task or type of task. Ultimately, your own algorithm needs to be evaluated in the context of other algorithms that have been trained to do similar tasks.

It's especially important to consider how your task differs from other, similar tasks when considering how your algorithm stacks up against other algorithms. For example, POS taggers trained on the Penn TreeBank and used on corpora with similar texts usually obtain accuracies in the upper 90s. However, when the same taggers are tested on bio-medical corpora, they get results that are much lower until they are also trained on tagged biomedical data (see Tsuruoka et al. 2005 and Fan et al. 2011 for more information on this topic). Using a different type of data for testing than training will probably cause a drop in performance, which can then lead to the annotation of a more relevant set of documents. But if you are the first person to explore a task in a different genre or subject, it's reasonable to expect that your scores will be lower than others who are working on improving their own scores with the same sets of data.

> Don't get too caught up on the word *test*. While we've compared the final evaluation scores to final exams for classes, there's no scale that determines if you "fail." Due to the huge variation in task difficulty, algorithm evaluation is more like being graded on a curve than on a line.

However, while POS tagging results are generally quite good (once appropriate data is being used for training), other tasks have accuracy numbers that are much lower, but that are still considered good for that task. Consider the TempEval-2 challenge, held as part of the 2010 SemEval (Verhagen et al. 2010). TempEval contains three main tasks:

event recognition, temporal expression recognition, and temporal relation annotation (which is further divided into subtasks). Because identifying temporal and event information in text requires much more interpretation of the data, most algorithms designed for this task had F-measures in the 80s for event recognition, and lower for relation annotation. But despite being comparatively lower than POS tasks, these scores are still considered good for the type of annotation they were working on. Thus, the evaluation of your algorithm must be done in the context of similar tasks, rather than on a strict scale from 0 to 100.

Problems That Can Affect Evaluation

While the methods of evaluation for algorithm accuracy are fairly straightforward to calculate, the numbers that you end up with won't necessarily show you all the sources of error that might be affecting your results. In this section we'll look at two of the common problems that affect algorithm evaluation and what to do about them.

Dataset Is Too Small

So far in this chapter we've talked about dividing the corpus into three sets: dev-training, dev-test, and final test. However, splitting up a corpus in this manner can be difficult if the corpus isn't very big. You want to make sure you have enough data to train on, but if your testing sets are too small, then even a few errors can make it seem as though your algorithm is doing a very poor job.

Fortunately, there is an approach you can use if you simply don't have enough data to properly train and test your algorithm. K-fold *cross-validation* is an analysis method that allows you to split your data into *k* different partitions (or *folds*), then train your algorithm on all the sections but one, and test it on the held-out section. You then choose a different partition to hold out and repeat the process, until all the partitions have been used as the test set. For example, if you divided your corpus into five partitions, (k = 5), you would take four of those in which to train your algorithm, and test it on the fifth. See Figure 8-2 for a visual representation of this method.

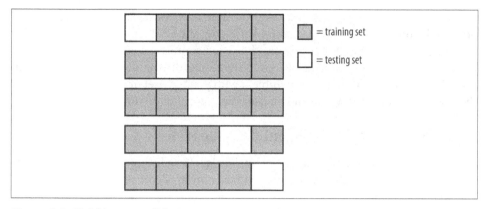

Figure 8-2. K-fold cross-validation

Once you have run your algorithm on all the subset variations of your testing and training data, you can evaluate the accuracy of each round of testing and give the average of all the results. There are other methods of dividing your test and training sets as well, such as performing a fixed number of tests but randomly selecting what documents will be in the training and testing sets each time. While the random selection method does help take care of some problems that can still be found using the k-fold method (e.g., if one of your folds randomly ended up with a set of documents that's very different from the rest of the folds), randomly selecting files means you can't be sure that every file will end up in both the testing and training sets at some point.

You can use Python to randomize your list of inputs and to select your folds. Assuming you have a list of files, f, you can call Python's shuf fle function over the list to randomize the order:

```
>>> import random
>>> random.shuffle(f)
```

If you're performing k-fold cross-validation and you want to use Python to select each fold, you can do that in a loop to create a list of the set of files in each fold:

```
>>> k = 20
>>> i=0
>>> folds = []
>>> while i<len(f):
>>>   folds.append(f[i:i+k])
>>>   i = i+k
```

Of course, you'll want to make sure you pick a *k* that doesn't leave your last set too small to use, so make sure the *k* you pick either divides the size of your list perfectly, or at least leaves a high enough remainder for the algorithm to be trained on.

Cross-validation is an excellent way to determine how consistent your dataset is and how stable your features are. If each round of testing and evaluation is returning roughly the same numbers, then you can infer that your corpus is consistent and that your evaluation results are accurate. However, if the results display a large amount of variation, then it could indicate a larger problem with your dataset or feature selection, and the results will not be very good if you use your algorithm on other datasets.

Algorithm Fits the Development Data Too Well

You might be wondering what we mean by the algorithm fitting the data too well: isn't that the whole point of selecting features and training an algorithm? While it's true that you want to have a feature set that does a good job of representing your corpus, it's possible to end up selecting features that exist disproportionately in your dev-training and dev-testing sets, which will mean your algorithm will not work as well on your final test set as it might otherwise. This problem is referred to as *overfitting*, and it generally occurs when you have too many features in your algorithm's model. Remember that the purpose of training an algorithm is to create a tool that can be used on new data, not only on your annotated corpus.

This is where the representativeness and balance of your corpus can really come into play, but it's also where the problem of attaining true representativeness and balance is brought to light. A corpus that can claim to be representative and balanced for the types of data it was created to represent will, in theory, lead to better ML results in the testing phase of the MATTER cycle, because there will be less variation in features between the training and testing datasets. However, in practice it will rarely be the case that all the features you are using to train with will appear in the same proportion as in the test data, simply from random chance in distributions.

So, how can you tell if your algorithm is overfit? Basically, if a feature adds accuracy during the test–eval phases, but is introducing errors during the final test phase, then your model is overfit to your training set. It's that simple, but overfitting your training data is a very easy trap to fall into, so watch out for it.

Keep track of your choices! The determination of how representative and balanced your corpus is will be highly influenced by what your corpus is intended to represent in the first place. This is why it's important to keep track of the methods you use to create your corpus and report them to those who might use your corpus or your algorithm. Let's say, for example, that you created a movie review corpus but only included reviews containing 200 words or more, and then took precautions to make sure the reviews were balanced across movie genres, polarity, and so on. You can claim that your corpus is representative of reviews over a certain length, but not that it's representative of all reviews—and that's fine! There can be good reasons for putting limits on what gets included in your corpus; the important thing is to be upfront about them so that others will understand what they're getting into when they use the resources you create.

Too Much Information in the Annotation

Sometimes your annotation task contains more information than a classifier actually needs. One way to test this is to remove features from your algorithm and see if the accuracy of the results changes significantly. Being able to achieve the same results with a smaller set of features helps you to focus in on what's really going on in the text, and how to best represent that to a computer. You can also examine each feature one at a time to help determine how much each one is adding to the accuracy of the overall results.

Final Testing Scores

To get the final accuracy numbers that you will report to other people for your algorithm, corpus, and annotation, you must run the trained algorithm over the final test set. However, there is a danger in evaluating over the test data too many times. First, the more times you run your algorithm over your final test data, the lower the statistical significance of your results becomes—running too many tests means that you're fishing for features and tweaks that will improve your final testing scores, but the act of fishing increases the likelihood that you'll stumble upon something that just happens to improve your scores, but doesn't actually reflect a true feature in the real world.

A second (but related) issue is that the more you tweak your features for your test data, the more danger you are in of overfitting your algorithm to your test data, which itself will be no more representative of data in the real world than the rest of your corpus.

Ideally, you would only run your algorithm on your final test data once. If you do run it more than once, be upfront about how many times it was run and what adjustments were made between runs. This not only keeps you honest (and safer from stats-savvy reviewers), but it also helps other people understand what problems they might encounter using similar datasets or systems.

Summary

In this chapter we discussed how to test and evaluate your ML algorithm's performance on your dev-test and final-test data. Some of the key points in this process are summarized here:

- Algorithms are tested multiple times over the development-training and development-testing sets of your corpus. After each run of the algorithm on the dev-test data, evaluation of the results is performed and the algorithm/features are adjusted as necessary.

- Creating a confusion matrix of your results is an excellent way to identify problems with your algorithm's performance, and also makes calculating accuracy scores much easier.

- Calculating the percentage accuracy for your algorithm provides a baseline level of evaluation, but it doesn't tell the whole story about how your algorithm is performing.

- Precision and recall are metrics used to compare the number of true positives, false positives, and false negatives that your algorithm is producing. A high precision score indicates that your algorithm is not returning many false positives; a high recall score indicates that it is not producing a lot of false negatives.

- Depending on the purpose of your algorithm, you may want to favor high recall over high precision, or vice versa.

- An F-measure is the harmonic mean of the precision and recall scores, and provides a more robust overall metric of your results.

- Other evaluation metrics such as ROC, chi-squared, t-tests, and ANOVA can be used to identify discrepancies and variables in your algorithm as well.

- The interpretation of evaluation scores is highly dependent on the current state of the art in research areas similar to what you are working on—you'll need to see how other, similar algorithms are performing to determine how yours stacks up.

- If your dataset is too small to divide into training and testing sets, you can use cross-validation to evaluate your algorithm.

- Beware of overfitting your algorithm to your training set!

- Run your algorithm over your final testing set as few times as possible (ideally, once), and make sure to report the evaluation metrics for that run, as well as any changes that you made between runs.

Revising and Reporting

Finally, we're at the "R" of the MATTER cycle—revising your project. Of course, you've probably been revising your project all along, as you worked your way through the MAMA cycle, and refit your algorithms through the training, testing, and evaluation stages of machine learning. However, while making adjustments at each step of the way, you may have focused only on the steps at hand, so in the first part of this chapter, we are going to take a step back and examine some of the "big picture" items that you may want to reconsider about your project. To that end, we'll discuss:

- Corpus modification
- Model and specs
- Annotation task and annotators
- Algorithm implementation

In the second part of the chapter we will discuss what information you should include about your task when you are writing papers, giving presentations, or just putting together a website so that people can learn about your project. Creating annotated corpora and leveraging those corpora into good machine learning (ML) algorithms are difficult tasks, and because so many variables affect the outcome of a project, the more open you are about the choices you made, the more other people will be able to learn based on your example. Some of the aspects of your project you need to consider reporting on are:

- Corpus size, content, and creation
- Annotation methods and annotator qualifications
- ML modifications and training adjustments
- Revisions to your project, both implemented and planned

Revising Your Project

Now that you've made it to the end of the MATTER cycle, it's a good time to step back and look at the big picture of your entire annotation and ML task. In this section we'll go over some of the aspects of your project that you might want to consider revisiting later.

 Just because you identify something you want to change doesn't mean it has to be changed immediately! We'll talk more about this in "Reporting About Your Work" on page 187, but when telling other people about your work, it's perfectly acceptable to say there are aspects of your project you are planning to change, and then report on what you have so far.

As you go through the first half of this chapter, it's a good idea to note the things that you *want* to revise, and the aspects of your project you *did* revise while working through the MATTER cycle. It will be much easier to report accurately on your annotation and ML task if you have a clear outline of everything that you actually changed as you worked, and everything that you would like to change in the future.

Corpus Distributions and Content

At this point we suggest going back and checking to see if your corpus is still representative and balanced with regard to your task. It's possible that your annotation model has changed enough that you need to collect some new data samples, or that during the training and testing phases you discovered some new features that you hadn't considered before and that are not well represented in your corpus.

However, don't forget the "balanced" part of "representative and balanced." If something is a useful feature for correctly creating an annotation but it doesn't appear in the wild with any frequency, you don't want to create an unbalanced corpus by having that feature over-represented in your corpus, because that will skew the balance of any ML algorithm trained on it.

Another task you may want to consider is testing your algorithm on a completely new corpus, to see how it performs on other data. This will be easiest if you can find a corpus that uses the same (or a similar) annotation scheme to the one that you are using. It's by no means required for you to do this, but it's always good to have an idea of new directions that your annotation and algorithm could go in the future.

Model and Specification

Now that you have the results of both the annotation and ML parts of your task, you can go back and examine the annotation model and specification in terms of the ML results. We're not suggesting that you completely change your annotation task to fit exactly with what your algorithm performed best at, of course—a corpus with linguistic subtleties is always a valuable resource, even if some of the aspects cannot be recreated reliably through machine learning or other computer systems. However, now is a good time to reevaluate how the features you used for machine learning tie in with the annotation you devised, and whether your corpus might benefit from reflecting more of those features.

At the same time, you can put some thought into whether all of the different tags and attributes truly form their own distinct categories, and whether it might be more sensible to conflate some of the information in your corpus. Sometimes during the MAMA cycle, when you've been looking closely at the texts, tags, and attributes, it's easy to become too wrapped up in minutiae, and once you've reached the end of the MATTER cycle, it's easier to see what parts of your annotation task may need to be culled. If, for example, you have a tag or attribute value that only gets used a handful of times in your corpus, it might be time to consider whether it's worth having annotators look for those specifically, or if they could be grouped in with something else.

 Just because a tag is rarely used doesn't necessarily mean you should get rid of it! It's also possible that something appears rarely simply because your corpus accurately represents distributions in the real world, and some things really do appear less frequently than others. For example, in the IMDb database of genres (as of April 20, 2012), there are 1,344,395 genre labels applied to all the titles in the database. Of those, "news" only appears 5,868 times—0.4% of all the labels used. But news is certainly distinct from all of the other genres that IMDb uses, so it wouldn't make a lot of sense to decide that the label shouldn't be used just because it only appears rarely. On the other hand, the "lifestyle" genre label is only used once, so it's probably fair to say that either that label should be phased out, or perhaps it's already being removed and there's just an artifact in the file somewhere.

Please note that we aren't suggesting there is a superior format for models or specs! Whether your task needs to add categories or take them away will depend greatly on your goal, data, and performance in the annotation and ML tasks, and there's no ideal number of categories, tags, attributes, or links that will apply to every task.

Annotation

When reviewing this stage of the MATTER cycle, we strongly recommend going back and writing down what you did, as well as what you want to change. While we recommend this for all aspects of the revision process, it is particularly important for this one because papers on annotation tasks tend to under-report details on the implementation of the annotation. But those details are some of the most important when it comes to giving readers a sufficient understanding of your annotation task, so it's important to have them available to others who will be using your data or trying to replicate your results.

Guidelines

Chances are you already fixed most of the problems with your annotation guidelines during the MAMA cycle, so don't worry too much about making corrections at this point. Definitely don't change your guidelines if you are planning to release the corpus and/or publish about the process—releasing a set of guidelines that are different from the ones used to annotate will only cause confusion. However, if you haven't already, you can always go back and poll your annotators to find out what aspects of the guidelines they found confusing, and make notes about that for future projects.

Also, if you've decided to move your annotation to a new corpus, or you've discovered aspects of your model that need to be changed, now is a good time to start making notes about parts of your guidelines that will need to be changed as well. Remember that if you are changing the type of documents in your corpus you will need to rework the examples to better reflect the new data, and any changes to the spec will need to be included as well.

Annotators

Another aspect of your task that you'll want to think about is who you hired to annotate your corpus. If you had a task requiring specialized knowledge to fully understand, did you hire people who had that knowledge already (e.g., did you hire people with training in linguistics to do a part-of-speech [POS] annotation task), or did you hire inexperienced people and train them? If you trained people from the beginning, were they able to pick up the task quickly and make a minimum of mistakes, and finally, was the training process ongoing throughout the annotation task? If you used Amazon's Mechanical Turk, were you able to obtain sufficiently high-quality annotations for your project, or did you have to spend a lot of time weeding out bad data?

Annotators are probably the most variable aspect of an annotation task, and it's worth taking the time to make sure your annotators can do the job you want them to do with a minimal amount of trouble. So when you're revising your project, take the time to consider whether there was anything about the annotators themselves (training, previous experience, etc.) that might have affected the quality of the annotation.

Tools

Finally, it's worth checking in with your annotators and adjudicators to see if the software you had them use to create your corpus is one that helped or hindered them in their task. While most annotation software has some limitations, it always helps to pick software that will support your annotation task rather than get in the way of it. But it's really up to your annotators, who spend the most time working with the software, to decide what the pros and cons are after they've finished their part of the MATTER cycle.

Training and Testing

If you're following the MATTER cycle in order, then you've reached the Revision stage right after going through a few turns of the Training–Evaluation cycle, so you're probably wondering what's left to evaluate. There's always more information to be found in a corpus, and now could be a good time to go back and examine more linguistic aspects of your corpus that could be useful for training and testing. In particular, if you focused on annotation-based features in your algorithm, maybe it's time to check to see if there are any structure-based aspects of your corpus that you can take advantage of. For example, do certain phrases that you're looking for tend to appear in noun groups or verb groups? If you don't know, try using a POS tagger or chunker or parser and then look for correlations in your annotation to different linguistic aspects of the text. If you do find correlations, you can make a note to add those aspects into future annotation tasks, or into the ML algorithms later on.

Other aspects of the texts that you can take into consideration are the structure of the document (are there section headers, or are important phrases more likely to appear at the beginning or end of paragraphs?), any meta-information such as genre or register (assuming that isn't what you're trying to figure out in the first place), the influence of prepositional phrases, and so on.

Now is also a good time to reconsider whether you're using the right algorithm—if you've found more features that would be useful, it's possible that you'll want to switch from one type of ML system to one that's better suited to the new aspects of your corpus that you're exploring.

Reporting About Your Work

Considering how much work goes into creating an annotated corpus and subsequently training an ML algorithm, you are probably going to want to tell people about what you did. You can submit papers to the same conferences and journals that you used for sources of inspiration for your annotation goal, or you can simply make the corpus, annotations, and your notes available on a website and let people know that the information is there. No matter how you decide to advertise the work you did, however, there are some basic pieces of information that will make it easier for other researchers to understand and make use of your materials.

At the moment there's no gold standard or ISO list of what information should be included about an annotated corpus, but in this chapter we're going to provide an overview of the information most people generally agree is helpful to have when using a new corpus or trying to understand how an ML algorithm was trained. In "Writing the Annotation Guidelines" on page 112, we mentioned a paper by Dipper et al. 2004 that examined annotation guidelines through the eyes of the different people who might be using the corpus and guidelines later. While we objected to the idea that all the information they suggested should be put in the annotation guidelines themselves, their suggestions for what information should be made available are excellent, and their categories of corpus users provide a useful overview of the types of people who might be interested in your work. These categories (summarized from Dipper et al. 2004) are:

Annotators
> These are the people who applied your model to the data and created your annotated corpus, and are interested mostly in the guidelines.

Corpus explorers
> These people are interested in using the collection of texts to explore linguistic hypotheses, and are most interested in how to find specific examples of linguistic phenomena and how to interpret the annotations.

Language engineers
> Language engineers are interested in using the corpus annotations to train their own ML algorithm.

Guideline explorers
> Theorctical linguists will want to know about the theory behind your annotation tasks, to understand the underlying assumptions in your guidelines, and other people looking to write annotation guidelines will also want to understand how you created the guidelines you used.

Guideline authors
> During the annotation process you probably referred to your own guidelines repeatedly to keep track of what you covered (or didn't cover) for your annotators.

While some of these categories may not seem extremely relevant at this point in the MATTER cycle (presumably you're already familiar with your own guidelines and the annotators have already put them away), remember that not only will people want to look at your work for inspiration, at some point you might want to go back to it as well, so the more carefully you compile and log your notes, the easier it will be to go back and start making revisions.

Other people who will be interested in your work are people who actually study factors that affect annotation and Inter-Annotator Agreement (IAA) scores: the science of annotation contains a lot of variables and unknowns, and the more information you share about your own task and process, the more others can learn about what works and what doesn't regarding annotation and ML projects. Bayerl and Paul 2011 recently published a journal article where they examined the factors that affect IAA scores (though they refer to them as inter-coder agreement scores) in which they identify several potential factors that will affect agreement. However, they also note that in many cases the information they need was not reported, which makes it difficult to make general statements about annotation tasks in general. In "About Your Annotation Task and Annotators" on page 190, we'll talk about the factors they identified as being relevant, so you'll know what to report on.

This part of the chapter isn't meant to be a how-to guide for writing articles for conferences or journals, so we're not going to go over when to cite your sources or how to structure a report about your work. If you're planning to publish a paper about your work, the best thing to do is to read other papers from the same source to get an idea of the expected tone and work from there. The rest of this section is intended as a guide for what information other people will find most useful and relevant for understanding the scope and implementation of your annotation and ML goal.

About Your Corpus

Ideally, you'll be able to make your corpus available for download—after all, you put a lot of work into collecting and annotating the data, so you should try to maximize the utility of it by sharing it with other researchers. However, be sure that you won't be violating any copyright or privacy laws if you give people the actual texts that you annotated.

Stand-off annotation is ideal for situations where you are unable to distribute a corpus yourself, but you have the ability to inform other people where to obtain the same texts—some websites, for example, don't want people to distribute portions of their databases without permission, but it would probably be acceptable for you to release the stand-off annotations and instructions for how to recreate the corpus that you used. If in doubt, however, ask permission first!

Even if you can make your corpus available, however, people will want to know what criteria you used to select what was included in your corpus, and what criteria you used to filter out unwanted texts. Furthermore, be sure to mention any changes that you made to the texts—if you changed the encodings or the formatting, or if you added or removed any information for your annotators. If you automated the corpus collection process, consider providing the code that you used as well—that way, if anyone wants to add more data or annotations to your corpus later, there won't be any discrepancies between the new and old files. Otherwise, consider posting a template for the data that other people can emulate.

If you used an existing corpus as a basis for your annotation, be sure to provide citation information and an explanation of why you chose that dataset.

About Your Model and Specifications

When we talk about providing the model and specs for your annotation task, we don't just mean posting the DTD (Document Type Definition) with the tag information and leaving it at that—although that's very important too! This is the information the "corpus explorers" want—not just the tags and attributes that you used, but the reasoning behind why you chose them, and what (if any) linguistic theories they were based on. If you performed a POS tagging task, what set of POS tags did you use? Did you make any modifications to those tags? If so, why? If you had to create your own set of tags, how did you divide the task into the categories that the tags represent? You should already know the answers to these questions—they're the same ones we asked you to think about in Chapter 4—but being able to explain your model and specs to other people so that they understand your reasoning will make your corpus significantly more useful to them, even if they disagree with your decisions or reasoning.

Remember that we previously described an annotation model as $M = <T,R,I>$, where T is a vocabulary of terms, R is the relations between these terms, and I is their interpretation. A lot of the information about these parts of the model will already be described in your annotation guidelines, but the reasoning behind them probably isn't, and that information is what people interested in the model and spec will want to know.

About Your Annotation Task and Annotators

Because so many variables can affect annotation tasks, it's important to be as clear as possible when reporting on how you created the annotations and gold standards. Publishing your annotation guidelines on your website or including them with the corpus will definitely help, but there are many other pieces of information that other researchers will consider important when evaluating your corpus. Bayerl and Paul 2011 in particular identified the following list of information that they believe should be included in any paper reporting on an annotation task:

- Number of annotators
- Type and amount of material annotated
- Number of categories in the scheme
- Criteria for selecting annotators
- Annotators' expert status (novices, domain experts, schema developers, native speakers, etc.)

- Type and intensity of training
- Type and computation of agreement index
- Purpose for calculating the agreement index (including whether the goal was to reach a certain threshold or achieve "highest-possible" agreement)

Everything on this list should be familiar to you, as they are aspects of the corpus, annotation, and evaluation that we encouraged you to consider throughout the MATTER cycle, so it should come as no surprise that other people will find this information useful as well. However, the list does not include all the factors that should be reported about your annotation task—there's lots of other information that other researchers will find useful when planning their own annotation task, such as:

- Annotation/adjudication tools that you used
- How the gold standard was adjudicated, and information about the adjudicators
- Any major revisions that your model or guidelines had to undergo during the MAMA cycle
- Information about the corpus, model, or other aspect of the annotation that may have affected agreement scores or annotation quality
- Major sources of confusion or disagreement among annotators or adjudicators

Naturally, neither of these lists covers everything that someone may find important to know about how your corpus was annotated, but providing this information offers a base of knowledge that people can use to understand your annotation task. If you're wondering what else you may want to include, think about things that you wish you'd known when you started the MATTER cycle yourself.

About Your ML Algorithm

Just as there are a lot of factors that can affect how your annotation task works out, there are a lot of factors that can affect how your ML algorithm is evaluated. At a minimum, we recommend reporting on:

- What type of algorithm you used (Naïve Bayes, decision tree, MaxEnt, etc.)
- The size of your training and testing corpus (or information about any cross-validation technique that you used)
- How you calculated accuracy scores
- The number of times you ran the algorithm on your final-evaluation test set
- What annotation-specific and structure-specific features you found most useful for training your algorithm

- Any other resources that you used (such as WordNet, other corpora, POS taggers, etc.)

Without this information, it will be difficult for other people to evaluate how well your algorithm actually performed or how it can be expected to perform on new data. If possible, we also encourage you to make your system available for download for other people to use—you went through all that work to create it, so you might as well get the credit for creating it!

About Your Revisions

Generally speaking, if you're writing a paper about your annotation task and ML results, any revisions that you made while working through the MATTER cycle would have been reported in the appropriate sections—they don't need to be reported in a separate section. However, if you have ideas for revisions that you would like to make in the future (such as ones you came up with during the Revision part of the MATTER cycle), it's common to put some notes about those in a "Future Work" section of a paper or website for the resource. Including this information both shows that your work has future applications and provides pointers for someone who might want to pick up where you left off once you've moved on to other projects.

Summary

In this chapter we discussed some of the important considerations that should be taken into account when revising your annotation task, or reporting the results to other researchers. In particular, we suggested the following:

- Once you've reached the Revision stage of the MATTER cycle, it's time to look back and consider what you could do differently, and how your annotations and algorithm can be used in the future.
- Consider whether there are any changes that you would make to the corpus, or whether the domain of the corpus could be expanded.
- If there were aspects of your model or specifications that annotators found difficult to implement or that weren't useful for machine learning, how would you change them? Or would you remove them entirely?
- Similarly, are there any tags or classes that you would add to your model or specification?
- Many different factors can affect annotation tasks, including annotation software, the guidelines, and the annotators themselves: is there anything about those aspects of your task that you would change?

- If you focused on annotation-based features during your ML training and testing, are there any structure-based features that you could look at adding next time? Or vice versa?

- As for reporting about your work, the more details that you make available to other researchers, the more useful they will find your corpus and annotations. If an annotation task is difficult to understand, it's unlikely to be used in other research.

- You don't have to publish a journal article or conference paper to make your corpus available—making your data available on a website is good too!

- When you're writing up the details of your annotation and ML task, consider all the different types of people who might be interested in your work: people looking to create their own annotation based on yours, people who want to do theoretical research on your corpus, people who want to train their own ML algorithms, and so on. Try to make available the relevant information that each of those groups will want to know about.

- Let people know how you created your corpus and what criteria you used to include (or exclude) certain texts.

- When explaining your model and specifications, don't just publish the DTD—make sure you explain where those tags and attributes came from and what theories they are grounded in.

- Because so many factors can affect an annotation task, it's important to report on as many details as you can, including information about the annotators, the software, how the IAA scores were calculated, and so on. That will allow readers to better compare your work to other corpora and annotations.

- Similarly, let people know how you trained your ML algorithm and which features were useful for you (and which ones weren't), as well as how you calculated the accuracy scores.

- If you have ideas about how you would revise your annotation or algorithm in the future, let people know! Ideas for expanding your corpus or annotation are always welcome, but it's also important to acknowledge places where you might have made a mistake that can be fixed later.

- Most important, the more information you share about your task, the more useful your task will be to other people, even if they don't always agree with the decisions you made.

Annotation: TimeML

Thus far in this book, we have been using TimeML as an example for annotation and machine learning (ML) tasks. In this chapter, we will discuss the development of TimeML as an annotation task, and guide you through the MAMA cycle, from its first conception to its application to the TimeBank corpus, to the ISO standard that it is today. We hope that by fully working through the MAMA cycle of a task as complex as TimeML, we will be able to give you a clear understanding of some of the decisions, problems, and successes that accompany a full-scale annotation task. Much of the content of this chapter has been discussed in other papers (particularly Pustejovsky et al. 2005 and Pustejovsky et al. 2003), but this is the first time a review of mistakes that were made and problems that were discovered in the development of the model and guidelines will be discussed in detail. In this chapter we'll go over:

- The goal of TimeML
- Some of the related research and theories that influenced the project
- The MAMA cycle that led to the TimeML specification
- The creation of TimeBank
- The changes that TimeML underwent to become an ISO standard
- Changes that will be applied to TimeML in the future

The ideas for TimeML stem from an ARDA workshop based on a proposal for a workshop to start thinking in terms of community standards for temporal expression and an accompanying corpus (Pustejovsky 2001).

At this point we need to acknowledge that the TimeML annotation task is clearly one that we are both deeply involved in. We didn't decide to focus on TimeML simply because we wanted to boast, however; these chapters detail many of the mistakes that were made in the creation of both TimeML and the TARSQI Toolkit, and they show just how messy an implementation of the MATTER cycle can be. While any annotation project will have similar problems and errors, we didn't want to air anyone else's dirty laundry by writing about their errors, so we decided to stick with ones we made ourselves. However, we hope that a discussion of some of the changes that had to be made to TimeML provides a useful perspective for any problems you might encounter with your own annotation task.

Many different people participated in the workshop, and many others have since contributed to TimeML and the accompanying corpus, TimeBank. For the sake of convenience, we will simply refer to the participants and contributors as the "working group."

The following people contributed to the creation of TimeML and TimeBank: James Allan, James Allen, Luc Belanger, Bran Boguraev, Michael Bukatin, Jose Castano, David Day, Lisa Ferro, John Fran, Rob Gaizauskas, Patrick Hanks, Jerry Hobbs, Robert Ingria, Graham Katz, Bob Knippen, Andrew Latto, Marcia Lazo, Penny Lehtola, Inderjeet Mani, Mark Maybury, Jessica (Littman) Moszkowicz, Bev Nunan, Jean Michel Pomareda, James Pustejovsky, Dragomir Radev, Erik Rauch, Anna Rumshisky, Antonio Sanfilippo, Roser Saurí, Len Schubert, Andrew See, Andrea Setzer, Amber Stubbs, Beth Sundheim, Svetlana Symonenko, Marc Verhagen, George Wilson, and Harris Wu.

The Goal of TimeML

The initial proposal for the workshop that created TimeML stated the following goals and research questions:

Goals:

(a) to examine how to formally distinguish events and their temporal anchoring in text (news articles); and (b) to evaluate and develop algorithms for identifying and extracting events and temporal expressions from texts.

Research questions:

1. Time stamping events (identifying an event and anchoring it in time);
2. Ordering events with respect to each other (relating more than one event in terms of precedence, overlap, and inclusion);
3. Reasoning about the ramifications of an event (what is changed by virtue of an event);

4. Reasoning about the persistence of an event (how long an event or the outcome of an event persists).

The proposal also stated that the working group would create a corpus, TimeBank, that would have 300–500 gold standard annotated documents.

 If you go to *http://timeml.org* and check out the document that was used to propose the workshop, you'll notice that it (and a few others) state the name of the project as "TenseML," which was the original name of the annotation language being created. However, the name was changed to TimeML because "tense" is an attribute that only verbs have, whereas events can also be nouns (and sometimes even adjectives). Also, "TenseML" sounded a bit like a treatment for anxiety, so it wasn't the best name, and "TimeML" was quickly adopted instead.

Related Research

With the stated goals in mind, the working group began looking into research that was related to their project. Specifically, they looked at existing computational linguistics research and projects to determine what aspects of their goals had already been implemented in some form, and then they looked at more theoretical treatments of the same problems to fill in the gaps of the existing research.

There was no completed version of anything like TimeML or TimeBank, but some aspects of the goals had been implemented in other annotation projects; for example, the TIMEX2 specification for marking times in texts had been developed the previous year as part of a DARPA program (*http://www.timexportal.info/timex2*), the work done on assigning timestamps to events in a document (Filatova and Hovy 2001), and Andrea Setzer's PhD dissertation work on annotating temporal information in newswire articles (Setzer 2001).

However, none of these annotation projects satisfied all the desiderata of the goal of TimeML, so the working group started to look at linguistic and temporal logic as well as quantitative temporal reasoning models. The working group wasn't looking only for the most famous theories, but rather for frameworks that lent themselves to being turned into models and annotations—work that could be represented consistently as tags and attributes.

For example, Reichenbach (1947) created a three-point system for describing the important times surrounding a statement of an event: the time of the event, E; the time of the statement, S; and the reference point of the statement, R. This provides a way to capture and reason with all the important information in a statement such as "By 9 p.m., everyone will have left the party." The statement about everyone leaving is being made prior to the event of their leaving, but the reference point of the event (9 p.m.) occurs after everyone has left (assuming that the speaker is correct). So we can interpret from this sentence that the speaking event, S, occurred before the action event, E, and that both of those occurred before the reference time, R. By providing clear reference points for each of the different times that influence how to interpret the events, each of these times can be tied neatly into an annotation system.

Some other theories that proved useful to the working group were event ontologies that distinguish between different types of events, such as activities, processes, and transitions (Vendler 1957; Kenny 1963); identifying linguistic features that determine what class an event belongs to (Dowty 1991; Jackendoff 1983); viewing events as grammatical objects (Tenny 2000); and subevent structures of identified events (Parsons 1990; Pustejovsky 1991). Some of these theories did not make it into TimeML—subevent structure, for example, wasn't included in the specification, and only now are people looking at including that information in a formal way.

The working group was also looking at the big-picture repercussions of the annotation scheme, and they were interested in making sure the logic of their system was consistent so that the annotations could be used for temporal reasoning. To that end, they examined linguistic theories of consistency and grammar (Montague 1970 ; Kamp 1988), as well as how the relations between events and times were being represented. The temporal interval problem was one that had received quite a bit of attention over the years, and the working group had a number of different proposals and implementations from early quantitative reasoning research to choose from (Allen 1984; Prior 1968; McDermott 1923; McCarthy and Hayes 1969). Eventually, the working group chose to use Allen's temporal interval logic, because the work has been consistently cited in the literature, so it was well known to all the participants, and Allen and his colleagues had made composition tables for the relations, so much of the work needed to turn the logic into an annotation-friendly format had already been done.

One aspect of representing time and events that the working group chose *not* to implement was the concept of *branching futures* (Belnap 1992), where events that may or may not happen in the future ("The class president candidate promised everyone would get free candy every day") are tracked in a separate timeline from events that are being discussed as already having happened. This type of modal representation was deemed to be outside the scope of the goals of the working group, and the task was set aside (or, perhaps, will be handled in a different branch in the future).

Once the working group had determined what theories and implementations were most useful to incorporate into TimeML, they were able to select a corpus and start working on the model and specification for the tasks, and begin working through the MAMA cycle.

Building the Corpus

The initial proposal for TimeML and TimeBank specified that TimeBank would be a gold standard corpus annotated with TimeML, and would contain "at least 300–500 articles, taken from either Reuters, the Factiva Media Base, or existing corpora such as TDT and TREC" (Pustejovsky 2001). During the course of the workshop, a second corpus was agreed upon—one of temporal queries. The effort to collect that corpus was spearheaded by Dragomir Radev, although in the end, this set of texts did not end up as part of TimeBank.

For the TimeBank corpus, the working group first planned to take 100 documents from the Automatic Content Extraction (ACE) corpus, 100 articles from the Document Understanding Conferences (DUC), 100 articles from PropBank, and 100 articles from the Reuters-21578 text collection.

However, throughout the course of the workshop and various annotation tasks, the working group found that 300–500 documents was far too much data to be annotated with a specification like TimeML, which not only usually identified multiple events and/ or times per sentence, but required detailed attribute information for each tag, as well as links between the annotated extents. As a result, the TimeBank corpus became smaller than was originally planned.

The current version of TimeBank (version 1.2) has 183 news reports collected from the ACE program and PropBank (TreeBank2) corpora. The articles from ACE are transcribed broadcast news articles from ABC, CNN, and other sources; ACE also supplied newswire texts from AP and the *New York Times*. Articles from the *Wall Street Journal* included in TimeBank come from PropBank. TimeBank is annotated with TimeML specification version 1.2.1 and is available for download at *http://www.timeml.org/site/ timebank/timebank.html*.

Model: Preliminary Specifications

The work that came closest to achieving the goals of the TimeML working group was that of Andrea Setzer (2001), whose dissertation research into annotating times and events provided a platform from which the TimeML group was able to work. Setzer's work came to be known as STAG (Sheffield Temporal Annotation Guidelines) by the working group, and it specified four types of extent tags: EVENT, Timex, SIGNAL, and DOA (Date of Article). The very first version of a TimeML specification is contained in the TimeML Historical Specification (version 0.2) (*http://www.timeml.org/site/terqas/docu mentation/TimeML-Draft2.8.html*), which we will describe here.

It should be noted that even though the document we are referring to is the "historical specification," it is still the result of more than one preliminary specification and annotation attempt. The modifications to the existing annotation guidelines weren't just made by people sitting around a table thinking very hard (though there was some of that too—and a lot of debating), but a lot of the modifications were made when the preliminary specifications were applied to a few articles to see how they worked.

Times

When the working group began looking into this problem, two existing tags were used for temporal annotation: the Timex tag, as described in STAG, and the TIMEX2 tag, which was the result of another workshop. However, neither of these tags contained as much information as the working group thought was needed, and so the working group proposed the creation of the TIMEX3 tag, which would be able to fully represent the temporal information in a phrase such as "the week before last," which is something that the Timex and TIMEX2 tags left underspecified.

For example, with the TIMEX2 specification the phrase "two days before the party" would be annotated as a single extent with an attribute that contained the calendar date being represented. The TimeML group, on the other hand, wanted to capture the different parts of that expression and recognize the "party" as an event, "two days" as a temporal expression, "before" as a temporal signal, and a relationship between "two days" and "party."

However, the full specifications for the TIMEX3 tag were not completed when the historical specification was released, and so it took a few more runs through the MAMA cycle before the tag really started to take shape, as we'll see later in this chapter.

Another temporal tag that was in STAG was the DOA or Date of Article tag, which was used to encode the date and time that the article was written, as that has special significance when interpreting a news article. However, the TimeML working group decided that rather than having a completely separate tag type for that temporal expression, it would be included in the TIMEX3 tag and be given a special attribute that designated the date as the DCT (Document Creation Time).

Signals

A temporal signal is a word in text that specifies a temporal relationship between two events, or a time and an event. As we mentioned in the preceding section, in the phrase "two days before the party," the word "before" is a temporal signal, because it indicates how two objects relate to each other. A SIGNAL tag existed in STAG, and the tag wasn't changed when it was adapted into TimeML. The only attribute was an ID that could be referenced by other tags.

Events

The EVENT tag in STAG contained a lot of attributes that captured the information about an event: there was a class attribute that denoted the type of event (occurrence, perception, etc.), `tense` and `aspect` attributes that denoted the verb form, a `related ToEvent` and `relatedToTime` attribute that designated what other event and/or time in the text the extent being annotated was related to, and `eventRelType` and `timeRel Type` attributes that indicated how the marked event was related to the indicated event or time ("before," "after," etc.).

However, the TimeML working group felt that too much information was being stored in an `EVENT` tag, and it was difficult to write guidelines that specified when the `related ToEvent`/`relatedToTime` and their accompanying `relType` tags should be filled out—if two events are connected in a sentence, which one should have that attribute information filled out? The first one? The second? Both of them? How would a system where only one event contained information that connected it to another event be programatically evaluated? Because of these concerns, the working group proposed that a new `LINK` tag be created to capture the relationship information between events and times without associating the relationship information with an extent in the text, which we will discuss in the next section.

At one point, the working group also proposed the creation of a `STATE` tag, for extents that indicated phrases that described an object or event, but that changed over the course of the document. The `STATE` tag was later folded into the `EVENT` tag, and `state` was added to the list of possible values for the `class` attribute.

Links

The `LINK` tag was given attributes that allowed it to represent the temporal relationship between two events, events and times, or two times (those attributes were removed from the `EVENT` tag, as they were no longer needed there). The `LINK` had three ID attributes: `eventID`, `timeID`, and `signalID`. It also had two attributes to indicate what type of object was being linked to: `relatedToEvent` and `relatedToTime`; and a `relType` attribute that contained an expanded set of relationships (based on Allen's work in temporal reasoning).

Not only did the `LINK` tag take the burden of expressing information about temporal relationships off of the `EVENT` tag, but it also made it possible for a (theoretically) unlimited number of relationships to be expressed in connection to a single event or time: this allowed for much more expressive temporal relations, and far more complete reasoning about the relationships between time and events.

Annotation: First Attempts

During the course of the workshop, a series of "annotation fests" were held, where participants in the working group annotated a small set of documents based on the current version of the specification. This proved to be an effective way to quickly find places where the theory outlined in the specification didn't quite line up with the reality of how times and events were actually expressed in the documents. While we don't have Inter-Annotator Agreement (IAA) scores to report from those annotation attempts, a few problems with the specifications did come to light as a result of the scores.

One thing the annotators noticed is that having one type of LINK tag didn't differentiate the different types of temporal relations: while it did allow for information about signals, the information in phrases such as "The boat began to sink" didn't really fit the LINK specification, and "began" isn't really a signal—it doesn't indicate a relationship between two different events, but rather where in the process of the "sinking" event the narrative takes place.

Another issue that was raised was how to indicate that a single text event might actually denote two events: in the sentence "John teaches on Monday and so does Mary," the "teaches" event is actually two events (in theory John and Mary could be teaching together, but that's not the standard interpretation of that phrasing), but it only has one instance in the text. Something needed to be done in the annotation that allowed an interpretive distinction of the two different events.

Not all of the problems discovered were with the specification—it was discovered that the software being used to create the annotation was making it difficult for the annotators to see the information in the LINK tags, and so the program itself had to be modified before a full annotation of the entire corpus could be completed.

Model: The TimeML Specification Used in TimeBank

TimeML 1.2.1 is the version of the specification that was used to annotate TimeBank, and is the most recent published version of the guidelines. Don't be fooled by the number, though: there were at least four "official" versions of the specifications through the years, and countless other interim versions, and more than one version of TimeBank. However, for this discussion we're going to roll up all those iterations of the MAMA cycle and just talk about the most recent version of TimeML and TimeBank. You can see the specifications at *http://bit.ly/SDblyF*.

Time Expressions

The TIMEX3 tag has been fleshed out to have many more attributes than the original Timex and TIMEX2 tags. The full set of attributes looks like this:

```
tid ::= ID
{tid ::= TimeID
TimeID ::= t<integer>}
type ::= 'DATE' | 'TIME' | 'DURATION' | 'SET'
beginPoint ::= IDREF
{beginPoint ::= TimeID}
endPoint ::= IDREF
{endPoint ::= TimeID}
```

```
quant ::= CDATA
freq ::= Duration
functionInDocument ::= 'CREATION_TIME' | 'EXPIRATION_TIME' |
                       'MODIFICATION_TIME' | PUBLICATION_TIME' |
                       ''RELEASE_TIME'| 'RECEPTION_TIME' |
                       'NONE' {default, if absent, is 'NONE'}
temporalFunction ::= 'true' | 'false' {default, if absent, is 'false'}
{temporalFunction ::= boolean}
value ::=  Duration | Date | Time | WeekDate | WeekTime | Season |
           PartOfYear | PaPrFu
valueFromFunction ::= IDREF
{valueFromFunction ::= TemporalFunctionID
TemporalFunctionID ::= tf<integer>}
mod ::= 'BEFORE' | 'AFTER' | 'ON_OR_BEFORE' | 'ON_OR_AFTER' |
        'LESS_THAN' | 'MORE_THAN' |'EQUAL_OR_LESS' |
        'EQUAL_OR_MORE' | 'START' | 'MID' | 'END' | 'APPROX'
anchorTimeID ::= IDREF
{anchorTimeID ::= TimeID}
comment ::= CDATA
```

As you can see, a lot of attributes help capture specific information about the time being annotated: when it begins, when it ends, how often it happens, as well as the actual value. The attribute functionInDocument helps encode a number of different ways that a temporal expression could affect the interpretation of the document, such as when it's created, published, released, or expires.

This is a much more complicated structure than other temporal expression representations, but the complexity of the information allows for the information to be used in much more robust temporal reasoning systems.

Events

Unlike the TIMEX3 tag, the EVENT tag became much simpler as compared to the STAG version. In this version of TimeML, it only has a few attributes: an ID, an event ID, a class, and an optional comment attribute (actually, all the tags have places to put comments—that has less to do with the semantics of representing time and events, and more to do with the fact that sometimes annotators need to explain why they made a particular decision).

```
eid ::= ID
{eid ::= EventID
EventID ::= e<integer>}
class ::= 'OCCURRENCE' | 'PERCEPTION' | 'REPORTING' | 'ASPECTUAL' |
          'STATE' | 'I_STATE' | 'I_ACTION'
comment ::= CDATA
```

Now, you've probably noticed that there's no way to annotate information such as verb tense and aspect, or other parts of an event that would be good to have available. That's because of the solution that the working group came up with to address the problem of single extents in text that actually encompass multiple events—the "John teaches on Monday and so does Mary" problem.

The solution to that problem was to create a tag called MAKEINSTANCE, as a way to distinguish between the linguistic mention of an event and how it was being used referentially. Every EVENT tag has at least one associated MAKEINSTANCE tag, or more if the semantics of the sentence call for it. The attributes for the MAKEINSTANCE tag look like this:

```
eiid ::= ID
{eiid ::= EventInstanceID
EventInstanceID ::= ei<integer>}
eventID ::= IDREF
{eventID ::= EventID}
signalID ::= IDREF
{signalID ::= SignalID}
pos ::= 'ADJECTIVE' | 'NOUN' | 'VERB' | 'PREPOSITION' | 'OTHER'
tense ::= 'FUTURE' | 'INFINITIVE' | 'PAST' | 'PASTPART' | 'PRESENT' |
          'PRESPART' | 'NONE'
aspect ::= 'PROGRESSIVE' | 'PERFECTIVE' | 'PERFECTIVE_PROGRESSIVE' | 'NONE'
cardinality ::= CDATA
polarity ::= 'NEG' | 'POS' {default, if absent, is 'POS'}
modality ::= CDATA
comment ::= CDATA
```

Not only does this tag encompass all the information needed for a verbal event, such as tense and aspect, but it also allows for the annotation of events that are nouns, adjectives, and prepositions. It also encodes the polarity of an event (in "did not go," the "go" event has a polarity of "neg" because the event is negated). When creating link tags, links are created between the IDs of the MAKEINSTANCE tags (called "event instance IDs") to keep the temporal relations as clear as possible.

Signals

Signal tags didn't actually change from the very first implementation in STAG (aside from the addition of a comment tag):

```
sid ::= ID
{sid ::= SignalID
SignalID ::= s<integer>}
comment ::= CDATA
```

What can we say? When something works, it works.

Links

Probably the biggest change from the starting STAG guidelines is how relationships between events and times are handled. The incorporation of the LINK tag at the very beginning was a pretty big change, but in this version of the TimeML specification, there are actually three different types of link tags: TLINKs, ALINKs, and SLINKs.

TLINKs encode relationships between temporal objects: event-event links, time-event links, event-time links, and time-time links.

```
attributes ::= [lid] [origin] (eventInstanceID | timeID) [signalID]
               (relatedToEventInstance | relatedToTime) relType [comment]
               [syntax]

lid ::= ID
{lid ::= LinkID
LinkID ::= l<integer>}
origin ::= CDATA
eventInstanceID ::= IDREF
{eventInstanceID ::= EventInstanceID}
timeID ::= IDREF
{timeID ::= TimeID}
signalID ::= IDREF
{signalID ::= SignalID}
relatedToEventInstance ::= IDREF
{relatedToEventInstance ::= EventInstanceID}
relatedToTime ::= IDREF
{relatedToTime ::= TimeID}
relType ::= 'BEFORE' | 'AFTER' | 'INCLUDES' | 'IS_INCLUDED' | 'DURING' |
            'SIMULTANEOUS' | 'IAFTER' | 'IBEFORE' | 'IDENTITY' |
            'BEGINS' | 'ENDS' | 'BEGUN_BY' | 'ENDED_BY' | 'DURING_INV'
comment ::= CDATA
syntax ::= CDATA
```

TLINKs are the most general-purpose of the links, and they also incorporate information about any signals that are influencing the relationship between the two objects. The relTypes are based on the temporal relationships defined by Allen (1984).

SLINKs don't actually have anything to do with the SIGNAL tag, which you might guess from the name. In fact, the S stands for "subordination," and these links are most commonly used to indicate that one verb takes a complement where another verb is subordinated. This usually happens with reporting verbs, as in "Harry said Sally went to the store." The "went" event is based on the "said" event—we can't know for sure that the "went" event actually happened. Similarly, events such as "want," "hope," "enjoy," "promise," and so on all introduce subordinating relationships. These types of relationships are marked specially to help keep track of the relationships that mark modality and intentionality. SLINKs have the following attributes:

```
lid ::= ID
{lid ::= LinkID
LinkID ::= l<integer>}
origin ::= CDATA
eventInstanceID ::= IDREF
{eventInstanceID ::= EventInstanceID}
subordinatedEventInstance ::= IDREF
```

```
{subordinatedEventInstance ::= EventInstanceID}
signalID ::= IDREF
{signalID ::= SignalID}
relType ::= 'MODAL' | 'EVIDENTIAL' | 'NEG_EVIDENTIAL' |
            'FACTIVE' | 'COUNTER_FACTIVE' | 'CONDITIONAL'
comment::= CDATA
syntax ::= CDATA
```

Initially, SLINKs were also used to mark modals and negatives, but sentences such as "John may not want to teach on Monday" would have had three SLINKs and proved far too difficult to annotate effectively or accurately.

The final new type of link tag is the ALINK, or aspectual link tag. These are used to take care of sentences such as "The boat began to sink" that we discussed before: they mark that the link being annotated has a temporal relationship, but they also mark what phase of the event is being discussed.

```
lid ::= ID
{lid ::= LinkID
LinkID ::= l<integer>}
eventInstanceID ::= ID
{eventInstanceID ::= EventInstanceID}
signalID ::= IDREF
{signalID ::= SignalID}
relatedToEventInstance ::= IDREF
{relatedToEventInstance ::= EventInstanceID}
relType ::= 'INITIATES' | 'CULMINATES' | 'TERMINATES' |
            'CONTINUES' | 'REINITIATES'
comment::= CDATA
syntax ::= CDATA
```

Confidence

A final addition to the TimeML specification is the CONFIDENCE tag, which is a non-consuming tag that was used to modify other tags. This, like the comment attribute on the other tags, was largely added as a way for the annotators to express their certainty about their annotations, and to indicate places where they weren't sure about an entire tag, or a specific attribute of an indicated tag.

```
tagType ::= CDATA
tagID ::= IDREF
attributeName ::= CDATA
confidenceValue ::= CDATA
{confidenceValue ::= 0 < x < 1}
comment ::= CDATA
```

The CONFIDENCE tag isn't a required part of the TimeML annotation, and since it's used to mark annotator's opinions about their own work, it's not included in IAA scoring.

Annotation: The Creation of TimeBank

Some of the articles in TimeBank have been annotated multiple times as the spec changed over the years; this is normal in a MAMA cycle, especially one where there have been multiple "official" specifications and guidelines. While we don't have agreement numbers on all of the different times each document was annotated, we do have numbers for the current TimeBank, version 1.2, annotated with TimeML specification version 1.2.1.

In "Reporting About Your Work" on page 187, we talked about the different parts of your annotation project that should be reported on to other people, and TimeML and TimeBank are no exception. We've already discussed the makeup and size of the corpus, and the specification has been gone over in a fair amount of detail here (and more detail is available online if you're interested). For annotators, the discussion gets a little bit complicated, as it says in the TimeBank documentation (*http://bit.ly/SDblyF*):

> The annotation of TimeBank has been a multi-step process. In the first phase, five annotators with varying backgrounds in linguistics took part. In addition to their annotation work, each participated in the development of the TimeML annotation scheme. This phase of the annotation took place during several annotation-intensive weeks. Throughout this time, the annotators met to discuss their work so that they could achieve a high level of annotator agreement.

> The annotation of each document during this phase of the effort began with a preprocessing step. This involved the tagging of some events and signals. When possible, preprocessing also attempted to supply the class, tense, and aspect of the tagged events. After preprocessing, one of the five annotators completed the annotation of the document including a check of the output from the preprocessing step.

> During this phase of the annotation effort, TimeML was still under development. Subsequent phases of annotation involved updating this early version of TimeBank to the current TimeML specification, version 1.2.1. This has been done automatically where possible and manually where needed.

> The most recent phase of the TimeBank development involved four annotators who have all previously participated in some TimeML annotation and are intimately familiar with the latest specification. Each annotator focused on a specific set of TimeML tags and used the TimeBank browser to check whether the annotation of his or her tags is accurate and complete. This current release of TimeBank reflects this work.

Because TimeML has been changed so many times, this partial-annotation approach is much more sensible than starting from scratch every time the specification is updated. However, taking this tack means that it is impossible to calculate IAA scores, because the additions to the corpus were made piecemeal. To obtain IAA scores, then, the working group tasked two annotators with experience in TimeML to annotate a subset of the TimeBank documents, and scores were computed by comparing one annotator's documents to the other to obtain accuracy scores.

One of the problems with comparing extent tags is determining how to compare tags that overlap but don't match perfectly. For example, if a sentence has the phrase "will have gone," and one annotator marks the entire phrase as an EVENT and another annotator marks only "gone" as an event, should they be counted as a match, or not? It's fairly common to report both sets of statistics, and that's what's done in the TimeBank documentation (see Table 10-1).

Table 10-1. IAA scores for TimeBank tags

TimeML tag	Exact match	Partial match
TIMEX3	.83	.96
SIGNAL	.77	.77
EVENT	.78	.81
ALINK	.81	
SLINK	.85	
TLINK	.55	

Partial matches can't be calculated for link tags, since it wouldn't make sense to consider two links to be a partial match if they share a single anchor, which is why those values are not provided in the table. The agreement for TLINKs is lower than for the other link tags because of the same problem we've been discussing regarding linking events and times: there are so many options for where links can be created, which makes creating such links very problematic.

Don't forget that when reporting on accuracy for tags, you also need to report on accuracy of attributes. Of course, you don't include the attributes of tags that don't match: only compare the attributes of tags that have matching extents (for extent tags) or matching anchors (for link tags). For TimeBank, these scores look like Table 10-2.

Table 10-2. IAA scores for TimeBank tag attributes

TimeML tag and attribute	Average precision and recall	Cohen's Kappa
TIMEX3.type	1.00	1.00
TIMEX3.value	.90	.89
TIMEX3.temporalFunction	.95	.87
TIMEX3.mod	.95	.73
EVENT.class	.77	.67
EVENT.pos	.99	.96
EVENT.tense	.96	.93
EVENT.aspect	1.00	1.00
EVENT.polarity	1.00	1.00
EVENT.modality	1.00	1.00

TimeML tag and attribute	Average precision and recall	Cohen's Kappa
`ALINK.relType`	.80	.63
`SLINK.relType`	.98	.96
`TLINK.relType`	.77	.71

As would be expected, the kappa scores for the attributes are lower than the average precision and recall scores, because kappa functions try to take into account the probability that annotators are agreeing by chance, rather than by choice.

Overall, however, these scores are good, especially considering how complex TimeML is (in terms of the number of tags and attributes) and how difficult temporal information in a document can be to interpret, even for native speakers.

TimeML Becomes ISO-TimeML

The transformation of TimeML into an ISO standard didn't happen overnight—in fact, the process actually took several months to get going, and several years for the specification to be approved. We won't go through all the gritty details of the process, but we will give an overview of some of the major changes as described in Pustejovsky et al. (forthcoming, 2010).

The first, and probably biggest, change for the specification was that it had to be made more abstract: the model for the original TimeML was rooted in the idea that all annotations using the TimeML specification would be using an XML format for their data, but that assumption couldn't be made for an international standard. Therefore, the ISO-TimeML model had to be expanded so that it could be represented in any number of formats, even very different ones such as a UML (Unified Modeling Language) diagram, or in different programming languages such as Lisp or Prolog. Doing this meant that the ISO-TimeML working group had to be able to clearly express the relationships between tags and their attributes, and how they could be connected to one another, so that those relationships could be modeled in other representations.

 Don't worry if your own model isn't quite as abstract as ISO-TimeML! While having a model that can be represented in many different ways without losing any data is definitely a perk that can make your annotation task more accessible to other people, it's not required —TimeBank was annotated before the ISO-TimeML abstraction was created, and it's still a very useful resource.

The next change that needed to be made was to make ISO-TimeML compliant with other ISO standards, such as the Linguistic Annotation Framework (LAF). Since the heavy lifting of creating a more abstract model had already been done, this primarily involved modifying the tags so that they could be used in a stand-off annotion format. The one used for ISO-TimeML is a token-based (rather than character-based) annotation.

Also, in terms of the tags and their attributes for ISO-TimeML, the ways that temporal relationships were handled had to be expanded so that the specification provided more coverage for three different characteristics:

Order
How an event or time is positioned in a timeline relative to other events or times

Measurement
The size of a temporal entity, such as an event's duration or the length of a temporal interval

Quantity
The number of events being described in a phrase

The original versions of TimeML actually handled the "order" characteristic quite well: TimeML already had a full set of temporal relations in the relType of the different link tags, so those remained unchanged in the ISO specification.

However, the "measure" characteristic of the text wasn't so fully covered. The original TimeML had a type='DURATION' option for the TIMEX3 tag, but that didn't fully capture the different types of meanings that a "duration" could imply. Consider the different interpretations of these two sentences: "Before leaving the house, I slept for two hours" and "Before getting my pilot's license, I flew for 300 hours." In the first sentence, we can reasonably interpret that the speaker slept for the full two-hour span, without any breaks. However, the same assumption decidedly cannot be made for the second sentence, despite the fact that both sentences have the same basic syntax. To more fully express the differences, a new type of link tag, the MLINK (measure link), was introduced in ISO-TimeML. Essentially, the MLINK is used to explicitly state that a Timex expression is used to "measure" the duration of an event.

The "quantity" characteristic was also somewhat underspecified in TimeML: as we mentioned in previous discussions, phrases where a single extent indicated that multiple events were taking place, such as "teach every Tuesday," are difficult to annotate. This is solved in ISO-TimeML by adding a "scopes" attribute to the TIMEX3 tag. This allows the tag to have a relationship with the "teaches" event that is not limited to the relType of the link, but rather provides a more open (but still semantically clear) interpretation of the expression.

One other major change from TimeML to ISO-TimeML is the removal of the MAKEIN STANCE tag. Annotators found the MAKEINSTANCE tag difficult to annotate, and so the attributes from that tag were placed back into the EVENT tag, which allowed for easier annotation, and the other additions to ISO-TimeML made up for the difference in how the different expressions were annotated.

Finally, since ISO-TimeML is, in fact, an international standard, some modifications had to be made to allow for the qualities of different languages besides English. For example, in Chinese, aspectual markers (words such as *begins*, *ends*, etc. in English) are not separate words, but rather are usually verbal suffixes. Also, some languages, such as Spanish, combine tense and aspect in a single verb form, rather than using modifying phrases. These and other cross-linguistic differences were accounted for in the ISO-TimeML standard.

Overall, ISO-TimeML provides a more robust way to annotate temporal information, and more accurate ways to encode temporal relationships for Question Answering tasks. However, remember that ISO-TimeML is still only a specification: if you want to apply it to your own annotation task, you'll still need to write the guidelines yourself!

Modeling the Future: Directions for TimeML

Even though it's now an international standard, TimeML isn't set in stone: as theories about temporal and event information in text are created and expanded, plans are being made to expand TimeML to make use of those new and improved ideas. Some of these possible additions are outlined in the following subsections.

Narrative Containers

One of the biggest hurdles in creating a TimeML-annotated document is creating the link tags, particularly TLINKs. As we discussed previously in this book, the sheer number of possible combinations of links between events and times makes creating a complete overview of the relationships in the text nearly impossible for human annotators. Another problem with the TLINKs as they exist in the text is that they often enforce the creation of relationships that are open-ended in terms of capturing boundaries on when an event can occur.

Consider a news article that begins with this: "The White House announced the president's intention…." In a standard TimeML annotation, the "announced" event would be given a "before" relationship with the document creation time. While this is technically true (clearly, the announcement couldn't have happened before the article was written), it's also extremely open-ended. How long before the writing of the article was the announcement made? Presumably it was made fairly close to the Document Creation Time (DCT) of the article—if it's being reported in a newspaper, then the event most likely occurred the day before. But a TLINK with a relType of before doesn't distinguish between an event occurring the previous day and an event occurring 100 years ago.

As a way to impose reasonable limits on when an event is likely to have occurred, the idea of *Narrative Containers* was introduced (Pustejovsky and Stubbs 2011). Essentially, a Narrative Container is a special type of time expression that acts like a bucket into which events can be placed. Consider the difference between knowing that an event occurred before January 13, 2012, and knowing that it occurred between January 11 and January 13, 2012. Having extra restrictions on where an event can be placed in a timeline allows for better temporal reasoning to be done over a document. Figure 10-1 shows the difference between the TimeBank annotation of a document for TLINKs, and a TLINK annotation using a Narrative Container instead of a DCT.

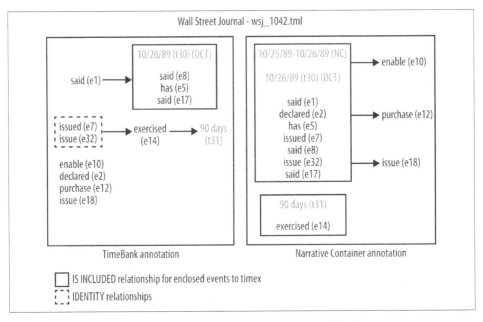

Figure 10-1. TimeML TLINKs versus Narrative Container TLINKs

The temporal value of a Narrative Container varies by genre: a daily newspaper will have a much smaller Narrative Container than a monthly magazine and a much bigger one than a broadcast on a 24-hour news service. However, the idea is both intuitive for annotators and extremely prevalent in news articles: an experimental annotation that incorporated Narrative Containers showed that nearly 50% of events in TimeBank were linked to their document's Narrative Container with an is_included relation type. Eventually, Narrative Containers will be included in the official TimeML specifications and guidelines.

Expanding TimeML to Other Domains

The original specifications for TimeML were designed for news articles, but temporal annotation of other types of documents is also needed. The THYME (Temporal Histories of Your Medical Event) Project is working to adapt the TimeML guidelines to the clinical domain so that electronic health records can be automatically processed [see the

THYME Project wiki (*https://clear.colorado.edu/TemporalWiki/index.php/ Main_Page*) for more information]. Because events and their relations in medical documents have some special properties that are important to encode, some changes must be made to TimeML to fully express what is being described by the document.

While the new guidelines are not out yet (as of summer 2012), a preliminary paper by Savova et al. (2009) outlines some of the suggested changes to TimeML that would make the system better for clinical documents, some of which we will describe here. For example, in traditional TimeML, the word *postoperative* would not be considered an event, but rather a temporal marker, yet for clinical notes, it should be considered an EVENT, along with other adjectives that indicate a person's state of health. Clearly, for the purposes of clinical notes, it is important to be able to determine what a person's condition is at any given time, and marking statements such as "patient is feverish" is a good way to incorporate their conditions into the temporal framework of the annotation.

Another change that was proposed is modifying the use of the EVENT tag's `tense` attribute. In TimeML, this was used to indicate the tense of the verb being annotated (as in "we went to the store" would have `tense='past'`, "we will go" would have `tense='future')`. However, most medical documents are written in the past tense, because they are written after the doctor meets with the patient, not while the meeting is taking place. Therefore, the majority of the verbs in the documents are in the past tense, regardless of whether they describe actions that occurred before the patient went to seek medical attention or actions that occurred during the visit. As a result, the tense of the verb doesn't help to determine when an action occurred in the timeline, and so the use of the `tense` attribute was modified to reflect the event's relationship to the time of the patient's meeting with the doctor instead of reflecting the syntactic tense of the verb. So, for example, "He *woke* with a headache" would be `tense='past'`, whereas "*rash* under right arm *observed*" would be `tense='present'`.

Whether or not an event caused another event to happen is also extremely important to record in an annotation of a clinical document, and while TimeML does have the tools to encode those relationships, the implementation and guidelines would need to be greatly expanded to have the full coverage needed for medical records.

In addition to making changes to TimeML, Savova et al. note that other resources will have to be expanded to the medical domain, such as PropBank (Palmer 2005), which is a resource that provides semantic roles for verbs, but does not have a large medical vocabulary. Similarly, part-of-speech (POS) and syntactic tree building systems will need to be retrained for the clinical domain, because many sentences in medical records are fragments rather than complete sentences.

The proposed changes to TimeML that we have outlined here based on Savova et al.'s preliminary work are not necessarily going to be implemented the same way in the THYME specifications and guidelines, but this discussion should give you an idea of what aspects of clinical notes would need to be accounted for to make TimeML fully useful for the clinical domain. The full set of specifications, when finished, will be posted on the THYME project wiki page, *https://clear.colorado.edu/TemporalWiki/index.php/Main_Page*.

Event Structures

We mentioned earlier that event structures didn't get included in the model for TimeML because of how difficult it would be to annotate all the information associated with them. An event structure is basically the information that can be inferred from an event's occurrence. For example, in the sentence "He gave the book to his brother yesterday," despite not knowing who the sentence is describing, we can state that the following subevents occurred:

- Prior to the giving event, "he" had the book.
- Prior to the giving event, his brother did not have the book.
- A giving event occurred.
- After the giving event, his brother had the book.
- After the giving event, he did not have the book.

Having access to this level of information makes any Question Answering System (QAS) vastly more robust, but the level of detail required to annotate all those stages makes the task nearly impossible for a manual annotation assignment.

While there are no plans to make event structure part of the annotation guidelines for TimeML, work is being done to create a TimeML-compliant framework that can be applied automatically to the EVENTs in an annotated document (Im and Pustejovsky 2010).

The approach being taken is to divide verbal events into aspectual classes (as described in Vendler [1967], Dowty [1979], and Pustejovsky [1995], and incorporated into the TimeML EVENT/MAKEINSTANCE tags), determine the verb's class and subclass (e.g., "state" or "change_of_location"), and then use that information to assign the event an Event Structure Frame (ESF). The ESF is essentially a more formalized version of the subevent list shown a few paragraphs up. With an event assigned an ESF, a lot more information is known about the different states and processes being described in the text. The ESF for the sentence we discussed earlier looks like this (Im forthcoming):

```
a. SENTENCE: He gave the book to his brother yesterday.
b. ESF of give
  se1: pre-state: have (he, the_book)
  se2: pre-state: not_have (his_brother, the_book)
  se3: process: giving (he, the_book)
  se4: post-state: not_have (he, the_book)
  se5: post-state: have (his_brother, the_book)
```

This is a fairly complicated example of an event structure, as a lot is going on in that one sentence. However, most verbs can be broken down into subevents, and so have similar subevents embedded within them. We won't go into a full description of exactly what the different types of ESFs look like, and how the verb classes affect the frames; that would be a book unto itself—or a dissertation; which, actually, it is! Check out (Im forthcoming) for a complete overview of the event structures and subevent classifications.

Summary

In this chapter we provided an overview of the MAMA cycle for TimeML, including a discussion of the changes in goal, model, and specification. In particular, we looked at the following:

- TimeML (formerly TenseML) was developed to provide a way to annotate events and their temporal anchorings in text, specifically news articles. The bulk of the TimeML specification development was done at a workshop in early 2002.

- One of the workshop's goals was to create a gold standard annotated corpus, called TimeBank. While initially TimeBank was going to contain 300–500 articles, the density of the TimeML annotation eventually left that to be cut down to 183. However, those articles are available for use as a resource from *http://timeml.org/*.

- TimeML didn't spring from the minds of the workshop's working group fully formed; it was based on some existing temporal and event annotations, and a lot of existing theories about linguistics and temporal reasoning.

- A primary source for TimeML was the dissertation work of Andrea Setzer, which resulted in the Sheffield Temporal Annotation Guidelines (STAG). The TIMEX2 tag was also an influencing factor, though eventually the working group created their own temporal annotation tag, TIMEX3.

- The specification for TimeML went through multiple iterations of the MAMA cycle, both during the course of the working group and afterward, as more refinements were made to the tags and attributes.

- During the workshop, periodic "annotation fests" were held, which allowed members of the working group to try out the current specifications on a small set of documents, which proved to be a very effective way of finding places where the spec wasn't suited to the reality of the texts.

- The final pre-ISO TimeML specification (version 1.2.1) consisted of tags: TIMEX3, EVENT, MAKEINSTANCE, SIGNAL, TLINK, ALINK, SLINK, and CONFIDENCE.

- Each of the TimeML tags has a set of attributes that is used to capture the relevant information about the text, such as the verb tenses, modality, relation type of the links, and value of the temporal expression (such as a calendar date or date relative to another event).

- The current version of TimeBank (version 1.2) is annotated with version 1.2.1 of TimeML. Because the specifications changed over the years, most of the annotations in the current TimeBank are modifications of the previous annotation efforts, which was more efficient than reannotating the entire corpus from scratch.

- ISO-TimeML is an expanded version of TimeML that allows for the annotation of temporal information in languages other than English, and provides more robust handling of complex temporal expressions. It is also compliant with other ISO standards, and provides more interoperability options for different annotation frameworks.

- Even though TimeML is currently an ISO standard, it is still undergoing changes as more research is done into temporal information and events. Some of these changes include adding new types of temporal objects, called Narrative Containers; adapting the TimeML specification and guidelines to new domains, such as clinical texts; and adding information about event classes and structures to TimeML-compliant resources.

Automatic Annotation: Generating TimeML

As you can see from the preceding chapter, modeling events, times, and their temporal relationships in an annotation is a large and complicated task. In this chapter we will discuss the TARSQI Toolkit, as well as other systems that were created to generate TimeML as part of the TempEval-2 challenge held in 2010. In this chapter, we will:

- Discuss how a complicated annotation can be broken down into different components for easier processing

- Provide an in-depth discussion of the first attempt to create a system for creating TimeML

- Show examples of how that system has been improved over the years

- Explain the approaches taken by other examples of systems designed to create TimeML

- Discuss the differences between rule-based and machine learning (ML) systems for complex annotation tasks

- Provide examples of ways that the TARSQI Toolkit could be expanded in the future

Overall, in this chapter we won't be going into detail about how each aspect of TimeML was automated; rather, we will provide a breakdown of how the task was approached, and give a sense of some of the different options available for tackling a complicated annotation.

The TARSQI Toolkit is not the creation of a single person, and we would like to acknowledge all of the people who have contributed to its creation and improvement (in alphabetical order): Alex Baron, Russell Entrikin, Catherine Havasi, Jerry Hobbs, Seo-Hyun Im, Seok Bae Jang, Bob Knippen, Inderjeet Mani, Jessica (Littman) Moszkowicz, Feng Pan, Jon Phillips, Alex Plotnik, James Pustejovsky, Alan Rubenstein, Anna Rumshisky, Roser Saurí, Amber Stubbs, and Ben Wellner. Special thanks go to Marc Verhagen, the curator of the TARSQI Toolkit, who provided and fact-checked much of the information in this chapter.

The TARSQI Components

When it comes to creating algorithms to perform automatic annotations, sometimes it's a good idea to break down a complicated task the same way that complicated annotations are performed: one tag at a time. This is the approach taken with the TARSQI Toolkit (TTK), the first system built for automatic creation of TimeML-annotated documents.

The TTK uses different components to create each of the different tags in TimeML. As with any project that's part of a Training–Evaluation cycle, the TTK has gone through various stages of existence and improvement over the years. In this chapter we'll walk you through the different components of the first version of the TTK, as well as some of the improvements that were made in later versions. We will also discuss some of the other systems that have been created to automatically annotate documents with TimeML.

The TARSQI (Temporal Awareness and Reasoning Systems for Question Interpretation) Project was a government-funded research initiative that aimed to create systems for enhancing documents with temporal and event information. The first versions of the TARSQI components were released in 2005. Technically speaking, they weren't actually a toolkit yet, as each component was created individually and then linked together later. TARSQI was a collaborative effort between Brandeis University, Georgetown University, and ISI (Information Sciences Institute, part of the University of Southern California). The primary paper on the components is from Verhagen et al. 2005.

Figure 11-1 shows the layout of the different components.

In the rest of this section, we'll discuss how the automated creation of TimeML got broken down into different components, and how each of those components works.

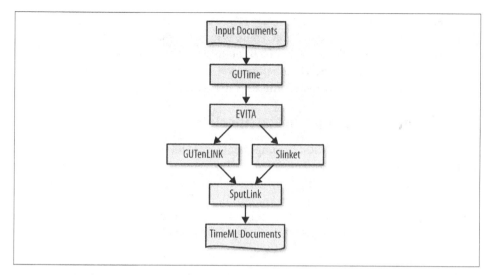

Figure 11-1. The TARSQI components in 2005

GUTime: Temporal Marker Identification

As we discussed in Chapter 10, temporal information in TimeML is marked with TIMEX3 tags, which not only encode time-related phrases in the text, but also contain other attributes such as date/time values for those expressions, which can be evaluated relative to other times in the text.

GUTime (Georgetown University Time) was used to create TIMEX3 tags as part of the TARSQI set of components. GUTime extended the TempEx tagger from MITRE, and used a rule-based system of regular expressions and phrase libraries to identify temporal expressions and provide them with normalized values. Therefore, it was able to identify and evaluate dates, such as "June 2, 2003," as well as relative phrases such as "yesterday" and "next month" (Verhagen et al. 2005).

Because GUTime was designed for newspaper articles, time expressions that relied on context to interpret, such as "today," were evaluated relative to the publication date of the article, like this (example from *http://www.timeml.org/site/tarsqi/modules/gutime/index.html*):

> In Washington **<TIMEX3 tid="t1" TYPE="DATE" VAL="PRESENT_REF" tempora-lFunction="true" valueFromFunction="tf1" anchorTimeID="t0">**today</TIMEX3>, the Federal Aviation Administration released air traffic control tapes from the night the TWA Flight eight hundred went down.

In TimeML-annotated news articles, VAL="PRESENT_REF" is evaluated as a reference to the publication date of the article, which here was given the TimeID of t0. You'll notice that the output from GUTime is in the form of inline annotation, rather than stand-off: most systems available around 2005 had not yet adapted stand-off annotation, so the practice has taken some time to become a standard.

EVITA: Event Recognition and Classification

TimeML EVENT tags in the TARSQI components were identified by EVITA—Events in Text Analyzer, described in Saurí et al. (2005). Because events in text can be verbs ("We **went** to the store"), nouns ("The **investigation** led to six arrests"), and even adjectives ("The water levels have been **high** for months"), EVITA takes in texts marked up with part-of-speech (POS) tags and syntactic chunks to identify parts of sentences likely to contain events, then evaluates EVENT candidates based on their part of speech.

Verbal chunks are evaluated based on their content to determine the head of the verb phrase, which is then checked to remove certain types of verbs, such as copular verbs like "is." Nominal events (i.e., nouns that function as events in the text) are identified in two steps. First, the head of the noun chunk is checked against WordNet to determine if it is a noun that is always associated with an event. If it isn't clear whether the noun is an event or not (words such as *party*, for example, can be events in the sense of "We had a party last night," or not, as in "The Republican Party"), then a determination of the noun's event status is made by a Bayesian classifier. Adjectives are rarely identified as events, unless they were marked as such in TimeBank.

EVITA gives identified events an EVENT tag as well as the EVENT's class type, and it also generates MAKEINSTANCE tags for each identified event and provides values for the MAKE INSTANCE tag attributes. Here is a sample of output from EVITA (provided by *http://www.timeml.org/site/tarsqi/modules/evita/index.html*):

> In Washington today, the Federal Aviation Administration **<EVENT eid="e1" class="OCCURRENCE">** released **</EVENT>** air traffic control tapes from the night the TWA Flight eight hundred **<EVENT eid="e2" class="OCCURRENCE">** went **</EVENT>** down.
>
> **<MAKEINSTANCE eventID="e1" eiid="ei1" pos="VERB" tense="PAST" aspect="NONE"/>**
>
> **<MAKEINSTANCE eventID="e2" eiid="ei2" pos="VERB" tense="PAST" aspect="NONE"/>**

EVITA also provides information about event polarity, aspect, and the other attributes that are part of the MAKEINSTANCE class.

GUTenLINK

TLINKs in the TARSQI Toolkit were created by GUTenLINK, as described in Verhagen et al. 2005. GUTenLINK used "hand-developed syntactic and lexical rules" (ibid.) to create TLINKs. It created TLINKs based on three sets of circumstances in the text:

- If an event and time expression were in the same clause and no signal was present. For example:

  The Olympics will be **held** in London **this year**.
  GUTenLINK: held **is_included** this year

- If an event was anchored to the Document Creation Time or DCT (such as reporting verbs in a news article). For example:

  Feb. 2, 2010
  The president **said** in a press release that…
  GUTenLINK: said **before** Feb. 2, 2010

- If the main event in one sentence is anchored to the main event in a previous sentence through clues such as tense or aspect. For example:

  The cat **woke up**. It **had been sleeping** all day.
  GUTenLINK: sleeping **before** woke up

Sample GUTenLINK output is shown here (from *http://www.timeml.org/site/tarsqi/modules/gutenlink/index.html*):

In Washington <TIMEX3 tid="t1" TYPE="DATE" VAL="PRESENT_REF" temporalFunction="true" valueFromFunction="tf1" anchorTimeID="t0"> **today** </TIMEX3>, the Federal Aviation Administration <EVENT eid="e1" class="OCCURRENCE"> **released** </EVENT> air traffic control tapes from the night the TWA Flight eight hundred <EVENT eid="e2" class="OCCURRENCE"> **went** </EVENT> down. There's nothing new on why the plane <EVENT eid="e3" class="OCCURRENCE"> **exploded** </EVENT>, but you <EVENT eid="e4" class="OCCURRENCE"> **cannot** </EVENT> <EVENT eid="e5" class="OCCURRENCE"> **miss** </EVENT> the moment. ABC's Lisa Stark <EVENT eid="e6" class="OCCURRENCE"> **has** </EVENT> more.

<MAKEINSTANCE   eventID="e1"   pos="VERB"   eiid="ei1"   tense="PAST" aspect="NONE"/>

<MAKEINSTANCE   eventID="e2"   pos="VERB"   eiid="ei2"   tense="PAST" aspect="NONE"/>

<MAKEINSTANCE   eventID="e3"   pos="VERB"   eiid="ei3"   tense="PAST" aspect="NONE"/>

<MAKEINSTANCE   eventID="e4"   pos="VERB"   eiid="ei4"   tense="PRESENT" aspect="NONE"/>

```
<MAKEINSTANCE eventID="e5" pos="VERB" eiid="ei5" tense="INFINITIVE"
aspect="NONE"/>

<MAKEINSTANCE eventID="e6" pos="NONE" eiid="ei6" tense="PRESENT"
aspect="NONE"/>


<TLINK eventInstanceID="ei1" relatedToTime="t1" relType="IS_INCLUDED"
rule="2-1" />

<TLINK eventInstanceID="ei2" relatedToTime="t1" relType="IS_INCLUDED"
rule="2-1" />

<TLINK eventInstanceID="ei1" relatedToEventInstance="ei3" relType="BEFORE"
rule="3-19" />

<TLINK eventInstanceID="ei3" relatedToEventInstance="ei4" relType="BEFORE"
rule="6-1" />

<TLINK eventInstanceID="ei3" relatedToEventInstance="ei6" relType="BEFORE"
rule="3-23" />
```

Slinket

The TARSQI component used to create SLINKs, or subordination links, was Slinket
(SLINK Events in Text) (Verhagen et al. 2005; Sauri et al. 2006). Slinket was a rule-based
system in which, once a subordinating event (such as *say, promise, plan*, etc.) was identified in the text, shallow syntactic parses were used to determine the scope of the subordination, and SLINKs were created between the subordinating event and any other
events deemed to be within its scope.

The SLINK also included information about the type of subordination being performed
and included that information in the relType attribute. Here is an example of the output
from Slinkct (from *http://www.timeml.org/site/tarsqi/modules/slinket/index.html*):

```
The Soviet Union <EVENT eid="e12" class="REPORTING">said</EVENT> today it
had <EVENT eid="e13" class="OCCURRENCE">sent</EVENT> an envoy to the Mid-
dle East.

<MAKEINSTANCE eventID="e12" eiid="ei12" tense="PAST" aspect="NONE"
pos="VERB"/>

<MAKEINSTANCE eventID="e13" eiid="ei13" tense="PAST" aspect="PERFECTIVE"
pos="VERB"/>

<SLINK lid="l2" relType="EVIDENTIAL" eventInstanceID="ei12" subordinatedE-
ventInstance="ei13"syntax="thatClause_NOT_that"/>
```

SputLink

SputLink is the TARSQI component that performed temporal closure calculations (Verhagen et al. 2005); that is to say, given the set of TLINKs and SLINKs created by GUTenLINK and Slinket, SputLink used interval algebra to infer relationships between events and times based on existing links, and to create new TLINKs based on what was already created.

In many ways, SputLink does what a human annotator can't do, in that it fills in all the possible relationships between events and times in the text (or at least, those that can be determined to be accurate). Remember in "Refining Your Goal: Informativity Versus Correctness" on page 35 when we used the example "On Tuesday, Pat jogged after leaving work. Then Pat went home, made dinner, and laid out clothes for the next day." We showed how difficult it would be to have a human create all the possible links between times and events that exist in those sentences. The diagram is shown in Figure 11-2.

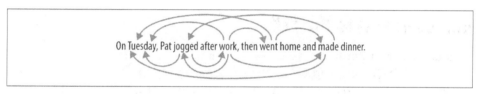

On Tuesday, Pat jogged after work, then went home and made dinner.

Figure 11-2. All temporal relations over events and times

It's clear why asking a human to create all those relations would be difficult, but it should also be clear why having all those relationships would be good for a Question Answering System (QAS): the greater number of relationships that were already worked out, the easier it would be to answer questions about any given pair. SputLink provided the ability to create most of those relationships without being trained on complicated annotations, or relying on complicated rule libraries in GUTenLINK and Slinket to create the TLINKs instead. Here is a sample of some TLINKs that SputLink could create:

On Tuesday, Pat jogged after work, went home and made dinner

Given: jogged AFTER work; went AFTER jogged; made AFTER went

SputLink: went AFTER work; made AFTER work; made AFTER jogged; etc…

Naturally, because temporal information in text can be vague, and because it's not always easy to determine what relationships can be extracted from a mixed set of TLINK relTypes, "complete" sets of links like the one in Figure 11-2 can't always be created. For a more in-depth discussion of how closure can be run over temporal links, please see Verhagen (2004).

Machine Learning in the TARSQI Components

You may have noticed that, aside from the nominal event classifier in EVITA, there are no ML algorithms in the TARSQI components. As we said in Chapter 7, sometimes it's a good idea to start with rule-based systems as a way to suss out what features would be good for an ML algorithm later on. There is also the fact that rule-based systems still outperform machine learning algorithms on some types of annotation tasks. As it happens, temporal expression annotation is one of them: as of the TempEval-2 challenge (Verhagen et al. 2010), the top-performing system for identifying and evaluating temporal events in text was HeidelTime, a purely rule-based system (*http://code.google.com/p/heideltime/*). However, more ML algorithms were incorporated into later versions of the TARSQI system, as we will see in the next section. In the TempEval challenges, different groups of researchers compete to create TimeML-generating systems, and different teams will use rule-based, ML, and combination architectures to obtain their results. We will discuss relative performances between the different types of systems in "TimeML Challenges: TempEval-2" on page 228.

Improvements to the TTK

Although we haven't provided details of the Training–Evaluation cycle for each component of TARSQI, we are providing an overview of the progression of the system as a whole. We won't go into excruciating detail about all the changes that have been made over the years, but in this section, we will provide information about how some of the individual components have changed, and how the system as a whole has been expanded since it was first released in 2005.

In 2008, a paper was published detailing the transformation of the TARSQI components into the pipeline that is now referred to as the TTK (TARSQI Toolkit) (Verhagen and Pustejovsky 2008), and over the years, further improvements have been made, resulting in the current TTK pipeline, which looks like the one shown in Figure 11-3 (Verhagen and Pustejovsky 2012).

Clearly, this diagram is a lot more complicated than the one we showed you earlier in the chapter, as it includes more stages before the TimeML processing starts, GUTime and GUTenLINK are no longer part of the system, and there are more temporal relation modules than there were before. Let's go through these one at a time.

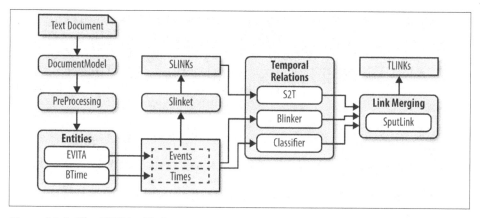

Figure 11-3. The TTK in 2012

Structural Changes

The new DocumentModel step cleans up input to the toolkit and provides support for encoding and metatags (Verhagen and Pustejovsky 2008). The preprocessing modules that provide the POS tags and chunks for EVITA are now part of the entire system, and the TTK has recently moved from using inline annotation to a stand-off representation that is compliant with the Linguistic Annotation Framework or LAF (Verhagen and Pustejovsky 2012).

While these changes don't directly affect the quality of the TimeML annotation that the system creates, they do provide more stability for the system and make processing the entire set of tags easier.

Improvements to Temporal Entity Recognition: BTime

In the newest release of the TTK, GUTime has been replaced with BTime, a temporal expression tagger developed at Brandeis University. While still rule-based, BTime uses a context-free grammar to create standardized representations of temporal expressions, which provides a code base that is much easier to keep updated than the regular expression libraries used in GUTime. While regular expressions are, of course, still a part of identifying temporal expressions, it is now much easier to convert a phrase in the text into a TIMEX3 tag. Here is a sample rule from the context-free grammar (Verhagen and Pustejovsky 2012):

```
date ->
   day month year (
       CalendarDate(_(2), _(1),_(0)  )
   | month day year (
       CalendarDate(_(2), _(0),_(1)  )
   |   day month "," year (
       CalendarDate(_(3), _(1),_(0)  )
```

This representation allows for various forms of a date to be transformed into a standardized representation: "13 January 1982", "January 13 1982", and "January 13, 1982" would all be turned into the calendar date form of "1982, January, 13" (or perhaps, "1982, 01, 13"). This format is also very easy to add to; if a document contained a string in the form "01-13-1982", a new variation of the "date" grammar could be added, like so:

```
|   month "-" day "-" year (
        CalendarDate(_(4), _(0),_(2)  )
```

BTime also includes a set of rules used to take underspecified TIMEX3s, such as those created for phrases like "yesterday" and "next month," and provide them with normalized values based on the most likely temporal anchor for those expressions (usually, this anchor is the DCT).

Temporal Relation Identification

In later versions of the TTK, the TLINK creator GUTenLINK was replaced with a suite of temporal processing components. First, Blinker was developed as a replacement for GUTenLINK. While Blinker is still rule-based, its library of rules has been expanded to account for even more temporal relationships (Verhagen and Pustejovsky 2008):

- An event and Timex in the same noun phrase:

  "**Saturday**'s **party**" —> party IS_INCLUDED Saturday

- An event being linked to the DCT:

  "The New York Times **reported** that…" —> reported BEFORE DCT

- Events and syntactically subordinated events:

  "The school board **says** they already **voted** on the matter" —> says AFTER voted

- Events in conjunctions:

  "We **swam** and **played** all day" —> swam IS_INCLUDED play

- Two main events in consecutive sentences:

  "I have **been running** from place to place all day. My cat, however, has **been sleeping** the whole time." —> running SIMULTANEOUS sleeping

- Timexes with other Timexes:

  "On **Monday** and **Wednesday** I went to the gym." —> Monday BEFORE Wednesday

In addition to Blinker, the S2T program takes the output from Slinket and turns the SLINKs into TLINKs through a set of predefined rules. For example, in the sentence "Mary **said** she **went** to the store," an SLINK exists between "said" and "went," but that would be turned into a TLINK with the relation set "went BEFORE said." The third addition to the set of TLINK-creation components was a Maximum Entropy (MaxEnt) classifier trained on the event relationships in TimeBank (Verhagen and Pustejovsky 2008).

Temporal Relation Validation

Naturally, with three different components creating TLINKs, the system needs some way to determine which links are most likely to be correct, since it's possible that Blinker, S2T, and the classifier would come up with different relationships between the same events. To deal with that possibility, the new TTK includes a Link Merging stage that first orders links by their confidence values, and then merges them into a graph of TIMEX3 and EVENT tag nodes with the TLINKs as edges. As each link is added, SputLink checks that the new edge will maintain the consistency of the graph. If it doesn't, the link is thrown out and the program proceeds to the next one (Verhagen and Pustejovsky 2012).

The confidence interval attached to each link is assigned to the links by the component that created it, with the rule-based systems having hardwired confidence scores and the classifier generating its own confidence scores based on the intervals. Finally, each score is weighted based on the general accuracy of each component.

Temporal Relation Visualization

TLINKs can be very difficult to validate due to how hard they are to read, and the problem becomes more difficult as the number of links in a document increases. As a way to deal with this problem, a program for visualizing links was added to the TTK. This program, called TBox, creates graphs of the document events and times and displays their relationships with arrows to indicate directionality. The created timelines are read left to right to indicate that the events on the left occurred before the events on the right; events occurring at the same time are put in boxes together, and events with no known relationship are stacked vertically. This system allows the output of the TTK to be much more easily validated than simply trying to read the TLINK texts. Figure 11-4 shows a TBox representation from Verhagen and Pustejovsky (2008).

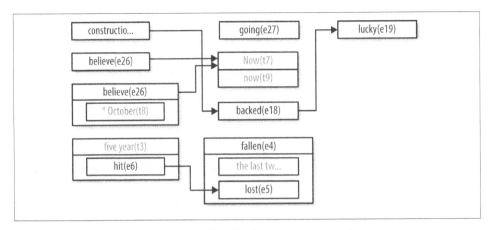

Figure 11-4. TBox representation of TLINKs between times and events

TimeML Challenges: TempEval-2

While so far we've only discussed the TTK as a way to create TimeML, other systems have been built to automatically generate temporal annotations. Many of them have been used at the TempEval challenges that were held as part of SemEval 2007 and SemEval 2010. These evaluation challenges are often held prior to conferences, with the results of the system's accuracy scores released at the conference, at which point papers on all the participating systems are also presented.

Because these challenges take place over the course of months rather than years, they often take advantage of smaller subsets of existing linguistic problems, as that allows participants to focus on particular aspects of a larger task. This is the approach that was used for the TempEval tasks, where TimeML was reduced to a smaller set of tags to test systems on only a few of the components of TimeML.

In particular, TempEval-2 (as described in Verhagen et al. 2010) used only `TIMEX3`, `EVENT`, and `TLINK` tags as part of the corpus that was provided to event participants. Additionally, the attribute values of those tags were cut down, as `TIMEX3` tags were limited to four temporal types—time, date, duration, and set—and the `TLINK` `relTypes` were limited to before, after, overlap, before-or-overlap, overlap-and-after, and vague.

The TempEval-2 challenge was split into six tasks:

- A: Find the text extent of time expressions in a text and determine their `type` and `val` attributes.
- B: Find the text extent of event expressions in a text and determine their class, tense, aspect, polarity, and modality attribute values.

- C: Determine the TLINK relationship between an event and a Timex in the same sentence.

- D: Determine the TLINK relationship between an event and the DCT.

- E: Determine the TLINK relationship between two main events in consecutive sentences.

- F: Determine the TLINK relationship between two events where one syntactically dominates the other.

Challenge participants could choose to participate in all the tasks or focus on the Timex (A), event (B), or TLINK tasks (C–F). Additionally, they could choose to build systems to create TimeML for Chinese, English, French, Italian, Korean, or Spanish (though not all aspects of the tasks were available for all languages).

For tasks A and B, evaluation was performed by calculating precision, recall, and F-measure for the TIMEX3 and EVENT tag locations, and the attributes were evaluated solely with percentage accuracy. Percentage accuracy was also used for calculating the results of the temporal relation tasks.

TempEval-2: System Summaries

Eight teams participated in TempEval-2, and combined, they submitted more than 18 systems, though only English and Spanish corpora were used for training and evaluation (Verhagen et al. 2010). Accuracy scores varied widely between systems, and in the rest of this section, we will go over how some of the participating groups created their systems and how well those systems performed. The systems are presented in alphabetical order.

Edinburgh-LTG (Grover et al. 2010)
This system participated in tasks A and B on the English corpus. It provides a pipeline of preprocessing modules that lemmatize, chunk, and provide POS tags for input data. For the TempEval-2 event and Timex recognition tasks they used rule-based systems to identify likely text extents and supply attribute information. Overall the system obtained .85 precision, .82 recall, and .84 F-measure for the TIMEX3 task (with .84 accuracy for the type attribute and .63 for value), and for the event recognition task, it obtained .75 precision, .85 recall, and .80 F-measure, with attribute values of .99, .99, .92, .98, and .76 for polarity, modality, tense, aspect, and class.

HeidelTime (Strötgen and Gertz 2010)
HeidelTime is a system for identifying temporal expressions and assigning values to them. It participated in task A of TempEval-2 on the English corpus. HeidelTime is a purely rule-based system that uses the UIMA framework to provide sentence boundaries, tokenization, and POS tags prior to identifying temporal expressions. HeidelTime was run over the evaluation data using two sets of rules: one to optimize

precision, the other to optimize recall. Both systems obtained F-measures of .86 for task A, making HeidelTime the most accurate system for temporal expression identification and evaluation in English that participated in the challenge.

JU_CSE_TEMP (Kolya et al. 2010)

This system participated in all the TempEval-2 tasks on the English corpus. For tasks A and B, it used rule-based systems to identify Timexes and events and to assign attribute values. For tasks C–F, the system builders used a Conditional Random Field (CRF) ML algorithm, and used combinations of POS tags and event attribute values (such as tense, polarity, class, etc.) as features. For the TIMEX3 task, JU_CSE_TEMP obtained precision, recall, and F-measure scores of .55, .17, and .26, respectively, but did not submit attribute values. For EVENTs, the system obtained precision, recall, and F-measure scores of .48, .56, and .52, with attribute scores of .98 for polarity and modality, .95 for aspect, .53 for class, and .30 for tense.

KUL (Kolomiyets and Moens 2010)

The KUL system participated in task A of TempEval-2 on the English corpus. The system uses a MaxEnt classifier to identify likely temporal expressions, then uses rules to normalize the output. A preprocessing step performs sentence detection, tokenization, POS tagging, and parsing. Feature candidates for the classifier were the last token in the selected phrase, lemma of the last token, POS tags, character patterns in the phrase and final token, syntactic depth of the phrase, and other syntactic features. Overall, the KUL system was run six times on the evaluation data, with the best run obtaining precision, recall, and F-measure values of .85, .84, and .84, and type and value attribute accuracy scores of .91 and .55, though other evaluation runs resulted in more variable scores.

NCSU (Ha et al. 2010)

NCSU participated in tasks C–F on the English corpus, with two systems, NCSU-indi and NCSU-joint. Both systems used a supervised ML system built on a Markov Model, but the NCSU-indi system had a classifier trained for each task, while the NCSU-joint system had one classifier trained for all four tasks combined. Each system used a combination of lexical features, syntactic features, and semantic relation features to train its algorithms. Overall, NCSU-indi obtained accuracy scores of .63, .68, .48, and .66 for tasks C, D, E, and F, and NCSU-joint obtained scores of .62, .21, .51, and .25 for the same tasks. NCSU-indi had the highest accuracy score for task F.

TERSEO + T2T3 (Saquete 2010)

This system participated in task A on the English corpus, and was a mix of the TIMEX2 recognition system, TERSEO, and the T2T3 system. TERSEO was a rule-based system for identifying temporal expressions as TIMEX2 tags in Spanish, which was then automatically extended to recognize temporal expressions in English and other languages. The T2T3 system was also rule-based, and provided a way to convert TERSEO's TIMEX2 tags into the TimeML TIMEX3 tags. Overall, this combination of systems obtained precision, recall, and F-measure scores of .76, .66, and .71 for TIMEX3 tag creation, and accuracy scores of .98 and .65 for the type and value attributes.

TIPSem (Llorens et al. 2010)

The TIPSem system participated in all of the TempEval-2 tasks in both Spanish and English, and used CRF models using morphological, syntactic, and event information as features, as well as semantic information such as semantic roles and governing verbs for TIMEX3 and EVENT recognition. For the TLINK relations, they used combinations of attribute values, syntactic information, and semantic roles about the Timexes and events participating in the links as classifier features. TIPSem was run twice over the evaluation data in both Spanish and English. It obtained the highest results for Spanish task A (against one other system), and was the only entry for the other Spanish corpus tasks (where it scored a .88 F-measure for task B, .81 for task C, and .59 for task D). For task A on the English corpus, it scored (.92, .80, .85, .92, and .65) and (.88, .60, .71, .88, and and .59) for precision, recall, F-measure, type, and value, respectively, for each run. For tasks C–F on the English corpus, it scored (.55, .82, .55, and .59) and (.54, .81, .55, and .60).

TRIPS and TRIOS (UzZaman and Allen 2010)

TRIPS and TRIOS were two different programs submitted by the same team of researchers, though both used combinations of Markov chains and CRF models trained on various syntactic and attribute features. The systems returned the same results for task A: .85 precision, .85 recall, .85 F-measure, .94 type accuracy, and .76 value accuracy. For task B, TRIOS obtained precision, recall, and F-measure values of .80, .74, and .77, while TRIPS scored .55, .88, and .68, respectively. TRIOS obtained the highest score (.65) for task C, while TRIPS obtained the highest score (.58) for task E.

UC3M (Vicente-Díez et al. 2010)

The UC3M system participated in task A for the Spanish corpus and used a rule-based system for both identifying temporal expressions and evaluating the expressions. Overall, the system obtained precision, recall, and F-measure scores of .90, .87, and .88, respectively, and .91 for type accuracy and .83 for value accuracy.

USFD2 (Derczynski and Gaizauskas 2010)

The USFD2 system participated in tasks A, C, and E in TempEval-2. The system uses a mix of rules and classifiers: a rule-based system identifies and evaluates temporal expressions, while a MaxEnt classifier is trained on features that describe temporal signals. For task A, the system obtained precision, recall, and F-measure values of .84, .79, and .82, with accuracy scores of .90 for type and .17 for value. It also scored .63 accuracy for task C and .45 accuracy for task E.

Overview of Results

Of the participating systems, there was a strong mix of rule-based and ML-based systems, with no clear winner as the "best" way to tackle automated TimeML annotation. While the classifier-based systems obtained the highest scores on the temporal relation tasks, not much can be drawn from that statement, because no rule-based systems participated in tasks C–F for TempEval-2 in the first place [although the best-performing system from the previous TempEval, which had tasks similar to C–F, was a mixed rule-based and statistical learning system (Puscasu 2007)].

For the temporal expression recognition task, the best-performing system was Heidel-Time, which is a purely rule-based system, whereas the ML system TIPSem obtained the best results on the event recognition task. However, it should also be noted that, due to the time constraints inherent in participating in a challenge like TempEval (or any of the SemEval challenges), the situation may favor ML algorithms, because they are much faster to select features for and train on different combinations in a short period of time, while rule-based systems take time to build.

Essentially, we would argue that for complex tasks, the question of whether rule-based or ML systems (or combinations of the two) are "best" has not been entirely settled, and we anticipate that the question will remain open for some time to come.

Future of the TTK

As with any ongoing project, the TTK is still undergoing improvements and being expanded, in terms of improving the quality of the output, increasing the flexibility of the system, adding to the domains where the TTK can be used, and incorporating new theories and the changes to TimeML that are still ongoing. In the rest of this section, we provide an overview of some of the proposed changes and improvements to the TTK, and some discussion of how those changes would be made (Verhagen 2012).

New Input Formats

Currently, the TTK is a start-to-finish pipeline: all the processing that needs to be done to a document to generate TimeML is already in the TTK, including tasks that are not directly TimeML-related but are necessary for some of the modules, such as POS tagging and syntactic chunking. However, because these systems are built into the TTK, other researchers who may wish to provide their own POS taggers, temporal expression recognizers, or other types of information have no way to do so short of rebuilding the TTK themselves.

Of course, building a system that can accept input from other algorithms is always a bit tricky, because it's difficult to ensure that the input data will be compatible with the rest of the pipeline. This is particularly difficult if, for example, a user wants to input inline annotations when the TTK has switched to using stand-off representations. Of course, the technical aspects of this modification to the TTK don't directly affect the MATTER cycle, so we won't go into much detail about them: suffice it to say that if you are interested in creating a processing pipeline like the TTK for your own task (or taking advantage of an existing pipeline or set of algorithms), ensuring compatibility between the components can be very tricky, so it's something to think about carefully before diving into a project.

Narrative Containers/Narrative Times

Just at TimeML and TimeBank are being augmented with Narrative Containers [as we discussed in "Narrative Containers" on page 211], there are also plans to add a new set of rules to the temporal linking components of the TTK to take advantage of the Narrative Container concept. Because Narrative Containers primarily influence where events and times in the text are anchored, most of the changes to the TTK to accommodate the idea would be in BTime and Blinker.

First of all, BTime's rules for assigning temporal values would have to be modified to incorporate the idea of Narrative Containers and Narrative Times. While in some cases this would be relatively trivial (e.g., changing the default anchor for times from the Document Creation Time to the Document Narrative Container), others require much more thought. Consider what rules would have to be written to resolve the values in this sentence:

> June 12, 2012
>
> **Last Sunday** was the closing day of *Pippin* at the local theater. The show, which ran from the **previous Sunday**…

Here, "Last Sunday" would be evaluated in relation to the DCT, which would give it a value of June 10. However, the phrase "previous Sunday" is referring to the Sunday before the 10th, which would be June 3; June 10 has been established as the local Narrative Time, and the interpretation of the second sentence relies on that information. How far the scope of a Narrative Time extends into the document is highly variable, however, and so it is not easy to write a set of rules that will determine what the anchor for each new temporal expression will be. Consider this alternate press release:

> June 12, 2012
>
> **Last Sunday** was the closing day of *Pippin* at the local theater. But **next Monday** a different group will start a run of *The Phantom Tollbooth*…

In this case, both temporal expressions must be given values relative to the DCT—the influence of "Last Sunday" as a Narrative Time does not extend to the next sentence. This may be a system where a robust set of rules could perform well at determining where a temporal expression's anchor should be, but it may also be the case that a classifier trained to examine other features could make a guess at what the Narrative Time is at each part of the document, which could then be used to inform BTime.

Similarly, Blinker would have to be modified to also take into account Narrative Times and containers so that correct temporal links could be produced. We'll talk a little more about the effect of Narrative Containers on linking tasks in the next section.

Medical Documents

As we mentioned previously, TimeBank is a set of news articles and transcripts that was annotated with TimeML. Therefore, the components of the TTK have been optimized to provide the best possible output for those document types. However, a new corpus often brings with it new challenges, and one of the goals for the TTK is to expand the different types of corpora that it can reliably process.

One of the first new areas that is being explored with the TTK is medical documents such as hospital discharge summaries. A preliminary study (Stubbs and Harshfield 2010) examined what would need to be done to make the TTK able to process electronic health records (EHRs). In particular, that study looked at what was needed to identify whether the TTK could be used to determine if the patient described in each record was taking a particular type of medication—cholesterol-lowering drugs called *statins*—when the patient was admitted to the hospital.

The necessary changes were not fully implemented in the TTK; rather, the gaps in the toolkit's capabilities were filled in with auxiliary Perl scripts so that results could be obtained more quickly. However, the study identified some important aspects of changes that would need to be made to the TTK to make it more useful in the medical domain.

 Using an existing system and adding to it from the outside is a perfectly valid way to test your own theories about what will and won't work with your own corpus and features. While ideally you would eventually build a complete system for your own task, sometimes it's best to find a workaround to make sure your idea will work.

One of the first problems that was encountered was that EVITA didn't have the vocabulary to recognize medical events, specifically drug prescriptions. To work around that, a list of statins was obtained from an MD, then augmented with alternative names and spellings from websites such as PubMedHealth (*http://www.ncbi.nlm.nih.gov/ pubmedhealth/s/drugs_and_supplements/a/*). Then this list was used to identify mentions of those drugs in the patient records and mark them using TimeML EVENT tags with the special attribute value class="MEDICINE".

The next aspect of the medical records that had to be addressed was the impact of the document structure on the interpretation of events. It is common for EHRs to be divided into sections, such as "Patient Medical History," "Current Medications," "Family History," "Course of Treatment," and so on. Naturally, these section headers have important temporal information regarding when the events occurred—they essentially provide a new Narrative Container for each section of the document. Therefore, a Perl script that recognized section headers was written, and each one was marked as a TIMEX3 tag with the modified attributes type="HEAD". The mod attribute was also given special values, which indicated whether the Narrative Container for that section occurred prior to hospital admission, during the hospital stay, after release from the hospital, or did not contain any temporal information.

To take advantage of the new EVENT and TIMEX3 tags in the documents, the Blinker component of the TTK was given a new set of rules that took into account the information about the Narrative Containers that were now part of the section headers. Blinker then created TLINKs for each medication EVENT tag related to the section headers, and those were evaluated by a small program to determine whether the patients in question were on statins at their hospital admission date.

Using these modifications compared to a human-annotated corpus the TTK had an accuracy rating of 84% overall, and 95% accuracy on the files that the human annotators found to be unambiguous. These results were promising, and there are plans to incorporate some of these changes into a version of the TTK that can be used in the medical domain.

Cross-Document Analysis

Currently, the TTK only analyzes a single document at a time, and TLINKs only connect events and times in each document as it's processed. However, there are many fields where being able to process multiple documents all at once, and generate relationships between the events and times in those documents, would be incredibly useful, particularly when evaluating the progress of news stories or medical records. Of course, by adding more times and events, the jobs of the temporal closure algorithms become even more complicated, and to provide the most useful information on these topics it would be best if the TTK was also able to perform cross-document event coreference resolution. But identifying two different events in two different articles (or even in the same article) as referring to the same event is not an easy task, and more work needs to be done in this area before cross-document analysis will be truly useful.

Summary

In this chapter we discussed the process used to automate the creation of TimeML-annotated texts through the building of the TARSQI Toolkit. In particular, we discussed the following:

- The TARSQI Toolkit (TTK) provides an example of a long-term production cycle for a system built to reproduce human annotation. While this chapter didn't go into details of the Training–Evaluation cycles of each individual component, it did provide a "big picture" look at a complex system.

- Each component in the TTK is designed to recreate a tag in the TimeML specification—and later versions of the TTK use multiple components for some of the tags.

- Using a divide-and-conquer approach may be the best way to approach your own annotation, especially if you have a task where some parts of the annotation rely on the existence of others (e.g., TLINKs can be made without TIMEX3 and EVENT tags already in the document).

- Rule-based systems can be an excellent way to try out ideas about how to automatically create your annotations, and in some cases will still outperform ML algorithms.

- The question of whether rule-based or statistics-based systems are superior for complicated tasks such as temporal processing has not yet been answered, as both systems tend to perform at nearly the same accuracy levels.

- There is always more that can be done to improve an automatic annotation system, whether it's simply improving accuracy, or expanding the genres or domains that the system can be used to annotate.

Afterword: The Future of Annotation

In this book we have endeavored to give you a taste of what it's like to go through the entire process of doing annotation for training machine learning (ML) algorithms. The MATTER development cycle provides a tested and well-understood methodology for all the steps required in this endeavor, but it doesn't tell you everything there is to know about annotation. In this chapter we look toward the future of annotation projects and ML algorithms, and show you some ways that the field of Natural Language Processing (NLP) is changing, as well as how those changes can help (or hurt) your own annotation and ML projects.

Crowdsourcing Annotation

As you have learned from working your way through the MATTER cycle, annotation is an expensive and time-consuming task. Therefore, you want to maximize the utility of your corpus to make the most of the time and energy you put into your task.

One way that people have tried to ameliorate the cost of large annotation projects is to use *crowdsourcing*—by making the task available to a large group of (usually untrained) people, it becomes both cheaper and faster to obtain annotated data, because the annotation is no longer being done by a handful of selected annotators, but rather by large groups of people.

If the concept of crowdsourcing seems strange, think about asking your friends on Facebook to recommend a restaurant, or consider what happens when a famous person uses Twitter to ask her followers for a piece of information, or their preferences for an upcoming event. These are examples of crowdsourcing—instead of just asking one person, or a focus group, the question is asked of as many people as can be reached, and the answer is extracted from there.

Naturally, asking questions about linguistic annotation on Facebook or Twitter isn't going to be a very efficient way of collecting the desired information. However, other platforms exist for just that purpose, and here we're going to go over a few of them. Each of these methods can be performed within the MATTER cycle—they still require coming up with an annotation goal, finding a specification, and defining guidelines for how the annotation will be applied, but the guidelines here aren't the traditional approach of writing an instruction manual and having the annotators read and apply what they learn.

Amazon's Mechanical Turk

One approach to crowdsourcing is this: rather than hire a small number of annotators to annotate a corpus at relatively high wages, the annotation task is divided into very small tasks, which are then distributed over a large number of people for very small amounts of money per task. The most widely used resource for this at the moment is Amazon's Mechanical Turk (*https://www.mturk.com/mturk/welcome*) (MTurk), where researchers (or businesses) create Human Intelligence Tasks (HITs) which are then posted on something like a job board, and Turkers (as the workers are called) have the option to take on a task, and get paid for completing it. Turkers are usually only paid a few cents for each HIT they complete, so it's easy to see why researchers are interested in using this system: paying a few cents per annotated phrase will almost always be cheaper than paying an hourly wage for annotators to perform the full annotation described in your specification and guidelines. Also, because the individual annotation tasks can be done in minutes or even seconds, annotations can be gathered very quickly, whereas full document annotation can take much longer when only a few annotators are working on the entire corpus and specification.

While the cost- and time-saving measures certainly make the MTurk paradigm sound ideal, the HIT system is by no means perfect. First of all, it requires that each annotation task be broken down into "microtasks" to present the Turkers with a simple and efficient interface. However, not all annotation tasks are suited to be turned into microtasks or are compatible with the HIT interface (e.g., it would be very difficult to design an interface that would make it easy to create syntactic trees). Even if an annotation specification can be turned into a series of microtasks, doing so may remove the annotator's ability to develop intuitions about the annotation, which may affect the results.

In addition to the interface problems, there may be problems with the quality of the data. A recent survey (Fort et al. 2011) of articles on the MTurk system showed that it was difficult for researchers to enforce requirements about their annotators (such as their native language being English), and that the quality of data varied greatly from Turker to Turker, which made it difficult to separate the good annotations from the bad.

Aside from the problems with data quality, Fort et al. also looked into the ethical issues surrounding the use of MTurk systems, and found that a significant number of Turkers use HITs as a main source of income. However, because each HIT only pays a few cents, the average income for a Turker is around $2/hour, so it's somewhat difficult to justify using the MTurk interface as a source of labor.

In terms of the MAMA cycle, the key to using MTurk is to test your HITs to make sure the annotation goal of each HIT is small enough to be performed quickly and accurately, and that the annotation guidelines are only a few sentences long. As with any project, it will take a few tries to get a HIT design that gets you the annotation you need in the degree of detail you want.

Games with a Purpose (GWAP)

Fortunately, other ways of crowdsourcing data also exist. One widely talked about method is that of using "games with a purpose"—essentially, computer games designed to make an annotation task fun so that people will do it voluntarily. A few successful annotation games are:

Phrase Detective (http://anawiki.essex.ac.uk/phrasedetectives/instructions.php)
Purpose: Collect information about coreference relations in text.

This game asks players to examine a short piece of text, with a section of the text (a word or phrase) highlighted in orange. The players are then asked if the phrase is referred to earlier in the text. An example given on the website for the game (using bold text instead of orange) is "'*It* is for *me*,' **he** said." The correct answer is to indicate that "he" refers to the same object as "me" in that sentence.

Sentiment Quiz (http://www.modul.ac.at/nmt/sentiment-quiz)
Purpose: Collect user intuitions about the sentiment (positive or negative) of phrases.

This game asks players to determine whether the word, phrase, or sentence expresses a positive, neutral, or negative emotion. For example, the website shows the sentence "We are headed down a path that is certain to end in the destruction of our experiment in democracy." The players use a scale of five options to rate the sentiment, and their answers are scored against the rest of the players to determine accuracy.

Guess What? (http://www.tiltfactor.org/metadata-games)
Purpose: Collect single-word descriptions of pictures for image recognition training.

From the website: "is a two-player game where players have to choose an image from an array of images based on clues sent to them by the networked partner. The partner sees only one image and what their partner is guessing."

ESP Game (http://www.gwap.com/gwap/gamesPreview/espgame/)
Purpose: Collect descriptions of pictures for image recognition training.

This game pairs up players anonymously and shows them both the same picture. Players are then given two and a half minutes to come up with the same word to describe 15 images. To increase the difficulty, the players are given a list of words that are "banned" for each picture, to get them to use less common descriptors.

These games avoid the potentially exploitative nature of MTurk, as they entice users to spend their free time providing the annotations because they enjoy the game. However, GWAPs may not completely avoid the problem of messy data. A well-designed game can put in place mechanisms that help curate content and reward players for inputting higher-quality data, but it can be difficult to design a game that executes these actions well.

 Effective GWAPs can be extremely difficult to design effectively, and even well-designed games don't produce perfect data. People will cheat at games to obtain higher scores, and they will often produce data that is incorrect or in other ways "dirty," and therefore needs to be cleaned up. For more information on this, see Speer et al. 2010.

Here, the MAMA cycle relies on the guidelines being incorporated into the rules and/or strategy of the games. Having a way to reward players for providing good data will help increase the quality of the annotations obtained.

A list of games with a purpose can be found at *http://semanticgames.org/category/text-annotation-games/* and *http://www.gwap.com/* (*http://www.gwap.com/gwap/gamesPreview/espgame/*).

User-Generated Content

Finally, another way to crowdsource data is to simply ask for it! The MIT Open Mind Common Sense (*http://commonsense.media.mit.edu/*) project is a website that allows users to input information they find to be "common sense"—that is, that relays knowledge about the world that wouldn't necessarily be stated in a text because "everybody knows it," such as the fact that a cat is an animal and can be a pet. This information will be used "to make indoor mobile robots that work in environments like homes and offices more intelligent."

Again, because this information is freely given by participants, it avoids the problems of exploitation. Like the GWAPs, however, users can input data that is false, though the fact that people aren't receiving any general benefit from the system (other than participating in research) may mean that users are less likely to input bad data. Like the other crowdsourcing paradigms described in this chapter, getting good annotations requires having a task and guidelines suited to the presentation, but also requires that the task is something people will be willing to spend time doing.

Handling Big Data

You already know that when it comes to corpora, bigger is better. However, the Big Data mantra comes with its own set of problems, particularly when it comes to annotating large amounts of data in accurate and useful ways. We just talked about some of the ways people are tackling the problem from the annotation side, but there are also some techniques that can be used on the ML side, particularly for corpora that are large, but perhaps not fully annotated.

Almost all of the techniques that attempt to handle Big Data in computational linguistics (and Artificial Intelligence in general) approach the phenomenon as an opportunity rather than a problem. With so much information, so this reasoning goes, is there some way to leverage particular properties of the dataset that will allow us to build even better learning algorithms? The strategy shared by all of the approaches we'll cover in this section is to try to make the best of as little annotated (training) data as possible, and to leverage different properties of the Big Data. As many ML researchers have pointed out, the content on the Web is highly redundant, and this can be used to the advantage of weak learners (as in boosting) or partial learners (as in co-training and other semi-supervised approaches).

Generally, people who talk about Big Data talk about the "3 Vs": volume, velocity, and variety. These were posited by Doug Laney (2001), and are generally taken to be:

Volume
> The size of the data that has been collected. Because this is "Big Data," the volume of a dataset is often measured in gigabytes or terabytes, rather than in number of documents or words.

Velocity
> The speed at which data can be collected and processed. The faster the data is collected and brought into the set, the more up-to-date and relevant the dataset becomes.

Variety
> Not only refers to collecting different types of web pages, or pages in different languages (though that is a factor), but also refers to collecting different types of data, from different sources and in different formats, to create as complete a picture of the state of your chosen field as possible.

Boosting

One approach that might be useful for handling the Big Data problem with applying learning algorithms over language data is called *boosting*. This is a *meta-algorithm*, that is, a strategy for directing supervised learning algorithms that tries to come up with a strong learner from a bunch of weak learners, given a dataset. The algorithm AdaBoost

(Freund and Schapire 1995), for example, has been used in conjunction with many different supervised learning classifiers for NLP purposes, and has been shown to work well when there are lots of noisy contexts, dirtying up the classifier dataset.

Boosting algorithms work by creating an overarching classification system that iteratively adds new, less accurate classifiers. As each new classifier is added, the results of each classifier are weighted based on the accuracy of all the classifiers. This allows the overarching system to obtain progressively better models for how to classify the data being examined, and each new classifier is trained in a way to focus on the data that the other algorithms are misclassifying. This allows the full system to have a set of classifiers that individually will only perform adequately over a set of data, but combined can create much more accurate classifications when the outputs of all the internal algorithms are weighted against one another.

Active Learning

Active learning is a kind of supervised learning where the learner can query the user to obtain information about the labeling of a sample that it is trying to identify. That is, the learning algorithm itself is able to choose the data from which it is learning, posing a query to a human annotator about an unlabeled instance. Figure 12-1 shows the active learning process.

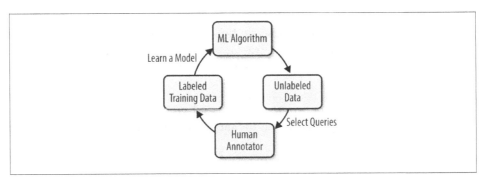

Figure 12-1. The active learning process (based on an illustration from Settles 2010)

The active learning process has been applied successfully to several areas of NLP, including information extraction, Named Entity (NE) recognition, part-of-speech (POS) tagging, text categorization, word sense disambiguation, and other areas (Settles 2010; Olsson 2009). The trick is for the learning algorithm to automatically figure out how to ask the most appropriate question to the oracle (the human annotator). There are several different strategies for selecting the next document to present to the annotator, such as the following (paraphrased from Settles 2010):

Uncertainty sampling

> Using this strategy, the learner selects the object for which he is least sure of the correct categorization to present to the user.

Query-by-committee

> Here, the "committee" is a set of models using different hypotheses about the data that get to "vote" on what is queried next by determining what parts of the corpus they disagree on the most.

Expected model change

> This strategy selects the query that would most affect the current algorithm if the label for the query was known; that is, the query that will add the most information to the model (as best as can be determined beforehand).

Expected error reduction

> This is similar to the preceding strategy, but this method selects the query that it deems will lead to the greatest reduction in the amount of error being generated by the learner. However, expected error reduction is usually very expensive (computationally) to calculate.

Variance reduction

> Rather than trying to reduce the amount of error, this method tries to reduce the amount of noise in the model.

Density-weighted methods

> These strategies use the idea of choosing the data that is most representative (feature-wise) of the rest of the pool, using the assumption that learning more about the features that most of the data shares will more quickly allow all the data to be classified.

One other method that can be used is to simply select the query randomly from the set of unlabeled data; while this method is certainly the fastest way of *choosing* a query, it does not improve the algorithm as quickly as some of the other methods can in terms of the number of times the human annotator is asked to provide input. Regardless of the selection strategy that you use, however, active learning can be an excellent way to train an algorithm to create the wanted annotations by direct user input (though it does require that the user have a good grasp of the annotation task at hand!).

Semi-Supervised Learning

We already described the methodology of semi-supervised learning (SSL) in "Semi-Supervised Learning" on page 163, but it's worth revisiting here. SSL is an excellent way to work with Big Data in an annotation/ML project, because it allows for a small annotated set to be used more effectively over a larger corpus. The co-training and "coupled training" approaches to SSL are particularly effective for datasets that already have some sort of user-generated annotation, such as data from Twitter or Flickr, where users tag their input themselves. This can function as the first set of input into a co-training algorithm, and then a MATTER-type annotation can be done by a researcher to capture other features of the data that would be useful in an ML model. Because so many different online platforms come with ways for users to tag or annotate their data in other ways, SSL techniques don't require that a researcher create and annotate two separate models over the data, since one of the models is already provided by the users (though there is, of course, always some messiness in user-generated content).

NLP Online and in the Cloud

The idea of cloud computing has been invading nearly every aspect of people's lives: from using cloud storage to store music and back up data to the return of the idea of distributed computers. Additionally, there has been a lot of movement to create central repositories, and more efforts to create interoperability standards as well as software that adheres to those standards. In this section we will examine some of the ways that cloud computing can affect NLP and annotation, and ways that the Internet is being used to organize NLP resources.

Distributed Computing

A common problem with NLP systems is that they are often very processing-intensive. Consider all the steps involved in the most recent version of the TARSQI Toolkit that we described in Chapter 11: starting from an unlabeled document, the text is separated into sentences, chunked and marked with POS tags, and examined for events and time expressions, the time expressions are evaluated, temporal signals are identified, SLINKs are created, three different systems are used to create TLINKs, those links are evaluated and merged, and then closure is run over the links that were kept. That requires a lot of steps, and when all of them are being run on a single machine, even a small document can take minutes to annotate, and a large corpus could take days.

Obviously, every year there are increases in the speed of computer CPUs and the memory available for processing, but the fact remains that a single computer running all of those processes is not going to be very fast. Even if you are only trying to train an ML algorithm, the process can still be very slow because of the "bigger is better" rule for corpora: a bigger dataset may be better for training a learning algorithm, but it's going to take even longer to use.

However, distributed computing frameworks such as Hadoop (*http:// hadoop.apache.org/*) make using multiple computers for the same task much more practical, and services such as the Amazon Elastic Compute Cloud (*http:// aws.amazon.com/ec2/*) make access to multiple powerful computers cheap and easy. Of course, the process to transfer NLP tools to distributed frameworks isn't trivial: among other problems (such as that most NLP tools are not optimized for distribution), NLP tools tend to be written in Python, while the Hadoop architecture is written entirely in

Java. Fortunately, work is already being done to distribute NLP programs over Hadoop networks (Madnani and Lin 2010), as well as the MapReduce framework (Lin and Dyer 2010).

Shared Language Resources

The Language Grid (*http://langrid.org/en/index.html*) is "an online multilingual service platform which enables easy registration and sharing of language services such as online dictionaries, bilingual corpora, and machine translators." In addition to providing a central repository for translation resources, it is affiliated with a number of language research projects, such as the Wikipedia Translation Project (*http://langrid.org/mwiki dev/demo_en/index.php/Main_Page*). The Grid is built around the idea of multilingual collaboration and interoperability for different types of multilanguage resources (Ishida 2011).

By making these resources available to a community, and encouraging the members of the community to share their own resources and research results, the entire field of NLP is enriched much more than it would be if everyone was working in isolation. The Language Grid focuses on translation projects and related language resources (such as dictionaries). Translation projects can be notoriously difficult, particularly when examining data that uses metaphors or other euphemistic language, or data that might be "dirty" (containing spelling or grammatical errors), so a repository for these types of resources is invaluable.

Shared Language Applications

The LAPPs (Language Applications) Grid (see Figure 12-2) is a project whose goal is to build a network of interoperable language processing resources (Ide and Pustejovsky forthcoming). It was inspired by the Language Grid, and will be built on the same software platform. It will also provide support for testing applications, application reuse, and error detection. The LAPPs Grid is still under construction at this time (summer 2012), but preliminary services should be available soon.

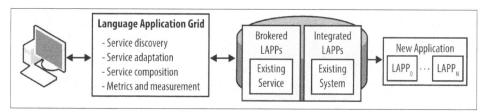

Figure 12-2. The LAPPs Grid system (Ide and Pustejovsky forthcoming)

Creating resources that are interoperable in some way is a difficult but necessary goal for NLP research. Just as the LAF and GrAF (Graph Annotation Framework) annotation standards try to provide a common ground for linguistic annotations, these concepts are being built into other projects as well, making progress in NLP much faster, as people no longer always have to build their own resources but can more reliably use those built by others.

And Finally...

In this chapter our goal was to show you the role that annotation is playing in cutting-edge developments in computational linguistics and machine learning. We pointed out how the different components of the MATTER development cycle are being experimented with and improved, including new ways to collect annotations, better methods for training algorithms, ways of leveraging cloud computing and distributed data, and stronger communities for resource sharing and collaboration.

Because of a lack of understanding of the role that annotation plays in the development of computational linguistics systems, there is always some discussion that the role of annotation is outdated; that with enough data, accurate clusters can be found without the need for human-vetted categories or other labels. But in fact, what we hope to have shown here is that the exact opposite is true. Namely, that only with a better understanding of how annotation reflects one's understanding of linguistic phenomena will a better set of features for the model and algorithm be created, whether it is rule-based or statistical.

List of Available Corpora and Specifications

This appendix was compiled primarily from the LRE Resource Map (*http://www.langua gelibrary.eu/lremap/*). Many thanks to Nicoletta Calzolari and Riccardo del Gratta for their help in creating this appendix, and for allowing us to reprint this information here.

Please note that this appendix does not represent a complete list of all the existing software for the various tasks listed here. It is intended to provide a general overview of the different corpora and specifications available, to give you an idea of what resources you can use in your own annotation and machine learning (ML) tasks. For the most up-to-date list of resources, check the LRE Resource Map, or just do a web search to see what else is available.

Corpora

A Reference Dependency Bank for Analyzing Complex Predicates
   Modality: Written

   Languages: Hindi/Urdu

   Annotation: Semantic dependencies

   URL: *http://ling.uni-konstanz.de/pages/home/pargram_urdu/main/Resources.html*

A Treebank for Finnish (FinnTreeBank)
   Modality: Written

   Language: Finnish

   Annotation: Treebank

   Size: 17,000 model sentences

   URL: *http://www.ling.helsinki.fi/kieliteknologia/tutkimus/treebank/index.shtml*

ALLEGRA (ALigned press reLEases of the GRisons Administration)
    Modality: Written

    Languages: German, Romansh, Italian

    URL: *http://www.latl.unige.ch/allegra/*

AnCora
    Modality: Written

    Language: Catalan

    Annotations: Lemma and part of speech, syntactic constituents and functions, argument structure and thematic roles, semantic classes of the verb, Named Entities, coreference relations

    URL: *http://clic.ub.edu/ancora/*

American Sign Language Lexicon Video Dataset
    Modality: Sign language

    Language: American Sign Language

    URL: *http://vlm1.uta.edu/~athitsos/asl_lexicon/*

Aozora Bunko
    Modality: Written

    Language: Word Sense Disambiguation Japanese

    URL: *http://www.aozora.gr.jp/*

Australian National Corpus
    Modality: Multimodal/multimedia

    Language: Australian English

    URL: *http://www.ausnc.org.au/*

BioInfer
    Modality: Written

    Language: English

    Annotation: Dependency parsing

    URL: *http://mars.cs.utu.fi/BioInfer/*

BioScope
   Modality: Written

   Language: English

   Annotations: Negation, speculation, linguistic scope

   URL: *http://www.inf.u-szeged.hu/rgai/bioscope*

British National Corpus (BNC)
   Modality: Speech/written

   Language: British English

   Size: 100 million words

   URL: *http://www.natcorp.ox.ac.uk/*

Brown Corpus
   Modality: Written

   Language: English

   Size: 1,014,312 words

   URL: *http://icame.uib.no/brown/bcm.html*

CALBC (Collaborative Annotation of a Large Biomedical Corpus) corpora
   Production status: Newly created–finished

   Language: English

   Annotations: Various

   URL: *http://www.ebi.ac.uk/Rebholz-srv/CALBC/corpora/resources.html*

CHILDES
   Modality: Multimedia

   Languages: Various

   Annotation: Transcriptions

   URL: *http://childes.psy.cmu.edu/*

CLC FCE (Cambridge ESOL First Certificate) dataset
   Modality: Written

   Language: English

   Size: 1,244 exam scripts

   URL: *http://ilexir.co.uk/applications/clc-fce-dataset/*

CoreSC/ART corpus
    Modality: Written

    Language: English

    Size: 225 papers

    Annotations: Scientific concepts

    URL: *http://www.aber.ac.uk/en/cs/research/cb/projects/art/art-corpus/*

Corpus de Referencia del Español Actual (CREA)
    Modality: Written

    Language: Spanish

    URL: *http://corpus.rae.es/creanet.html*

Corpus del Español
    Modality: Written

    Language: Spanish

    Size: 100 million words

    URL: *http://www.corpusdelespanol.org/*

Cross Language Entity Linking in 21 Languages (XLEL-21)
    Modality: Written

    Languages: 21 non-English languages, plus English

    Size: 55,000 queries

    URL: *http://hltcoe.jhu.edu/datasets/*

DUC (Document Understanding Conferences)
    Modality: Written

    Language: English

    Annotation: Document summarization

    URL: *http://duc.nist.gov/*

EASC (Essex Arabic Summaries Corpus)
    Modality: Written

    Language: Arabic

    Size: 153 articles, 765 human-generated summaries

    URL: *http://privatewww.essex.ac.uk/~melhaj/easc.htm*

Enron Email Corpus
    Modality: Written

    Language: English

    Size: 500,000 messages

    URL: *http://sgi.nu/enron/*

Estonian Reference Corpus
    Modality: Written

    Language: Estonian

    URL: *http://www.cl.ut.ee/korpused/segakorpus/index.php?lang=en*

Europarl—A Parallel Corpus for Statistical Machine Translation
    Modality: Written

    Languages: French, Italian, Spanish, Portuguese, Romanian, English, Dutch, German, Danish, Swedish, Bulgarian, Czech, Polish, Slovak, Slovene, Finnish, Hungarian, Estonian, Latvian, Lithuanian, Greek

    URL: *http://www.statmt.org/europarl/*

FrameNet
    Modality: Written

    Language: English

    Annotation: Semantic frames

    URL: *https://framenet.icsi.berkeley.edu/fndrupal/*

GENIA Corpus
    Modality: Written

    Language: English

    Annotations: Coreference, syntactic, semantic, part-of-speech, Treebank

    URL: *http://www.nactem.ac.uk/genia/*

Genre Collection Repository
    Modality: Written

    Language: English

    Annotations: Various

    Size: Various

    URL: *http://www.webgenrewiki.org/index.php5/Genre_Collection_Repository*

GRID
> Modality: Multimodal/multimedia
>
> Language: English
>
> URL: *http://www.dcs.shef.ac.uk/spandh/gridcorpus/*

Icelandic Parsed Historical Corpus (IcePaHC)
> Modality: Written
>
> Language: Icelandic
>
> Annotation: Treebank
>
> Size: 1,002,390 words
>
> URL: *http://www.linguist.is/icelandic_treebank/*

Irony Detection
> Modality: Written
>
> Language: English
>
> Annotations: Sarcasm and irony
>
> URL: *http://storm.cis.fordham.edu/~filatova/SarcasmCorpus.html*

Italian CCG Treebank (CCG-TUT)
> Modality: Written
>
> Language: Italian
>
> Annotation: Treebank
>
> URL: *http://www.di.unito.it/~tutreeb/CCG-TUT/*

JRC-Acquis Multilingual Parallel Corpus
> Modality: Written
>
> Languages: Bulgarian, Czech, Danish, German, Greek, English, Spanish, Estonian, Finnish, French, Hungarian, Italian, Lithuanian, Latvian, Maltese, Dutch, Polish, Portuguese, Romanian, Slovak, Slovene, Swedish
>
> Size: Average of 18,833 aligned documents per language
>
> URL: *http://langtech.jrc.ec.europa.eu/JRC-Acquis.html*

La Repubblica
> Modality: Written
>
> Language: Italian
>
> URL: *http://dev.sslmit.unibo.it/corpora/corpus.php?path=%26name=Repubblica*

Large Movie Review Dataset
  Modality: Written

  Language: English

  Size: 50,000 reviews

  URL: *http://www.andrew-maas.net/data/sentiment*

Leipzig Corpus-Based Monolingual Dictionaries
  Modality: Written

  Languages: 155 different languages

  URL: *http://corpora.uni-leipzig.de/*

LIPS 2008 Speech Synthesis AV Corpus
  Modality: Multimodal/Multimedia

  Language: English

  URL: *http://lips2008.org/*

MASC (Manually Annotated Sub-Corpus)
  Modality: Speech/written

  Language: American English

  Size: 500,000 words

  Annotations: Various

  URL: *http://www.anc.org/MASC/Home.html*

Message Understanding Conference (MUC) Corpora
  Modality: Written

  Language: Information Extraction Information Retrieval English

  URL: *http://www-nlpir.nist.gov/related_projects/muc/*

Movie Review Dataset
  Modality: Written

  Language: English

  Annotation: Movie ratings

  URL: *http://www.cs.cornell.edu/people/pabo/movie-review-data/*

MPQA Opinion Corpus
  Modality: Written

  Language: English

Annotation: Opinion

URL: *http://www.cs.pitt.edu/mpqa/*

Multi-Domain Sentiment Dataset 2.0
Modality: Written

Language: English

Annotations: Positive and negative reviews

URL: *http://www.cs.jhu.edu/~mdredze/datasets/sentiment/*

Multilingual UN Parallel Text 2000–2009 (MultiUN)
Modality: Written

Languages: English, French, Spanish, Arabic, Russian, Chinese, German

Size: 300 million+ words per language

URL: *http://www.euromatrixplus.net/multi-un/*

Multimodal Russian Corpus (MURCO)
Modality: Multimodal/multimedia

Language: Russian

Size: 300 million+ words

URL: *http://www.ruscorpora.ru*

NAIST Text Corpus
Modality: Written

Language: Japanese

Annotations: Anaphoric relations, coreference

URL: *http://cl.naist.jp/nldata/corpus/*

National Corpus of Polish
Modality: Written

Language: Polish

URL: *http://nkjp.pl*

Near-Identity Relations for Co-reference (NIdent) CA
Modality: Written

Languages: English, Catalan

Annotation: Near-identity relations

URL: *http://clic.ub.edu/corpus/nident*

NLEL corpora
> Modality: Written
>
> Languages: Various
>
> Size: Various
>
> Annotations: Various
>
> URL: *http://users.dsic.upv.es/grupos/nle/?file=kop4.php*

Online Database of Interlinear Text (ODIN)
> Modality: Written
>
> Languages: 1,274 languages
>
> Size: 2,017 documents
>
> URL: *http://odin.linguistlist.org/*

OntoNotes
> Modality: Written
>
> Languages: English, Chinese, Arabic
>
> Size: Varies by language
>
> URL: *http://www.bbn.com/ontonotes/*

Open American National Corpus (OANC)
> Modality: Speech/written
>
> Language: American English
>
> Size: 14 million+ words
>
> Annotations: Structural markup, sentence boundaries, part-of-speech annotations, noun chunks, verb chunks
>
> URL: *http://www.anc.org/OANC*

OPUS (Open Parallel Corpus)
> Modality: Written
>
> Use: Machine Translation
>
> Languages: Various
>
> URL: *http://opus.lingfil.uu.se/*

PAN-PC-11 Plagiarism Detection Corpus
  Modality: Written

  Language: English

  URL: *http://www.uni-weimar.de/medien/webis/research/events/pan-11/pan11-web/plagiarism-detection.html*

Penn TreeBank Project
  Modality: Written

  Language: English

  Annotation: Treebank

  URL: *http://www.cis.upenn.edu/~treebank/*

Persian Treebank (PerTreeBank)
  Modality: Written

  Language: Persian

  Annotations: Part-of-speech, Treebank

  URL: *http://hpsg.fu-berlin.de/~ghayoomi/PTB.html*

PiTu—Danish Nonsense Syllable Project
  Modality: Speech

  Language: Danish nonsense syllables

  URL: *http://amtoolbox.sourceforge.net/pitu/*

Polish Sejm Corpus
  Modality: Multimodal/multimedia

  Use: Language modeling

  Language: Polish

  Annotations: Segmentation, tokenization, lemmatization, disambiguated morpho-syntactic description, syntactic words, syntactic groups, Named Entities

  URL: *http://clip.ipipan.waw.pl/PSC*

PropBank
  Modality: Written

  Language: English

  Annotation: Semantic role labeling

  URL: *http://verbs.colorado.edu/~mpalmer/projects/ace.html*

Real Word Error Corpus
    Modality: Written

    Language: English

    Size: 833 dyslexic real-word errors in context

    URL: *http://www.dcs.bbk.ac.uk/~jenny/resources.html*

Recognising Textual Entailment (RTE) 2 Test Set
    Modality: Written

    Language: English

    Annotations: Textual entailments

    URL: *http://pascallin.ecs.soton.ac.uk/Challenges/RTE2/*

Reuters-21578 Text Categorization Collection
    Modality: Written

    Language: English

    Annotation: Categories

    URL: *http://kdd.ics.uci.edu/databases/reuters21578/reuters21578.html*

RODRIGO
    Modality: Written

    Use: Handwriting recognition

    Language: Old Spanish

    URL: *http://prhlt.iti.upv.es/rodrigo.php*

RWTH-Fingerspelling
    Modality: Sign language

    Language: German Sign Language

    URL: *http://www-i6.informatik.rwth-aachen.de/aslr/*

Sighan 2005 Bakeoff Data
    Modality: Written

    Language: Word segmentation Chinese

    Annotation: Word segmentation

    URL: *http://www.sighan.org/bakeoff2005/*

South-East European Times—parallel corpus of Balkan languages
    Modality: Written

    Languages: Balkan languages

    Size: 72 files

    URL: *http://opus.lingfil.uu.se/SETIMES.php*

Spanish Learner Language Oral Corpora (SPLLOC)
    Modality: Speech

    Language: Spanish

    Size: 1000+ hours

    URL: *http://www.splloc.soton.ac.uk/index.html*

The Switchboard-1 Telephone Speech Corpus
    Modality: Spoken

    Language: English

    Size: 2,400 conversations

    URL: *http://www.ldc.upenn.edu/Catalog/CatalogEntry.jsp?catalogId=LDC97S62*

Syntax-oriented Corpus of Portuguese Dialects (CORDIAL-SIN)
    Modality: Written

    Languages: Portuguese dialects

    Annotations: Part-of-speech and syntactic annotations

    URL: *http://www.clul.ul.pt/english/sectores/variacao/cordialsin/projecto_cordial sin_corpus.php*

TalkBank
    Modality: Multimodal/multimedia

    Languages: Various

    Size: Various

    URL: *http://talkbank.org*

Tamil Dependency Treebank (TamilTB)
    Modality: Written

    Language: Tamil

    Size: 600 sentences

    Annotation: Morphology and dependency syntax

URL: *http://ufal.mff.cuni.cz/~ramasamy/tamiltb/0.1/*

Text_Classification_Reuters_Corpus
    Modality: Written

    Language: English

    Size: 22 files

    Annotation: Categories

    URL: *http://kdd.ics.uci.edu/databases/reuters21578/reuters21578.html*

The 4 Universities Data Set
    Modality: Websites

    Language: English

    Size: 8,282 pages

    Annotation: Categories

    URL: *http://www.cs.cmu.edu/afs/cs.cmu.edu/project/theo-20/www/data*

The basic dictionary of FinSL example text corpus (Suvi)
    Modality: Sign language

    Languages: Finnish, Sign Language

    URL: *http://suvi.viittomat.net*

The CONCISUS Corpus of Event Summaries
    Modality: Written

    Languages: Spanish, English

    URL: *http://www.taln.upf.edu/pages/concisus/*

The EMIME Mandarin/English Bilingual Database
    Modality: Speech

    Languages: Finnish/English, German/English, Mandarin/English

    URL: *http://www.emime.org/participate/emime-bilingual-database*

The Quranic Arabic Corpus
    Modality: Written

    Language: Arabic

    Annotations: Grammar, syntax, morphology

    URL: *http://corpus.quran.com*

The Wenzhou Spoken Corpus
   Modality: Transcribed speech

   Language: Wenzhou

   Size: 150,000 words

   URL: *http://corpora.tapor.ualberta.ca/wenzhou/aboutCorpus.html*

TIGER Corpus
   Modality: Written

   Language: German

   Size: 50,000 sentences

   URL: *http://www.ims.uni-stuttgart.de/projekte/TIGER/TIGERCorpus/*

TimeBank
   Modality: Written

   Language: English

   Size: 183 articles

   Annotation: TimeML

   URL: *http://www.timeml.org/site/timebank/timebank.html*

TimeBankPT
   Modality: Written

   Language: Portuguese

   Size: 70,000 words

   Annotation: TimeML

   URL: *http://nlx.di.fc.ul.pt/~fcosta/TimeBankPT/*

TREC Corpora
   Modality: Written

   Language: English

   Annotations: Various

   URL: *http://trec.nist.gov/*

TRIOS-TimeBank corpus
   Modality: Written

   Language: English

   Annotation: TimeML

URL: *http://www.cs.rochester.edu/u/naushad/trios-timebank-corpus*

TUT (Turin University Treebank)
Modality: Written

Language: Italian

Size: 2,860 sentences

URL: *http://www.di.unito.it/~tutreeb*

Tycho Brahe Parsed Corpus of Historical Portuguese
Modality: Written

Language: Portuguese

Size: 53 texts

URL: *http://www.tycho.iel.unicamp.br/~tycho/corpus/en/*

TYPO (misspelling) CORPUS
Modality: Written

Language: English

Size: 19,000+ errors

URL: *http://luululu.com/tweet/*

UIUC Question Classification Dataset
Modality: Written

Use: Question Answering

Language: English

Size: 15,500 questions

URL: *http://l2r.cs.uiuc.edu/~cogcomp/Data/QA/QC*

University of Maryland Parallel Corpus Project: The Bible
Modality: Written

Languages: Cebuano, Chinese, Danish, English, Finnish, French, Greek, Indonesian, Latin, Spanish, Swahili, Swedish, Vietnamese

URL: *http://www.umiacs.umd.edu/~resnik/parallel/bible.html*

USENET corpus
Modality: Written

Use: Language modeling

Language: English

Size: 30 billion+ words

URL: *http://www.psych.ualberta.ca/~westburylab/downloads/usenetcorpus.download.html*

Utsunomiya University Spoken Dialogue Database for Paralinguistic Information Studies

Modality: Speech

Language: Japanese

URL: *http://uudb.speech-lab.org/*

W2C–Web To Corpus

Modality: Written

Languages: 120

Size: Varies per language

URL: *http://ufal.mff.cuni.cz/~majlis/w2c/*

Webcorpora

Modality: Written

Languages: Catalan, Croatian, Czech, Danish, Dutch, Finnish, Indonesian, Lithuanian, Norwegian, Polish, Portuguese, Romanian, Serbian_sh, Serbian_sr, Slovak, Spanish, Swedish

Size: Varies by language

URL: *http://hlt.sztaki.hu/resources/webcorpora.html*

WikiWars

Modality: Written

Size: 22 documents

Language: English

Annotation: TIMEX2

URL: *http://www.timexportal.info/wikiwars*

WikiWoods

Production status: Newly created–in progress

Modality: Written

Size: 1.3 million+ articles

Language: English

URL: *http://www.delph-in.net/wikiwoods/*

World Wide English Corpus
   Modality: Written

   Language: English

   Size: 200,000-word web-corpora

   URL: *http://www.comp.leeds.ac.uk/eric/wwe.shtml*

Specifications, Guidelines, and Other Resources

ACE Entity and Relation Annotation Guidelines
   Use: Entity (Person, Organization, Location, Facility, and Geo-Political Entity, with subtypes) and relation (ordered pairs of entities, modality, tense) annotation

   Languages: English, Arabic

   URL: *http://projects.ldc.upenn.edu/ace/annotation/*

CoreSC Annotation Guidelines
   Use: Scientific concept annotation

   Language: English

   URL: *http://www.aber.ac.uk/en/cs/research/cb/projects/art/art-corpus/* (guidelines available upon request)

EAGLES Recommendations for the Morphosyntactic and Syntactic Annotation of Corpora
   Use: Morphosyntactic annotation

   Languages: Various

   URL: *http://www.ilc.cnr.it/EAGLES96/browse.html*

FrameNet
   Use: Semantic frames

   Languages: Various

   URL: *https://framenet.icsi.berkeley.edu/fndrupal/home*

GALE (Global Autonomous Language Exploitation) annotation guidelines
   Use: Data collection, transcription, translation, word alignment

   Languages: Chinese, English, Arabic

   URL: *http://projects.ldc.upenn.edu/gale/index.html*

GALE LDC translation guidelines
Use: Translation guidelines

Languages: Arabic, Chinese

URL: *http://projects.ldc.upenn.edu/gale/Translation/*

GENIA Annotation Guidelines
Use: Biomedical text annotations

Language: English

URL: *http://www.nactem.ac.uk/genia/*

Grammatical Framework
Use: Programming language for multilingual grammar applications

Languages: Amharic (partial), Arabic (partial), Bulgarian, Catalan, Danish, Dutch, English, Finnish, French, German, Hindi (fragments), Interlingua, Italian, Latin (fragments), Latvian, Nepali, Norwegian bokmål, Persian, Polish, Punjabi, Romanian, Russian, Spanish, Swedish, Thai, Turkish (fragments), Urdu

URL: *http://www.grammaticalframework.org*

Guidelines for the Syntactic Annotation of Latin and Greek Treebanks
Use: Syntactic Treebank annotation

Language: Latin (written in English and Spanish)

URL: *http://nlp.perseus.tufts.edu/syntax/treebank/index.html*

International Phonetic Alphabet
Use: Phonetic transcription/notation

Language: Language-independent

URL: *http://www.langsci.ucl.ac.uk/ipa/ipachart.html*

ISO 639-3
Use: Codes for the representation of names of languages

Languages: Various

URL: *http://www.sil.org/ISO639-3/default.asp*

ISO-Space
Use: Annotating spatiotemporal information in text

Language: English

URL: *https://sites.google.com/site/wikiisospace/*

Language-Independent Named Entity Recognition
    Use: Named Entity annotation

    Language: Language-independent

    URL: *http://www.cnts.ua.ac.be/conll2003/ner/*

LinES guidelines
    Use: Swedish–English parallel Treebanking

    Languages: English, Swedish

    URL: *http://www.ida.liu.se/~lah/transmap/Corpus/*

Prague Dependency Treebank annotation guidelines
    Use: Morphological, analytical, tectogrammatical

    Language: Czech (written in English)

    URL: *http://ufal.mff.cuni.cz/pdt2.0/doc/pdt-guide/en/html/ch02.html*

PropBank Annotation Guidelines
    Use: Propositional annotation over parse trees

    Languages: Hindi, Chinese, English

    URL: *http://clear.colorado.edu/compsem/index.php?page=annotation&sub=prop bank*

Simple Named Entity Guidelines
    Use: Named Entity annotation

    Language: Language-independent

    URL: *http://projects.ldc.upenn.edu/LCTL/Specifications/*

SpatialML
    Use: Annotation of named and nominal references to places in text

    Language: English

    URL: *http://www.lrec-conf.org/proceedings/lrec2008/summaries/106.html*

Stuttgart-Tbingen Tagset of German
    Use: Part-of-speech tagging

    Language: Linguistic Research German

    URL: *http://www.sfs.uni-tuebingen.de/Elwis/stts/stts.html*

Syntactic Annotation Guidelines for the Quranic Arabic Dependency Treebank
    Use: Part-of-speech tagging

    Language: Quranic Arabic

URL: *http://corpus.quran.com*

TAC Knowledge Base Population Annotation and Assessment Guidelines
Use: Question Answering, information extraction

Languages: English, Chinese

URL: *http://nlp.cs.qc.cuny.edu/kbp/2011*

TimeML/ISO TimeML
Use: Event, time, temporal relation annotation

Languages: English, various (adapted for other languages)

URL: *http://www.timeml.org/site/publications/specs.html*

TreeBank Annotation Guidelines for Biomedical Text
Use: Treebanking biomedical texts

Language: English

URL: *http://clear.colorado.edu/compsem/documents/treebank_guidelines.pdf*

WordNet
Use: Lexical database

Language: English

URL: *http://wordnet.princeton.edu/*

WordNet–FrameNet Annotations
Use: Consolidating WordNet and FrameNet annotations

Language: English

URL: *http://www.anc.org/MASC/WordNet_Annotations.html*

Representation Standards

Graph Annotation Framework (GrAF, ISO TC37SC4 working group 1)
Use: Graphical representation of linguistic annotations

Language: Language-independent

URL: *http://www.cs.vassar.edu/~ide/papers/LAW.pdf*

Lexical Markup Framework (LMF) (ISO-24613:2008)
Use: Standardization of Natural Language Processing lexicons and machine-readable dictionaries

Language: Language-independent

URL: *http://www.lexicalmarkupframework.org/*

Linguistic Annotation Framework (LAF) (ISO 24612)
  Use: Representing annotation information over corpora

  Language: Language-independent

  URL: *http://www.iso.org/iso/iso_catalogue/catalogue_tc/catalogue_detail.htm?
  csnumber=37326, http://www.cs.vassar.edu/~ide/papers/ide-romary-clergerie.pdf*

MLIF/MultiLingual Information Framework (ISO 24616-2011)
  Use: Specification platform for computer-oriented representation of multilingual
  data

  Language: Language-independent

  URL: *http://mlif.loria.fr*

Text Encoding Initiative (TEI)
  Use: Standard for the representation of texts in digital form

  Language: Language-independent

  URL: *http://www.tei-c.org/index.xml*

Unicode Character Database
  Use: Cross-linguistic written character representation

  Language: Multilingual

  URL: *http://unicode.org/ucd/*

List of Software Resources

This appendix was compiled primarily from the LRE Resource Map (*http://www.langua gelibrary.eu/lremap/*). Many thanks to Nicoletta Calzolari and Riccardo del Gratta for their help in creating this appendix, and for allowing us to reprint this information here.

Please note that this appendix does not represent a complete list of all the existing software for the various tasks listed here. It is intended to provide a general overview of the different tools available, to give you an idea of what resources you can use in your own annotation and machine learning (ML) tasks. For the most up-to-date list of resources, check the LRE Resource Map, or just do a web search to see what else is available.

Annotation and Adjudication Software

Multipurpose Tools

GATE

>   Modality: Written

>   Use: Corpus creation and management, automatic annotation, manual correction of annotation, part-of-speech tagging, Named Entity recognition, word sense disambiguation, etc.

>   Languages: Various

>   URL: *http://gate.ac.uk/*

NLTK

>   Modality: Written

>   Use: Classification, tokenization, stemming, tagging, parsing, semantic reasoning, machine learning

>   Languages: Various, language-independent

URL: *http://nltk.org/*

OpenNLP (Apache)
Modality: Written

Use: Tokenization, sentence segmentation, part-of-speech tagging, Named Entity extraction, chunking, parsing, coreference resolution

Languages: Various

URL: *http://opennlp.apache.org*

WordFreak
Modality: Written

Use: Hand annotation, automated annotation

Language: Language-independent

URL: *http://wordfreak.sourceforge.net/*

Corpus Creation and Exploration Tools

Djangology: A lightweight web-based tool for distributed collaborative text annotation
Modality: Written

Use: Distributed collaborative text annotation

Language: Language-independent

URL: *http://sourceforge.net/projects/djangology/*

Ellogon
Modality: Written

Use: Hand annotation, machine annotation, project management

Language: Language-independent

URL: *http://www.ellogon.org/*

Unitex
Modality: Written

Use: Corpus processing

Language: Language-independent

URL: *http://www-igm.univ-mlv.fr/~unitex/*

Wikipedia Miner
   Modality: Written

   Use: Corpus collection

   Language: Language-independent

   URL: *http://wikipedia-miner.cms.waikato.ac.nz*

Manual Annotation Tools

ANVIL tool
   Modality: Video

   Use: Manual annotation

   URL: *http://www.anvil-software.de*

BAT (Brandeis Annotation Tool)
   Modality: Written

   Use: Corpus annotation

   Language: Language-independent

   URL: *http://timeml.org/site/bat/*

Callisto
   Modality: Written

   Use: Annotation

   Language: Language-independent

   URL: *http://callisto.mitre.org/*

Djangology: A lightweight web-based tool for distributed collaborative text annotation
   Modality: Written

   Use: Distributed collaborative text annotation

   Language: Language-independent

   URL: *http://sourceforge.net/projects/djangology/*

ELAN
   Modality: Video/audio

   Use: Manual annotation

   Language: Language-independent

   URL: *http://www.lat-mpi.eu/tools/elan/*

Ellogon
    Modality: Written

    Use: Hand annotation, machine annotation, project management

    Language: Language-independent

    URL: *http://www.ellogon.org/*

EMU Speech Database System
    Modality: Speech

    Use: Speech annotation

    Language: Language-independent

    URL: *http://emu.sourceforge.net*

EXMARaLDA (Extensible Markup Language for Discourse Annotation)
    Modality: Multimodal/multimedia

    Use: Discourse annotation

    Language: Language-independent

    URL: *http://www.exmaralda.org*

feat (Flexible Error Annotation Tool)
    Modality: Speech/written

    Use: Error transcription

    Language: Language-independent

    URL: *http://ufal.mff.cuni.cz/~hana/feat.html*

FOLKER
    Modality: Speech

    Use: Transcription

    Language: Language-independent

    URL: *http://agd.ids-mannheim.de/folker_en.shtml*

GATE
    Modality: Written

    Use: Corpus creation and management, automatic annotation, manual correction of annotation, part-of-speech tagging, Named Entity recognition, word sense disambiguation, etc.

    Languages: Various

URL: *http://gate.ac.uk/*

Jubilee

    Modality: Written

    Use: PropBank annotation editor

    Languages: English, Arabic, Chinese

    URL: *http://code.google.com/p/propbank/*

Knowtator

    Modality: Written

    Use: Manual annotation

    Language: Language-independent

    URL: *http://knowtator.sourceforge.net/index.shtml*

MAE (Multipurpose Annotation Environment)

    Modality: Written

    Use: Manual annotation

    Language: Language-independent

    URL: *http://code.google.com/p/mae-annotation/*

MMAX2

    Modality: Written

    Use: Manual annotation

    Language: Language-independent

    URL: *http://www.eml-research.de/english/research/nlp/download/mmax.php*

PALinkA (Perspicuous and Adjustable Links Annotator)

    Modality: Written

    Use: Manual link annotation

    Language: Language-independent

    URL: *http://clg.wlv.ac.uk/projects/PALinkA/*

Praat

    Modality: Speech

    Use: Manual annotation

    Language: Language-independent

    URL: *http://www.praat.org*

Sanchay

    Modality: Written

    Use: Manual annotation

    Languages: South Asian languages

    URL: *http://sanchay.co.in/*

SAPIENT: Semantic Annotation of Papers Interface and Enrichment Tool

    Modality: Written

    Use: Manual semantic annotation of scientific concepts

    Language: Document Classification Text categorization English

    URL: *http://www.aber.ac.uk/en/cs/research/cb/projects/sapienta/software/*

Scheherazade

    Modality: Written

    Use: Manual semantic annotation

    Language: Discourse English

    URL: *http://www.cs.columbia.edu/~delson/software.shtml*

Sextant (Standoff EXMARaLDA Transcription Annotation Tool)

    Modality: Speech

    Use: Manual transcription annotation

    Language: Language-independent

    URL: *http://exmaralda.org/sextant/*

SSI (Social Signal Interpretation)

    Modality: Multimodal/multimedia

    Use: Manual human behavior annotation

    Language: Language-independent

    URL: *http://mm-werkstatt.informatik.uni-augsburg.de/ssi.html*

SMORE

    Modality: Written

    Use: OWL markup of websites

    Language: Language-independent

    URL: *http://www.mindswap.org/2005/SMORE/*

TrEd
> Modality: Written
>
> Use: Treebank creation/annotation
>
> Language: Language-independent
>
> URL: *http://ufal.mff.cuni.cz/tred/*

WebAnnotator
> Modality: Websites
>
> Use: Web annotation
>
> Language: Language-independent
>
> URL: *http://www.limsi.fr/Individu/xtannier/en/WebAnnotator/*

WordAligner
> Modality: Written
>
> Use: Machine Translation word alignment
>
> Language: Language-independent
>
> URL: *http://www.bultreebank.bas.bg/aligner/index.php*

Automated Annotation Tools

Multipurpose tools

fnTBL
> Modality: Written
>
> Use: Part-of-speech tagging, base noun phrase chunking, text chunking, end-of-sentence detection, word sense disambiguation
>
> Languages: Various
>
> URL: *http://www.cs.jhu.edu/~rflorian/fntbl/*

FreeLing
> Modality: Written
>
> Use: Tokenization, sentence splitting, morpheme identification, Named Entity detection, part-of-speech tagging, shallow parsing, Named Entity classification, nominal coreference resolution
>
> Languages: Spanish, Catalan, Galician, Italian, English, Russian, Portuguese, Welsh, Austrian
>
> URL: *http://nlp.lsi.upc.edu/freeling*

GATE
Modality: Written

Use: Corpus creation and management, automatic annotation, manual correction of annotation, part-of-speech tagging, Named Entity recognition, word sense disambiguation, etc.

Languages: Various

URL: *http://gate.ac.uk/*

Illinois NLP tools
Modality: Written

Use: Part-of-speech tagging, chunking, coreference, Named Entity tagging, semantic role labeling

Language: Language-independent

URL: *http://cogcomp.cs.illinois.edu/page/software*

MADA + TOKAN
Production status: Existing–used

Modality: Written

Use: Tokenization, diacritization, morphological disambiguation, part-of-speech, tagging, stemming, and lemmatization

Language: Arabic

URL: *http://www1.ccls.columbia.edu/~cadim/*

MorphAdorner
Modality: Written

Use: Tokenizing text, recognizing sentence boundaries, extracting names and places

Language: English

URL: *http://morphadorner.northwestern.edu/*

NLTK
Modality: Written

Use: Classification, tokenization, stemming, tagging, parsing, semantic reasoning, machine learning

Language: English

URL: *http://nltk.org/*

RACAI web service
Modality: Written

Use: Tokenization, sentence splitting, C-tagset part-of-speech tagging, MSD-tagset part-of-speech tagging, lemmatization, identify language (57 languages)

Languages: English, Romanian

URL: *http://www.racai.ro/webservices*

Standford NLP tools
Modality: Written

Use: Parsing, part-of-speech tagging, Named Entity recognition, word segmentation, tokenizing, temporal tagging, topic modeling

Language: English

URL: *http://nlp.stanford.edu/software/*

Phonetic annotation

FOLKER
Modality: Speech

Use: Transcription

Language: Language-independent

URL: *http://agd.ids-mannheim.de/folker_en.shtml*

Julius
Modality: Speech

Use: Speech Recognition/understanding

Language: Japanese

URL: *http://julius.sourceforge.jp/*

SPPAS (SPeech Phonetization Alignment and Syllabification)
Modality: Speech

Use: Automatic phonetic transcription and segmentation

Language: Basque

URL: *http://www.lpl-aix.fr/~bigi/sppas/*

Part-of-speech taggers/syntactic parsers

Alpino

    Modality: Written

    Use: Dependency parser

    Language: Dutch

    URL: *http://www.let.rug.nl/vannoord/alp/Alpino/*

Apertium-kir

    Modality: Written

    Use: Machine Translation

    Languages: Various

    URL: *http://sourceforge.net/projects/apertium/*

Automatic Syntactic Analysis for Polish Language (ASA-PL)

    Modality: Written

    Use: Syntactic analysis

    Language: Polish

    URL: *http://seagrass.man.poznan.pl/~michzimny/asa-pl/*

Berkeley Parser

    Modality: Written

    Use: Parsing

    Languages: Various

    URL: *http://code.google.com/p/berkeleyparser/*

BitPar

    Modality: Software

    Use: Syntactic parsing

    Language: English

    URL: *http://www.ims.uni-stuttgart.de/tcl/SOFTWARE/BitPar.html*

C&C Toolkit

    Modality: Written

    Use: Parsing, tagging

    Language: English

    URL: *http://svn.ask.it.usyd.edu.au/trac/candc/wiki*

Charniak Parser
    Modality: Written

    Use: Parsing

    Language: English

    URL: *http://www.cs.brown.edu/people/ec/#software*

CombiTagger
    Modality: Written

    Use: Part-of-speech tagging

    Language: Language-independent

    URL: *http://combitagger.sourceforge.net*

Dependency Shift Reduce parser (DeSR)
    Modality: Written

    Use: Dependency parsing

    Language: English

    URL: *http://sites.google.com/site/desrparser/*

DepPattern
    Production status: Newly created–in progress

    Modality: Written

    Use: Grammar compiler, part-of-speech tagger, dependency-based parser

    Languages: English, Spanish, Galician, French, Portuguese

    URL: *http://gramatica.usc.es/pln/tools/deppattern.html*

DeSR
    Modality: Written

    Use: Parsing

    Languages: Various

    URL: *http://desr.sourceforge.net/doc/*

Enju
    Modality: Written

    Use: Syntactic parser

    Language: English

    URL: *http://www-tsujii.is.s.u-tokyo.ac.jp/enju/*

Granska tagger
    Modality: Written

    Use: Part-of-speech tagger

    Language: Swedish

    URL: *http://www.csc.kth.se/tcs/humanlang/tools.html*

Greek POS Tagger
    Modality: Written

    Use: Part-of-speech tagger

    Language: Koine Greek

    URL: *http://nlp.cs.aueb.gr/software.html*

Hunpos
    Modality: Written

    Use: Part-of-speech tagger

    Languages: Various

    URL: *http://mokk.bme.hu/resources/hunpos*

IceNLP
    Modality: Written

    Use: Tokenization, part-of-speech tagging, parsing

    Language: Icelandic

    URL: *http://icenlp.sourceforge.net/*

J-Safran (Java Syntaxico-semantic French Analyser)
    Modality: Written

    Use: Syntactic dependency parsing

    Language: French

    URL: *http://rapsodis.loria.fr/jsafran/index.html*

KyTea, the Kyoto Text Analysis Toolkit
    Modality: Written

    Use: Word segmentation, tagging

    Languages: Japanese, Chinese

    URL: *http://www.phontron.com/kytea*

LGTagger
    Modality: Written

    Use: Part-of-speech tagging

    Language: French

    URL: *http://igm.univ-mlv.fr/~mconstan/research/software/*

Linguistica
    Modality: Written

    Use: Morpheme recognition

    Language: Language-independent

    URL: *http://linguistica.uchicago.edu/linguistica.html*

Link Parser
    Modality: Written

    Use: Syntactic parsing

    Language: English

    URL: *http://www.link.cs.cmu.edu/link/*

LX-Parser
    Modality: Written

    Use: Text parsing

    Language: Portuguese

    URL: *http://lxparser.di.fc.ul.pt*

MaltParser
    Modality: Written

    Use: Parsing

    Language: Language-independent

    URL: *http://maltparser.org/*

MiniPar
    Modality: Written

    Use: Parsing

    Language: English

    URL: *http://www.cs.ualberta.ca/~lindek/minipar.htm*

Mogura

    Modality: Written

    Use: Syntactic parsing

    Language: English

    URL: *http://www-tsujii.is.s.u-tokyo.ac.jp/enju/*

Morče

    Modality: Written

    Use: Czech morphological tagger

    Language: Czech

    URL: *http://ufal.mff.cuni.cz/morce/*

MSTParser (maximum spanning tree parser)

    Modality: Written

    Use: Parsing

    Language: Language-independent

    URL: *http://sourceforge.net/projects/mstparser*

MuNPEx

    Modality: Written

    Use: Noun phrase extraction

    Languages: English, German, French, Spanish

    URL: *http://www.semanticsoftware.info/munpex*

Pantera-tagger

    Modality: Not applicable

    Use: Morphosyntactic tagging

    Languages: Various

    URL: *http://code.google.com/p/pantera-tagger/*

RASP

    Modality: Written

    Use: Parsing

    Language: English

    URL: *http://www.informatics.sussex.ac.uk/research/groups/nlp/rasp/*

RelEx
> Modality: Written

> Use: Semantic dependency parsing

> Language: English

> URL: *http://opencog.org/wiki/RelEx*

SEMAFOR 2.0
> Modality: Written

> Use: Shallow semantic parsing

> Language: English

> URL: *http://www.ark.cs.cmu.edu/SEMAFOR/*

Shalmaneser
> Modality: Written

> Use: Automatic semantic parsing

> Languages: English, German

> URL: *http://www.coli.uni-saarland.de/projects/salsa/shal/*

SVMTool
> Modality: Written

> Use: Part-of-speech tagging and chunking

> Languages: Various

> URL: *http://www.lsi.upc.edu/~nlp/SVMTool/*

SET (Syntax in Elements of Text)
> Modality: Written

> Use: Syntactic parsing

> Language: Czech

> URL: *http://nlp.fi.muni.cz/trac/set*

TreeTagger
> Modality: Written

> Use: Part-of-speech tagging

> Language: Language-independent

> URL: *http://www.ims.uni-stuttgart.de/projekte/corplex/TreeTagger/*

upparse
> Modality: Written
>
> Use: Partial parsing
>
> Language: Language-independent
>
> URL: *http://elias.ponvert.net/upparse*

WMBT
> Modality: Not applicable
>
> Use: Morphosyntactic tagging
>
> Language: Polish
>
> URL: *http://nlp.pwr.wroc.pl/redmine/projects/wmbt/wiki*

Word clAss taGGER (WAGGER)
> Modality: Written
>
> Use: Part-of-speech tagging
>
> Languages: English, Portuguese
>
> URL: *http://www.inf.pucrs.br/afonso.sales/wagger*

Tokenizers/chunkers/stemmers

JOS ToTaLe text analyser
> Modality: Written
>
> Use: Morphological disambiguation and lemmatization
>
> Language: Slovenian
>
> URL: *http://nl.ijs.si/jos/analyse/*

MMSEG
> Modality: Written
>
> Use: Word segmentation
>
> Language: Chinese
>
> URL: *http://code.google.com/p/pymmseg-cpp/*

MorphTagger
> Modality: Written
>
> Use: Morpheme annotation
>
> Language: Arabic
>
> URL: *http://www-i6.informatik.rwth-aachen.de/~mansour/MorphSegmenter/*

Snowball
    Modality: Written

    Use: Stemming

    Language: English

    URL: *http://snowball.tartarus.org/download.php*

Yet Another Multipurpose CHunk Annotator (YamCha)
    Modality: Written

    Use: Text chunking

    Language: English

    URL: *http://chasen.org/~taku/software/yamcha/*

Other

BART Anaphora Resolution Toolkit
    Modality: Written

    Use: Coreference/anaphora resolution

    Language: English

    URL: *http://www.bart-coref.org/*

GIZA++
    Modality: Written

    Use: Machine Translation

    Languages: Various

    URL: *http://code.google.com/p/giza-pp/*

Google Translate
    Modality: Written

    Use: Machine Translation

    Languages: Various

    URL: *http://www.translate.google.com*

HeidelTime
    Modality: Written

    Use: Temporal expression tagger

    Languages: Various

    URL: *http://dbs.ifi.uni-heidelberg.de/heideltime*

Illinois Coreference Package
    Modality: Written

    Use: Coreference resolution

    Language: English

    URL: *http://cogcomp.cs.illinois.edu/page/software_view/18*

MAZEA-Web
    Modality: Written

    Use: Rhetorical structure annotation

    Language: Discourse English

    URL: *http://www.nilc.icmc.usp.br/mazea-web/*

TARSQI Toolkit
    Modality: Written

    Use: Temporal expression and event tagging, temporal linking

    Language: English

    URL: *http://www.timeml.org/site/tarsqi/toolkit/*

Machine Learning Resources

GATE (General Architecture for Text Engineering)
    Modality: Written

    Use: Corpus creation and management, automatic annotation, manual correction of annotation, part-of-speech tagging, Named Entity recognition, word sense disambiguation, etc.

    Languages: Various

    URL: *http://gate.ac.uk/*

MALLET (MAchine Learning for LanguagE Toolkit)
    Modality: Written, graphical (with add-on)

    Use: Document classification, clustering, topic modeling, information extraction, other machine learning applications

    Language: Language-independent

    URL: *http://mallet.cs.umass.edu/*

NLTK (Natural Language Toolkit)
  Modality: Written

  Use: Classification, tokenization, stemming, tagging, parsing, semantic reasoning, machine learning

  Languages: Various, language-independent

  URL: *http://nltk.org/*

OpenNLP Toolkit
  Modality: Written

  Uses: Tokenization, sentence segmentation, part-of-speech tagging, Named Entity extraction, chunking, parsing, and coreference resolution; Maximum Entropy and perception-based machine learning

  URL: *http://incubator.apache.org/opennlp/*

WEKA
  Modality: Written

  Use: Data preprocessing, classification, regression, clustering, association rules, visualization, machine learning

  Language: Language-independent

  URL: *http://www.cs.waikato.ac.nz/ml/weka/*

MAE User Guide

MAE (Multipurpose Annotation Environment) was written by Amber Stubbs, and is provided free for use from *http://code.google.com/p/mae-annotation/*. Although many other annotation tools are available for use, MAE provides a simple interface that requires little setup, and so we are providing the user guide here for those readers who would like to start annotating right away.

Input to MAE is in the form of DTD-like files that describe the task name, elements, and attributes. A sample task definition is included with the MAE distribution, and instructions for creating your own tasks are included in this appendix. MAE was written in Java on an Ubuntu Linux system, and has been tested on Windows XP, Windows 7, and Mac OS X. It uses the SQLiteJDBC Java driver (more information is available at *https://github.com/crawshaw/sqlitejdbc*).

MAE is free software: you can redistribute it and/or modify it under the terms of the GNU General Public License as published by the Free Software Foundation, either version 3 of the License, or (at your option) any later version. This program is distributed in the hope that it will be useful, but *without any warranty*; without even the implied warranty of *merchantability* or *fitness for a particular purpose*. See the GNU General Public License for more details (*http://www.gnu.org/licenses/*).

Installing and Running MAE

MAE requires Java to run. On Windows and Unix systems, it should be used with the most recent version of Java 6 (it must have at least update 14 to run properly on Windows and Unix), though it can also be compiled under Java 5, so it can also be run on older Macs. To run MAE on any operating system, open a terminal and navigate to the directory where the *.jar* file exists, then run this command:

```
java -jar MAEversion.jar
```

On most platforms, it is also possible to open the program by double-clicking on the *.jar* file. However, doing so will not allow all error messages to be displayed, so using the terminal is recommended. On all systems, you should see the window shown in Figure C-1.

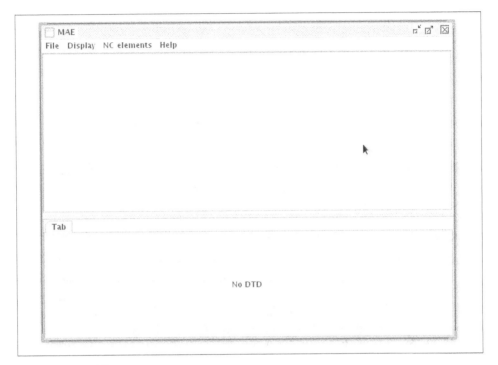

Figure C-1. MAE startup screen

Loading Tasks and Files

Loading a Task

To use MAE, you must load both a task definition file (*.dtd*) and a file to be annotated (*.txt* or *.xml*). The task definition must be loaded first, by selecting Load DTD from the File menu. Once the DTD is loaded, the lower section of the MAE window will be filled with tabs representing the different elements. The MAE distribution includes a sample DTD and file for annotation, located in the *samples* directory.

Loading a File

Once the task is loaded, it is now possible to annotate files. To load a file for annotation, use the Load File option in the File menu. The easiest way to begin annotating is to load a UTF-8 encoded text file that contains only the text you wish to annotate. You may also, of course, load a file that has been previously annotated in MAE or in any other program, as long as it adheres to the following format:

```
<TaskName>
<TEXT><![CDATA[
this is the text that will be annotated.

More text to be annotated.
]]></TEXT>
<TAGS>
<tag1... />
<tag2... />
</TAGS>
</TaskName>
\end{verbatim}
```

When the input file is loaded, the text for annotation will appear in the top MAE window. The file being loaded must use UTF-8 encoding, especially if you are trying to annotate files in languages that use characters other than those in the English alphabet.

Annotating Entities

Entity annotation is done with the mouse. Simply highlight the word to be annotated with the left mouse button. With the word highlighted, right-click with the mouse to open a menu of possible entity tags. Select the desired tag from the menu, and the information about the tag will be added to the appropriate tab at the bottom of the screen. The ID, start, end, and text features are automatically generated by MAE, and are best left unmodified. The other features can be changed by the annotator as needed.

Attribute information

Once a tag has been created and appears in the table at the bottom of the screen, it is possible to set values for the different attributes contained in the tag. Depending on the task, the attribute values can either be entered as free text or be selected from a list, as shown in Figure C-2.

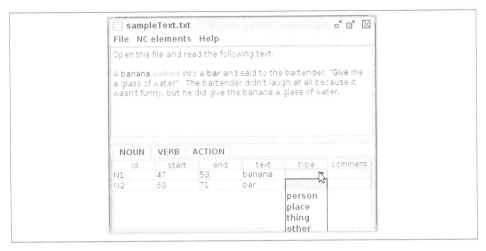

Figure C-2. Annotation in MAE

Nonconsuming tags

It is possible in MAE to have annotation schemes that have entity tags that do not require extents to be associated with them. This can be useful for entities that are implied, but not explicitly mentioned. Nonconsuming tags can be added to the annotation by selecting the tag type from the "Nonconsuming tags" menu at the top of the MAE window. These will be given ID tags, but the start and end elements will be set to –1. All nonconsuming tags will be listed as options for linking to and from in the link creation window.

Annotating Links

To create links between two entities, simply make sure the text window is active (left-clicking anywhere on the text will suffice for that), hold down the Ctrl key (or the Command key, if you are on a Mac), and left-click each entity that will be included in the link, in the order you want them to appear in the link. Once this is done, a window will pop up that will allow you to select where the link starts and where it ends, and the type of link that you want to create between them. When you click on the "Create link" button at the bottom of the pop-up window, the link will be added to the appropriate table, where you can fill in the rest of the information about it.

Deleting Tags

There are two ways to delete entity tags. One way is to highlight all or part of the tagged text in the window, and right-click on it. The pop-up menu will list all the tags at that location, with the option to remove each of them. The other way to remove an extent tag also works for links and nonconsuming tags: just select the row of the tag that you want to remove in the table, and right-click. You will have the option to remove all the highlighted rows in the active tab. When an extent tag is removed, all the link tags that it is a part of are removed as well to maintain consistency. The reverse is not true for link tags—removing a link tag will have no effect on extent tags. Please note that there is no undo function.

Saving Files

To save the information you have annotated, select "Save as XML" from the File menu. This will create a file that contains the text and the tags that you have created, with the tags in stand-off format. Once you have created this file, you will be able to load it back into MAE to continue, or edit existing annotations. There is another option in the File menu called Create RTF. This option *will not* save all the information about the tags and annotation you created, but it is a handy way to look at the annotation of each word.

Defining Your Own Task

Creating an annotation task for MAE is fairly straightforward. The format of the input is similar to DTDs (Document Type Definitions) used for XML. There are three main parts of task creation: the task name, the tag names, and the tag attributes. DTDs are simply text files with a *.dtd* extension—you can create them in any text editing program. The specifics of how these lines should be formatted might not work well in a *.pdf* file, so please refer to the included sample DTD (*samples/sampleTask.dtd*) for help if necessary.

Task Name

The task name is defined with the !ENTITY tag. If you wanted to create a task called "myTask", then you would create the !ENTITY line with name and the name of the task in quotes. The line to do so would look like this:

```
<!ENTITY name "myTask">
```

This simply provides a name to be used in the output files.

Elements (a.k.a. Tags)

Elements (defined by !ELEMENT tags) are used to define the names of the tags being used in your annotation task. MAE recognizes two types of tags: extent tags (tags used to label actual words in the document) and link tags (tags that identify a relationship between two extent tags). To define an extent tag for your task, the line in your DTD will look like this:

```
<!ELEMENT TagName ( #PCDATA ) >
```

while a link tag will look like this:

```
<!ELEMENT LinkName EMPTY >
```

The (#PCDATA) marker indicates that the tag will have extents, while the EMPTY indicates that the tag will be used for linking. You cannot have two tags with the same name, even if they are of different types.

 Currently, there is a limited number of font colors that are being assigned to tags—the colors will repeat, which may make annotation confusing if you have more than 11 tags.

Attributes

Attributes (defined by the !ATTLIST tags) contain the information associated with each tag. Some attributes are predefined by MAE—extent tags will always have start, end, text, and id attributes, even if they are not defined in the DTD. Link tags will always have to, from, toText, fromText, and id attributes. Attributes must include the name of the element that they refer to, followed by the name of the attribute and the type of the attribute, like so:

```
<!ATTLIST TagName attribute1 ( YES | NO ) #IMPLIED >
<!ATTLIST TagName attribute2 CDATA #IMPLIED >
```

In the following subsections I will go over the details of the attribute descriptions.

id attributes

If no id attribute is created, then MAE will assume by default that the prefix for the ids for that tag will be the first letter of that tag name. So, for example, a tag called Verb will have the ids V1, V2, V3, and so on. ID values are automatically assigned by the program to help prevent two tags from having the same ID. If you want to specify your own prefix, add prefix="MC" to your element attribute, like so:

```
<!ATTLIST TagName id ID prefix="MC" #REQUIRED >
```

In a future version of MAE, the \#REQUIRED and \#IMPLIED values will have an impact on how the files are output to XML (whether an exception will be thrown if a required attribute is left blank), but at the moment, they don't actually do anything, except when used for the start attribute.

start attribute

As previously mentioned, all extent tags have an attribute called start, which denotes where the tag begins in the text. It is possible in MAE to create a nonconsuming extent tag—an extent tag that doesn't actually cover any text, but instead exists as a placeholder. By default, MAE will not allow a tag to be nonconsuming, but by putting a line for the `start` attribute with the value \#IMPLIED, the tag that the `start` attribute belongs to will be added to the list of nonconsuming tags. For example, this line:

```
<!ATTLIST Tag1 start #IMPLIED >
```

will make it so that the tag `Tag1` is allowed to be nonconsuming. If you do not want to allow a tag to be nonconsuming, it is not necessary to mention the `start` attribute in the DTD at all.

Attribute types

It is possible in MAE to have a set of options for an attribute value, rather than asking the annotators to fill in their own values each time. If you want to have a list of values, create the attribute and include a list of options in parentheses, separated by "| ", like so:

```
<!ATTLIST TagName attribute1 ( YES | NO ) #IMPLIED >
```

If, on the other hand, you want the annotator to be able to enter her own values into the field for that attribute, assign the #CDATA value:

```
<!ATTLIST TagName attribute2 CDATA #IMPLIED >
```

Again, the #IMPLIED and #REQUIRED values for these attributes don't currently have an impact on how MAE operates, and it is fine to not include them.

Default attribute values

Starting in version 0.9, MAE allows you to set default values for any attribute by placing the desired value in quotes at the end of the attribute definition, like so:

```
<!ATTLIST TagName attribute1 ( YES | NO ) #IMPLIED "YES">
<!ATTLIST TagName attribute2 CDATA #IMPLIED "default">
```

Please note that if a list of options is defined in an attribute but the default value does not appear in the list, MAE will not provide that default value when creating a new tag.

Frequently Asked Questions

What does it mean when text is underlined?
   Text in the annotation window is underlined when there is more than one extent tag at that location. I experimented with mixing the colors of the two (or more) overlapping tags, but the colors were muddy and difficult to distinguish. Underlining seemed like a more recognizable visual clue.

Why doesn't MAE do XYZ?/Hey, this doesn't work!
   MAE is a work in progress. If you find any bugs or have any suggestions for improvement, please contact the creator, Amber Stubbs, at *astubbs@cs.brandeis.edu.*

Can MAE do multilevel annotations?

MAE is much more suited for single-layer annotation tasks. If you want to create an annotation involving multiple layers, you should look at a more complex annotation tool. See Appendix B for suggestions.

MAI User Guide

MAI (Multidocument Adjudication Interface) was created as a companion program to the annotation tool MAE (Multipurpose Annotation Environment). MAI was written by Amber Stubbs, and is provided free for use from *http://code.google.com/p/mai-adjudication/*. While many other annotation and adjudication tools are available for use, MAI was designed specifically for use in adjudicating the output from MAE, and so we are providing the user guide here for those readers who would like to start annotating and adjudicating right away.

Input to MAI is in the form of annotated stand-off XML files that are the output of MAE, as well as the DTD file used to create the annotations. Sample files are included with the MAI distribution, and instructions for adjudicating annotated files are included in this appendix. MAI was written in Java on an Ubuntu Linux system, and has been tested on Windows XP, Windows 7, and Mac OS X. It uses the SQLiteJDBC Java driver (more information is available at *https://github.com/crawshaw/sqlitejdbc*).

MAI is free software: you can redistribute it and/or modify it under the terms of the GNU General Public License as published by the Free Software Foundation, either version 3 of the License, or (at your option) any later version. This program is distributed in the hope that it will be useful, but *without any warranty*; without even the implied warranty of *merchantability* or *fitness for a particular purpose*. See the GNU General Public License for more details (*http://www.gnu.org/licenses/*).

Installing and Running MAI

MAI requires Java to run. On Windows and Unix systems, it should be used with the most recent version of Java 6 (it must have at least update 14 to run properly on Windows and Unix), though it can also be compiled under Java 5, so it can also be run on older Macs. To run MAI on any operating system, open a terminal and navigate to the directory where the *.jar* file exists, then run this command:

```
java -jar MAIversion.jar
```

On most platforms, it is also possible to open the program by double-clicking on the *.jar* file. However, doing so will not allow all error messages to be displayed, so using the terminal is recommended. On all systems, you should see the window shown in Figure D-1.

Figure D-1. MAI with a DTD loaded

Loading Tasks and Files

Loading a Task

To use MAI, you must load both a task definition file (*.dtd*) and the files to be adjudicated (*.xml*). The task definition must be loaded first, by selecting Load DTD from the File menu. Once the DTD is loaded, the left side of the screen will contain the names of the different tags in the DTD.

Loading Files

Once the DTD is loaded, it is possible to adjudicate files. To start a new adjudication task, go to the File menu and select "Start new adjudication," then load the first file that you want to adjudicate. The text of the file will be loaded in the center window, and a table will be created to the right that will show the tag attributes of a selected extent.

To add a file to an adjudication task, go to the File menu and select "Add file to adjudication." The file that is added *must* have the same base text as the other files being adjudicated; otherwise, it cannot be loaded. That is to say, all the text in the files between the <TEXT> and </TEXT> tags cannot be different; otherwise, the character locations will be different and the tags cannot be matched up.

To add a gold standard file to the task (i.e., a file where the tags have already been vetted by an adjudicator), go to the File menu and select "Add gold standard file." Please note that a gold standard file cannot be added to the adjudication unless another file with the same text has already been loaded (if you want to only view the gold standard file, you can load it first as a regular adjudication file, then again as a gold standard file). Any tags that have already been added to the gold standard prior to loading the file will still exist, so be careful of ID overlaps.

Adjudicating

The MAI Window

Each tag type is adjudicated individually. Select the tag that will be adjudicated from the options on the left. The text will be highlighted according to the agreement for each character.

For extent tags:

Blue
> All the annotators agree that the selected tag should be at that location (this does not mean that the annotators all agree on the values of the tag attribute).

Red
> At least one annotator believes that the tag should be at a location, but not all of them do.

Black
> No annotator placed the selected tag at that location.

Green
> A tag has been placed at this location in the gold standard.

For link tags:

Blue
> All the annotators agree that the text at that location is either a `to` or `from` anchor in a link of the selected type.

Red
> At least one annotator believes that the text at that location is either a `to` or `from` anchor in a link of the selected type.

Black
> No gold standard extent tag that is participating in the selected link tag exists at that location.

Green
> The text at that location is either a `to` or `from` anchor in a link of the selected type in the gold standard.

Light gray
> The text at this location is included in a tag that is in the gold standard, but none of the files being adjudicated have an extent tag that is participating in a link at the same location.

Magenta
> Areas of the text that have been viewed by the adjudicator for the selected tag are displayed in magenta to help the adjudicator keep track of the locations in the text that have been adjudicated.

Adjudicating a Tag

For all tag types, when a tag from a file being adjudicated is copied to the gold standard, the information from the copied tag is automatically assigned a gold standard ID and added to the database. If you wish to change an attribute on a gold standard tag, you must only make the appropriate changes and then click the "Add/modify" button in the rightmost table column. Changes are not saved automatically, however—modifications to attributes are only committed when the button is clicked.

Extent Tags

By selecting an extent where a tag exists in at least one of the annotations, the information for all the tags at that location will populate the table at the bottom of the screen. There, if you agree with an annotator about the location and attributes of a tag, you can copy the contents of the annotator's tag by clicking the "Copy to gold standard" button in the annotation column. This will copy the contents of the link to the gold standard, and generate a new ID for that tag in the gold standard file.

Once a tag has been added to the gold standard, you may modify any of the tag's attributes except for the filename. It is, however, generally not advisable to change the computer-generated ID of the tag, as this may cause problems with the database.

Link Tags

If a link tag is selected from the lefthand display, the interface behaves slightly differently than when displaying information about an extent tag. The colors are displayed according to the preceding guide. It should be noted that information about any link is only displayed if the to and from anchors for the tags in the files being adjudicated overlap with extents of the same type in the gold standard. This is so that the adjudicator's screen will not be cluttered with information about links pertaining to extents that he has not placed in the gold standard.

When a span of text is selected in the window, the link information displayed in the table, while originating from the files being adjudicated, will have the attribute information in the fromID and toID and fromText and toText fields replaced with the corresponding information from the gold standard tags at those locations. This ensures that there will not be any errors pertaining to text spans or ID numbers.

Nonconsuming Tags

Tags that have the option of being nonconsuming (if they are described so in the DTD; see the MAE User Guide for details) are added to the bottom of the tag list on the left side of the screen as NC-(tagname). When one of these is selected from the left side of the screen, all nonconsuming tags of that type are displayed in the tag table.

Adding New Tags

You may also add a tag to the gold standard that does not exist in any of the files being adjudicated. The functionality of this feature is much like that of MAE. To add a new extent tag, use the mouse to highlight the text where the tag should be placed, then right-click and select the tag name from the pop-up menu. This will add the tag to the table at the bottom of the MAI window, where the adjudicator can enter any missing attribute information.

To add a link tag, you must select the text window, then hold down the Ctrl key (or the Command key, if using a Mac), and left-click each entity that will be included in the link, in the order you want them to appear in the link (i.e., the first entity that is clicked on will be in the "from" position, and the second will be in the "to" position). Once this is done, a window will pop up that will allow you to select where the link starts and where it ends, and the type of link that you want to create between them. When you click on the "Create link" button at the bottom of the pop-up window, the link will be added to the appropriate table, where you can fill in the rest of the information about it.

If you wish to add a new nonconsuming tag, you must simply highlight an area of the text and right-click, then proceed as with adding a regular extent tag (the area selected doesn't matter, as the start and end will both be set to –1).

Deleting tags

Tags may be deleted from the gold standard (not from the files being adjudicated) by selecting the row in the table of the tag that should be deleted and right-clicking. You will have the option to remove all the highlighted rows in the table.

When an extent tag is removed, all the link tags that it is a part of are removed as well to maintain consistency in the database. The reverse is not true for link tags—removing a link tag will have no effect on extent tags.

Please note that there is no undo function.

Saving Files

To save the information you have annotated, select "Save as XML" from the File menu. This will create a file that contains the text and the tags that you have created, with the tags in stand-off format.

APPENDIX E
Bibliography

Allen, James. 1984. "Towards a General Theory of Action and Time." *Artificial Intelligence* 23:123–154.

Artstein, Ron, and Massimo Poesio. December 2008. "Inter-coder agreement for computational linguistics." *Computational Linguistics* 34(4):555–596.

Atkins, Sue, and N. Ostler. 1992. "Predictable Meaning Shift: Some Linguistic Properties of Lexical Implication Rules." In *Lexical Semantics and Commonsense Reasoning.* J. Pustejovsky and S. Bergler (Eds.). New York: Springer-Verlag.

Baroni, M. 2009. "Distributions in text." In Anke Lüdeling and Merja Kytö (eds.), *Corpus linguistics: An international handbook*, Volume 2, Berlin: Mouton de Gruyter: 803–821.

Bayerl, Petra Saskia, and Karsten Ingmar Paul. December 2011. "What Determines Inter-Coder Agreement in Manual Annotations? A Meta-Analytic Investigation." *Computational Linguistics* 37(4):699–725.

Belnap, Nuel. 1992. "Branching Space-Time." *Synthese* 92:385–434.

Biber, Douglas. 1993. "Representativeness in Corpus Design." *Literary and Linguistic Computing* 8:243–257.

Bird, Steven, Ewan Klein, and Edward Loper. 2010. *Natural Language Processing with Python.* Sebastopol, CA: O'Reilly.

Blum, Avrim, and Tom Mitchell. 1998. "Combining labeled and unlabeled data with co-training." In *COLT: Proceedings of the Workshop on Computational Learning Theory.* Madison, WI: Morgan Kaufmann.

Blunsom, Phil. 2004. "Maximum Entropy Markov Models for Semantic Role Labelling." In *Proceedings of the Australasian Language Technology Workshop.*

Brill, Eric. December 1995. "Transformation-Based Error-Driven Learning and Natural Language Processing: A Case Study in Part of Speech Tagging." *Computational Linguistics* 21(4):543–565.

Carlson, Andrew, Justin Betteridge, Richard C. Wang, Estevam R. Hruschka Jr., and Tom M. Mitchell. 2010. "Coupled Semi-Supervised Learning for Information Extraction." In *Proceedings of the 3rd ACM International Conference on Web Search and Data Mining (WSDM).*

Chomsky, Noam. 1957. *Syntactic Structures*. Paris: Mouton.

Chuzhanova, N.A., A.J. Jones, and S. Margetts.1998. "Feature selection for genetic sequence classification. "*Bioinformatics* 14(2):139–143.

Culotta, Aron, Michael Wick, Robert Hall, and Andrew McCallum. 2007. "First-Order Probabilistic Models for Coreference Resolution." In *Proceedings of the Human Language Technology Conference of the North American Chapter of the Association of Computational Linguistics (HLT/NAACL).*

Derczynski, Leon, and Robert Gaizauskas. 2010. "USFD2: Annotating Temporal Expressions and TLINKs for TempEval-2." In *Proceedings of the 5th International Workshop on Semantic Evaluation.*

Dipper, Stefanie, Michael Götze, and Stavros Skopeteas. 2004. "Towards User-Adaptive Annotation Guidelines." In *Proceedings of the COLING Workshop on Linguistically Interpreted Corpora, LINC-2004*, pp. 23–30, Geneva.

Dowty, David. 1979. *Word Meaning and Montague Grammar*. Dordrecht, The Netherlands: Kluwer.

Dowty, David. 1991. "Thematic proto-roles and argument selection." *Language* 67:547–619.

Fan, Jung-wei, Rashmi Prasad, Rommel M. Yabut, Richard M. Loomis, Daniel S. Zisook, John E. Mattison, and Yang Huang. 2011. "Part-of-speech tagging for clinical text: Wall or bridge between institutions?" In *Proceedings of the AMIA Annual Symposium*, pp. 382–391.

Filatova, Elena, and Eduard Hovy. 2001. "Assigning Time-Stamps to Event-Clauses." In *Proceedings of the ACL Workshop on Temporal and Spatial Reasoning*, Toulouse, France.

Fort, Karën, Gilles Adda, and K. Bretonnel Cohen. 2011. "Amazon Mechanical Turk: Gold Mine or Coal Mine?" *Computational Linguistics* 37(2):413–420.

Francis, W.N., and H. Kucera. 1964 (Revised 1971 and 1979). *Brown Corpus Manual*. Available online: *http://khnt.aksis.uib.no/icame/manuals/brown/*. Accessed Aug. 2011.

Freund, Yoav, and Robert E. Schapire. 1995. "A Decision-Theoretic Generalization of On-Line Learning and an Application to Boosting. In *EuroCOLT '95 Proceedings of the 2nd European Conference on Computational Learning Theory*.

Goldman, Sally, and Yah Zhou. 2000. "Enhancing supervised learning with unlabeled data." In *Proceedings of the 17th International Conference on Machine Learning*, pp. 327–334. San Francisco: Morgan Kaufmann.

Grant, Barry Keith. 2007. *Film Genre: From Iconography to Ideology*. London: Wallflower Press.

Grover, Claire, Richard Tobin, Beatrice Alex, and Kate Byrne. 2010. "Edinburgh-LTG: TempEval-2 System Description." In *Proceedings of the 5th International Workshop on Semantic Evaluation*.

Ha, Eun, Alok Baikadi, Carlyle Licata, and James Lester. 2010. "NCSU: Modeling Temporal Relations with Markov Logic and Lexical Ontology." In *Proceedings of the 5th International Workshop on Semantic Evaluation*.

Hanks, Patrick, and James Pustejovsky. 2005. "A Pattern Dictionary for Natural Language Processing." In *Revue Française de Linguistique Appliquee*.

Herzig, Livnat, Alex Nunes, and Batia Snir. 2011. "An Annotation Scheme for Automated Bias Detection in Wikipedia." In *Proceedings of the 5th Linguistic Annotation Workshop*.

Ide, Nancy, and James Pustejovsky. "The Language Application Grid: A Framework for Rapid Adaptation and Reuse." *Language, Resource, and Evaluation*, submitted. Forthcoming.

Ide, Nancy, and Laurent Romary. 2004. "International standard for a linguistic annotation framework." *Journal of Natural Language Engineering* 10(3–4):211–225.

Ide, Nancy, and Laurent Romary. 2006. "Representing Linguistic Corpora and Their Annotations." In *Proceedings of the 5th Language Resources and Evaluation Conference (LREC)*, Genoa, Italy.

Im, Seohyun. *Generator of the Event Structure Lexicon (GESL): Automatic Annotation of Lexically Entailed Subevents for Textual Inference Tasks*. PhD dissertation, Brandeis University. Forthcoming.

Im, Seohyun, and James Pustejovsky. 2010. "Annotating Lexically Entailed Subevents for Textual Inference Tasks." In *Proceedings of FLAIRS 23*, Daytona Beach, FL, May 17–20, 2010.

Ishida, Toru (Ed.). 2011. *The Language Grid*. New York: Springer.

Jackendoff, Ray S. 1983. *Semantics and Cognition*. Cambridge, MA: The MIT Press.

Jurafsky, Daniel, and James H. Martin. 2008. *Speech and Language Processing* (2 ed.). Upper Saddle River, NJ: Pearson Prentice Hall.

Kamp, Hans. 1988. "Discourse Representation Theory: What it is and where it ought to go." In A. Bläser (Ed.), *Natural Language and the Computer*. Berlin: Springer.

Kenny, Anthony. 1963. *Action, Emotion and Will*. London: Routledge & Kegan.

Kolomiyets, Oleksandr, and Marie-Francine Moens. 2010. "KUL: Recognition and Normalization of Temporal Expressions." In *Proceedings of the 5th International Workshop on Semantic Evaluation*.

Kolya, Anup Kumar, Asif Ekbal, and Sivaji Bandyopadhyay. 2010. "JU_CSE_TEMP: A First Step Towards Evaluating Events, Time Expressions and Temporal Relations." In *Proceedings of the 5th International Workshop on Semantic Evaluation*.

Kuhn, Thomas. 1961. *The Function of Measurement in Modern Physical Science*. Chicago: The University of Chicago Press.

Lafferty, J., A. McCallum, and F. Pereira. 2001. "Conditional random fields: Probabilistic models for segmenting and labeling sequence data." In *Proceedings of the ICML-01*, pp. 282–289.

Landis, J.R., and G. Koch. 1977. "The measurement of observer agreement for categorical data." *Biometrics* 33(1):159–174.

Laney, Douglas. February 2001. *3D Data Management: Controlling Data Volume, Velocity and Variety. MetaGroup*. Available online: *http://blogs.gartner.com/doug-laney/files/2012/01/ad949-3D-Data-Management-Controlling-Data-Volume-Velocity-and-Variety.pdf*. Retrieved Aug. 7, 2012.

Leech, Geoffrey. 1991. "The state of the art in corpus linguistics." In *English Corpus Linguistics: Linguistic Studies in Honour of Jan Svartvik*. London: Longman, pp. 8–29.

Leslie, Christina, Eleazar Eskin, and William Stafford Noble. 2002. "The spectrum kernel: A string kernel for SVM protein classification." In *Pacific Symposium on Biocomputing*, pp. 566–575.

Lim, Joon-Ho, Young-Sook Hwang, So-Young Park, and Hae-Chang Rim. 2004. "Semantic role labeling using maximum entropy model." In *Proceedings of the CoNLL-2004 Shared Task*.

Lin, Jimmy, and Chris Dyer. 2010. *Data-Intensive Text Processing with MapReduce*. Morgan & Claypool Publishers. Available at *http://bit.ly/RckgZ8*.

Liu, Bing. 2012. *Sentiment Analysis and Opinion Mining*. Morgan & Claypool Publishers. Available at *http://bit.ly/Vgq8pp*.

Llorens, Hector, Estela Saquete, and Borja Navarro. 2010. "TIPSem (English and Spanish): Evaluating CRFs and Semantic Roles in TempEval-2." In *Proceedings of the 5th International Workshop on Semantic Evaluation*.

Madnani, Nitin. 2007. "Getting Started on Natural Language Processing with Python." *ACM Crossroads* 13(4). Updated version available at *http://www.desilinguist.org/*. Accessed May 16, 2012.

Madnani, Nitin, and Jimmy Lin. *Natural Language Processing with Hadoop and Python.* *http://www.cloudera.com/blog/2010/03/natural-language-processing-with-hadoopand-python/*. Posted March 16, 2010.

Mani, Inderjeet, Marc Verhagen, Ben Wellner, Chong Min Lee, and James Pustejovsky. 2006. *Proceedings of Machine Learning of Temporal Relations.* ACL 2006, Sydney, Australia.

Manning, Chris, and Hinrich Schütze. 1999. *Foundations of Statistical Natural Language Processing.* Cambridge, MA: The MIT Press.

Manning, Christopher D., Prabhakar Raghavan, and Hinrich Schütze. 2008. *Introduction to Information Retrieval* (1 ed.). Cambridge, UK: Cambridge University Press.

Marcus, Mitchell P., Beatrice Santorini, and Mary Ann Marcinkiewicz. 1994. "Building a Large Annotated Corpus of English: The Penn Treebank." *Computational Linguistics* 19(2):313–330.

McCallum, D. Freitag, and F. Pereira. 2000. "Maximum entropy Markov models for information extraction and segmentation." In *Proceedings of ICML 2000*, Stanford, CA: pp. 591–598.

McCarthy, John, and Patrick J. Hayes. 1969. "Some Philosophical Problems from the Standpoint of Artificial Intelligence." In B. Meltzer and D. Michie (Eds.), *Machine Intelligence* 4, pp. 463–502. Edinburgh, Scotland: Edinburgh University Press.

McDermott, Drew. 1923. "A Temporal Logic for Reasoning about Processes and Plans." *Cognitive Science* 6:101–155.

McEnery, Tony, Richard Xiao, and Yukio Tono. 2006. *Corpus-based Language Studies: An Advanced Resource Book.* London and New York: Routledge.

McLachlan, Geoffrey J., and Thriyambakam Krishnan. 1996. *The EM Algorithm and Extensions.* New York: Wiley-Interscience.

Mitchell, Tom. 1997. *Machine Learning.* New York: McGraw-Hill.

Montague, Richard. 1970. "English as a Formal Language." In Bruno Visentini (Ed.), *Linguaggi nella società e nella tecnica.* Milan: Edizioni di Comunità, pp. 189–224. Reprinted in Montague (1974), pp. 188–221.

Ng, Vincent, and Claire Cardie. 2002. "Improving Machine Learning Approaches to Coreference Resolution." In *Proceedings of the 40th Annual Meeting of the Association for Computational Linguistics.*

Ng, Vincent, and Claire Cardie. 2003. "Bootstrapping Coreference Classifiers with Multiple Machine Learning Algorithms." In *Proceedings of the 2003 Conference on Empirical Methods in Natural Language Processing (EMNLP-2003)*, Association for Computational Linguistics.

Nigam, Kamal, John Lafferty, and Andrew McCallum. 1999. "Using maximum entropy for text classification." In *Proceedings of the IJCAI-99 Workshop on Machine Learning for Information Filtering*, pp. 61–67.

Olsson, Fredrik. 2009. *A literature survey of active machine learning in the context of natural language processing*. [SICS Report]

Palmer, Martha, Dan Gildea, and Paul Kingsbury. 2005. "The Proposition Bank: A Corpus Annotated with Semantic Roles." *Computational Linguistics Journal* 31(1):71–106.

Panchenko, Alexander, Sergey Adeykin, Alexey Romanov, and Pavel Romanov. 2012. "Extraction of Semantic Relations between Concepts with KNN Algorithms on Wikipedia." In *Proceedings of Concept Discovery in Unstructured Data 2012*, Leuven, Belgium, May 10, 2012.

Pang, Bo, and Lillian Lee. 2004. "A sentimental education: Sentiment analysis using subjectivity summarization based on minimum cuts." In *Proceedings of the 42nd Annual Meeting of the Association for Computational Linguistics* (ACL '04), Stroudsburg, PA, Article 271.

Pang, Bo, Lillian Lee, and Shivakumar Vaithyanathan. 2002. "Thumbs Up? Sentiment Classification Using Machine Learning Techniques." In *Proceedings of the ACL-02 Conference on Empirical Methods in Natural Language Processing* (vol. 10, EMNLP '02, pp. 79–86), Stroudsburg, PA; Association for Computational Linguistics.

Parsons, Terence. 1990. *Events in the Semantics of English: A Study of Subatomic Semantics*. Cambridge, MA: The MIT Press.

Pomikálek, Jan, Miloš Jakubíček, and Pavel Rychlý. 2012. "Building a 70-billion word corpus of English from ClueWeb." In *Proceedings of the 8th International Conference on Language Resources and Evaluation (LREC)*.

Pradhan, Sameer, Kadri Hacioglu, Wayne Ward, James H. Martin, and Daniel Jurafsky. 2003. "Semantic Role Parsing: Adding Semantic Structure to Unstructured Text." In *Proceedings of the International Conference on Data Mining (ICDM-2003)*, Melbourne, FL, Nov. 19–22, 2003.

Prior, Arthur. 1968. *Papers on Time and Tense*. Oxford, UK: Oxford University Press.

Puscasu, Georgiana. 2007. "WVALI: Temporal Relation Identification by Syntactico-Semantic Analysis." In *Proceedings of the 4th International Workshop on Semantic Evaluation*.

Pustejovsky, James. 1991. "The Syntax of Event Structure." *Cognition* 41(1–3):47–81.

Pustejovsky, James. 1995. *The Generative Lexicon*. Cambridge, MA: The MIT Press.

Pustejovsky, James. 2001. *ARDA Workshop Proposal: Temporal Issues*. Archived at *http://www.timeml.org/site/terqas/documentation/ARDA-proposal3.html*.

Pustejovsky, James. 2006. "Unifying Linguistic Annotations: A TimeML Case Study." In *Proceedings of the Text, Speech, and Dialogue Conference*.

Pustejovsky, James, José Castaño, Robert Ingria, Roser Saurí, Robert Gaizauskas, Andrea Setzer, and Graham Katz. 2003. "TimeML: Robust Specification of Event and Temporal Expressions in Text." In *Proceedings of IWCS-5, the 5th International Workshop on Computational Semantics*.

Pustejovsky, James, Robert Knippen, Jessica Littman, and Roser Sauri. 2005. "Temporal and Event Information in Natural Language Text." *Language Resources and Evaluation* 39(2):123–164.

Pustejovsky, James, Kiyong Lee, Harry Bunt, and Laurent Romary. 2010. "ISO-TimeML: An International Standard for Semantic Annotation." In *Proceedings of LREC 2010*, Malta, May 18–21, 2010.

Pustejovsky, James, Kiyong Lee, Harry Bunt, and Laurent Romary. "ISO-TimeML: A Standard for Annotating Temporal Information in Language." Submitted to the *Journal of Language Resources and Evaluation*: Special Issue on Standards. Forthcoming.

Pustejovsky, James, Patrick Hanks, and Anna Rumshisky. 2004. "Automated Induction of Sense in Context." In *Proceedings of ACL-COLING*, Geneva.

Pustejovsky, James, and Amber Stubbs. 2011. "Increasing Informativeness in Temporal Annotation." In *2011 Proceedings of the Linguistic Annotation Workshop V, Association of Computational Linguistics*, Portland, OR, July 23–24, 2011.

Quirk, Randolph, Sidney Greenbaum, Geoffrey Leech, and Jan Svartik.1985. *A Comprehensive Grammar of the English Language*. London and New York: Longman.

Randell, David A., Zhan Cui, and Anthony G. Cohn. 1992. "A spatial logic based on regions and Q17 connections." In M. Kaufmann (Ed.), *Proceedings of the 3rd International 905 Conference on Knowledge Representation and Reasoning*, San Mateo, CA: pp. 165–176.

Reichenbach, Hans. 1947. *Elements of Symbolic Logic*. New York: Macmillan Co.; New York: Dover Publications, 1980 (reprint).

Rumshisky, Anna. 2008. *Verbal Polysemy Resolution through Contextualized Clustering of Arguments*. PhD Dissertation, Brandeis University.

Russell, David A. 2011. *Mining the Social Web*. Sebastopol, CA: O'Reilly.

Saquete, Estela. 2010. "ID 392:TERSEO + T2T3 Transducer. A System for Recognizing and Normalizing TIMEX3." In *Proceedings of the 5th International Workshop on Semantic Evaluation.*

Saurí, Roser, Robert Knippen, Marc Verhagen, and James Pustejovsky. 2005. "Evita: A Robust Event Recognizer for QA Systems." In *Proceedings of HLT/EMNLP 2005.*

Saurí, Roser, Marc Verhagen, and James Pustejovsky. 2006. "SlinkET: A Partial Modal Parser for Events." In *Proceedings of LREC 2006*, Genoa, Italy, May 23–26, 2006.

Savova, Guergana, Steven Bethard, Will Styler, James Martin, Martha Palmer, James Masanz, and Wayne Ward. 2009. "Towards Temporal Relation Discovery from the Clinical Narrative." In *Proceedings of the AMIA 2009 Symposium.*

Settles, Burr. "Active Learning Literature Survey." *Computer Sciences Technical Report 1648*, University of Wisconsin-Madison. Updated Jan. 26, 2010.

Setzer, Andrea. 2001. *Temporal Information in Newswire Articles: An Annotation Scheme and Corpus Study.* PhD thesis. University of Sheffield, UK.

Sinclair, J. 2005. "Corpus and Text: Basic Principles." In M. Wynne (Ed.), *Developing Linguistic Corpora: A Guide to Good Practice.* Oxford, UK: Oxbow Books, pp. 1–16. Available online: *http://ahds.ac.uk/linguistic-corpora/.* Accessed June 18, 2012.

Singh, Aarti, Robert Nowak, and Xiaojin Zhu. 2008. "Unlabeled data: Now it helps, now it doesn't." In Proceedings of *Neural Information Processing Systems (NIPS)* 22:1513–1520.

Speer, Robert, Catherine Havasi, and Harshit Surana. "Using Verbosity: Common Sense Data from Games with a Purpose." In *Proceedings of the 23rd International FLAIRS Conference.*

Strötgen, Jannik, and Michael Gertz. 2010. "HeidelTime: High Quality Rule-Based Extraction and Normalization of Temporal Expressions." In *Proceedings of the 5th International Workshop on Semantic Evaluation.*

Stubbs, Amber. *A Methodology for Using Professional Knowledge in Corpus Annotation.* Doctoral dissertation. Brandeis University, August 2012; to be published February 2013.

Stubbs, Amber, and Benjamin Harshfield. 2010. "Applying the TARSQI Toolkit to augment text mining of EHRs." BioNLP '10 poster session: In *Proceedings of the 2010 Workshop on Biomedical Natural Language Processing.*

Tenny, Carol. 2000. "Core events and adverbial modification." In J. Pustejovsky and C. Tenny (Eds.), *Events as Grammatical Objects.* Stanford, CA: Stanford: Center for the Study of Language and Information, pp. 285–334.

Tsuruoka, Yoshimasa, Yuka Tateishi, Jin-Dong Kim, Tomoko Ohta, John McNaught, Sophia Ananiadou, and Jun'ichi Tsujii. 2005. "Developing a Robust Part-of-Speech Tagger for Biomedical Text." *Advances in Informatics: 10th Panhellenic Conference on Informatics* (vol. 3746, pp. 382–392).

UzZaman, Naushad, and James Allen. 2010. "TRIPS and TRIOS System for TempEval-2: Extracting Temporal Information from Text." In *Proceedings of the 5th International Workshop on Semantic Evaluation.*

Vendler, Zeno. 1957. "Verbs and Times." *The Philosophical Review* 66(2):143–160.

Vendler, Zeno. 1967. *Linguistics in Philosophy.* Ithaca, NY: Cornell University Press.

Verhagen, Marc. 2004. *Times Between the Lines.* PhD thesis. Brandeis University.

Verhagen, Marc. 2012. *TTK Wish List.* Internal document, Brandeis University.

Verhagen, Marc, Inderjeet Mani, Roser Sauri, Robert Knippen, Seok Bae Jang, Jessica Littman, Anna Rumshisky, John Phillips, and James Pustejovsky. 2005. "Automating Temporal Annotation with TARSQI." In *Proceedings of the ACL 2005 on Interactive Poster and Demonstration Sessions.*

Verhagen, Marc, and James Pustejovsky. 2008. "Temporal processing with the TARSQI Toolkit." In *Proceedings of COLING '08, the 22nd International Conference on Computational Linguistics: Demonstration Papers.*

Verhagen, Marc, and James Pustejovsky. 2012. "The TARSQI Toolkit." In *Proceedings of the 8th International Conference on Language Resources and Evaluation (LREC'12), European Language Resources Association (ELRA).*

Verhagen, Marc, Roser Sauri, Tommaso Caselli, and James Pustejovsky. 2010. "SemEval-2010 Task 13: TempEval-2." In *Proceedings of the 5th International Workshop on Semantic Evaluation.*

Vicente-Díez, María Teresa, Julián Moreno-Schneider, and Paloma Martínez. 2010. "UC3M System: Determining the Extent, Type and Value of Time Expressions in TempEval-2." In *Proceedings of the 5th International Workshop on Semantic Evaluation.*

Wellner, Ben, Andrew McCallum, Fuchun Peng, and Michael Hay. 2004. "An Integrated, Conditional Model of Information Extraction and Coreference with Application to Citation Matching." In *Proceedings of the Conference on Uncertainty in Artificial Intelligence (UAI),* July 2004, Banff, Canada.

Wiebe, Janyce, Theresa Wilson, and Claire Cardie. 2005. "Annotating expressions of opinions and emotions in language." *Language Resources and Evaluation* 39(2–3): 165–210.

References for Using Amazon's Mechanical Turk/ Crowdsourcing

Aker, Ahmet, Mahmoud El-Haj, M-Dyaa Albakour, and Udo Kruschwitz. 2012. "Assessing Crowdsourcing Quality through Objective Tasks." In *Proceedings of the 8th International Conference on Language Resources and Evaluation (LREC'12)*, Istanbul, Turkey.

Filatova, Elena. 2012. "Irony and Sarcasm: Corpus Generation and Analysis Using Crowdsourcing." In *Proceedings of the 8th International Conference on Language Resources and Evaluation (LREC'12)*, Istanbul, Turkey.

Fort, Karën, Gilles Adda, and K. Bretonnel Cohen. 2011. "Amazon Mechanical Turk: Gold Mine or Coal Mine?" *Computational Linguistics* 37(2):413–420.

Kittur, E.H. Chi, and B. Suh. 2008. "Crowdsourcing user studies with Mechanical Turk." In *Proceedings of CHI '08: The 26th Annual SIGCHI Conference on Human Factors in Computing Systems.*

Kunchukuttan, Anoop, Shourya Roy, Pratik Patel, Kushal Ladha, Somya Gupta, Mitesh M. Khapra, and Pushpak Bhattacharyya. 2012. "Experiences in Resource Generation for Machine Translation through Crowdsourcing." In *Proceedings of the 8th International Conference on Language Resources and Evaluation (LREC'12)*, Istanbul, Turkey.

Marujo, Luís, Anatole Gershman, Jaime Carbonell, Robert Frederking, and Joaĩfo P. Neto. 2012. "Supervised Topical Key Phrase Extraction of News Stories using Crowdsourcing, Light Filtering and Co-reference Normalization." In *Proceedings of the 8th International Conference on Language Resources and Evaluation (LREC'12)*, Istanbul, Turkey.

Rumshisky, Anna. 2011. "Crowdsourcing Word Sense Definition." In *Proceedings of the 5th Linguistic Annotation Workshop (LAW-V)*, ACL-HLT 2011, Portland, OR.

Rumshisky, Anna, Nick Botchan, Sophie Kushkuley, and James Pustejovsky. 2012. "Word Sense Inventories by Non-Experts." In *Proceedings of the 8th International Conference on Language Resources and Evaluation (LREC'12)*, Istanbul, Turkey.

Scharl, Arno, Marta Sabou, Stefan Gindl, Walter Rafelsberger, and Albert Weichselbraun. 2012. "Leveraging the Wisdom of the Crowds for the Acquisition of Multilingual Language Resources." In *Proceedings of the 8th International Conference on Language Resources and Evaluation (LREC'12)*, Istanbul, Turkey.

Snow, Rion, Brendan O'Connor, Daniel Jurafsky, and Andrew Y. Ng. 2008. "Cheap and Fast—But Is It Good? Evaluating Non-Expert Annotations for Natural Language Tasks." In *Proceedings of EMNLP-08*.

Sorokin, Alexander, and David Forsyth. 2008. "Utility data annotation with Amazon Mechanical Turk." In *Proceedings of the Computer Vision and Pattern Recognition Workshops*.

Index

Symbols

(κ) Kappa scores, 28
    Cohen's Kappa (κ), 127–128
    Fleiss's Kappa (κ), 128–131
X-squared (chi-squared) test, 176

A

A Standard Corpus of Present-Day American
    English (Kucera and Francis) (see Brown
    Corpus)
active learning algorithms, 242
adjudication, 135
    MAI as tool for, 297–302
Allen, James, 80, 198
Amazon Elastic Compute Cloud, 244
Amazon's Mechanical Turk (MTurk), 107
American Medical Informatics Association
    (AMIA), 42
American National Corpus (ANC), 7
Analysis of variance (ANOVA) test, 176
Analyzing Linguistic Data: A Practical Intro-
    duction to Statistics using R (Baayen), 54
annotated corpus, 2
annotation environments
    annotation units, support for, 125
    chosing, 124
    MAE (Multipurpose Annotation Environ-
    ment), 289–296

process enforcement in, 125
    revising, 187
annotation guideline(s), 27, 112
    categories, using in, 117
    classifications, defining and clarifying, 113
    labels, importance of clear definitions for,
        116
    limits on number of labels, effects of, 116
    link tags, 120
    list of available, 263–266
    multiple lables, use of and considerations
        needed for, 115
    named entities, defining, 119
    and outside information, 118
    reproducibility, 117
    revising, 186
    revising, need for, 109
    semantic roles, 120
    specifications vs., 108
    writing, 112
annotation standards, 80–84, 87–102
    community-driven, 83
    data storage format and, 84
    date format and, 84
    ISO standards, 80–83
    LAF (Linguistic Annotation Framework)
        standard, 102
    linked extent annotation, 101
    naming conventions and, 84

We'd like to hear your suggestions for improving our indexes. Send email to index@oreilly.com.

classifier algorithms, 144–159
   decision tree learning, 145–147
   macro-averaging, 159
   micro-averaging, 159
closure rules, 36
Cloud computing and NLP, 244–246
   distributed computing, 244
   shared language resources, 245, 245
ClueWeb09 corpus, 14
clustering, 162
   classification vs., 162–165
   exclusive clustering, 162
   hierarchical clustering, 162
   overlapping clustering, 162
   probabilistic clustering, 162
clustering algorithms, 22
Cohen's Kappa (κ), 127–128
   and confusion matrices, 171
   Fleiss's Kappa (κ), 129
   interpreting, 131–135
   skewed data, potential for, 133
collocations, 62
concordances, 10
   Corpus Pattern Analysis, 11
   Key Word in Context index (KWIC), 10
condition-action pair, 143
conditional probability, 56
Conditional Random Field models (CRF), 22,
   161
Conference on Computational Linguistics
   (COLING), 42
Conference on Natural Language Learning
   (CoNLL) Shared Task (Special Interest
   Group on Natural Language Learning of the
   Association for Computational Linguistics),
   43
confusion matrix, 127, 171
consuming tags, 27
corpus analytics, 53–65
   joint probability distributions, 55–57
   language models, 63
   lexical statistics for, 58–63
   probability principles for, 54–58
      (see also probability)
corpus linguistics, 5–14
   history of, 5–8
Corpus of Contemporary American English
   (COCA), 7
Corpus Pattern Analysis, 11

corpus, corpora
   analyzing, 53–65
   assembling, 43–47
   balanced sampling in, 8
   balanced sampling, importance of, 45
   concordances, 10
   current usage of, 13
   defined, 2, 8
   distribution of sources, 49
   gold standard corpus, 28
   Google Ngram corpus, 13
   guidelines for creating, 43
   and the Internet, 14
   Internet, collecting data from, 45
   legal concerns with eliciting data from peo-
      ple, 46
   linguists, as source for preassembled, 41
   list of available corpora, 247–263
   NLP challenges, as sources for preassembled
      corpora, 42
   organizations/conferences, as source for pre-
      assembled, 42
   people, eliciting data from, 46
   read vs. spontaneous speech in, 46
   reporting on, 189
   representative sampling in, 8
   representative sampling, importance of, 44
   resources for existing, 40–43
   revising distributions/content of, 184
   size considerations with, 47
   size, comparing with other corpora, 48
   TimeML, building for, and evolution of, 199
crowdsourcing (of annotation tasks), 107, 237–
   240
   Games with a Purpose (GWAP), 239–240
   Mechanical Turk (MTurk), 238
   user-generated content, 240

D

DARPA (Defense Advanced Research Projects
   Agency), 197
Data Category Registry (DCR), 81
data preparation for annotation, 110–113
   metadata and the potential for bias in, 110
   preprocessed data, advantages/concerns
      with, 110
   splitting files for annotation/testing, 111
data sparseness problem, 153
dataset (see corpus, corpora)

DCR (Data Category Registry), 81
decision tree, 22
decision tree learning, 145–147
development corpus, 29
development-test set, 29
directed acyclic graph (DAG), 17
distributed method of annotation, 105
document annotation, 25
document classification, 5
Document Type Definition (see DTD (Document Type Definition)
Document Understanding Conferences (DUC), 199
DTD (Document Type Definition), 68, 118
    attributes, 69
    linking element, 69

E

Edinburgh-LTG, TempEval-2 system, 229
ELRA (European Language Resources Association), 41, 83
entropy, 149
ESP Game (GWAP), 239
European Language Resources Association (ELRA), 42
evaluating annotations, 126–135
    Cohen's Kappa (κ), 127–128
    confusion matrix, 127
    Fleiss's Kappa (κ), 128–131
    Kappa (κ) scores, interpreting, 131–135
    skewed data, potential for, 133
evaluation, 170–182
    confusion matrix, 171
    final scores, 181
    scores, calculating, 172–178
evaluation score(s), 172–178
    Analysis of variance (ANOVA) test, 176
    F-measure, 175
    interpreting, 177
    percentage accuracy, 172
    precision and recall, 173
    Receiver Operator Characteristic (ROC) curves, 177
    T-test, 176
    X-squared (chi-squared) test, 176
evaluation set, 170
Event Structure Frame (ESF), 214
events, 26
EVITA—Events in Text Analyzer (TTK), 220

exclusive clustering, 162
Expectation-Maximization (EM) algorithm, 163
extent annotation (see text extent annotation)

F

F-measure evaluation score, 30, 175
F-score (see F-measure evaluation score)
F1 score (see F-measure evaluation score)
Facebook, as text corpora, 7
Factiva Media Base, 199
false negative0, 173
false positive, 173
feature selection, 141
Feature-based sequence classification, 160
Film Genre: From Iconography to Ideology (Grant), 117
Fleiss's Kappa (κ), 128–131
    Cohen's Kappa (κ), 129
    interpreting, 131–135
    skewed data, potential for, 133
FrameNet, 77
Francis, W. Nelson, 8
frequency spectrum metric, 60
Fuzzy C-Means (FCM), 22

G

Georgetown University, 218
GNU General Public License, 289
goals (of annotation), 33–40
    corpus, determining scope of, 39
    desired outcomes, 38
    informativity vs. correctness, 35
    process, defining, 40
    purpose, 38
    scope of task, 36
    statement of purpose, 34
gold standard data set, 28, 135
Google, 13, 116, 116
Google Ngram corpus, 7, 13
    English subsets available in, 14
    languages available in, 14
Google Ngram Viewer, 13
grammar, 3
Grammar of English, 6
Guess What? (GWAP), 239
guidelines (see annotation guidelines)
GUTenLINK (TTK), 221
GUTime (Georgetown University Time), 219

H

Hadoop, 244
Hanks, Patrick, 11
hapax legomena, 60
HeidelTime, TempEval-2 system, 229, 232
Hidden Markov Models (see HMMS (Hidden Markov Models))
hierarchical clustering, 22, 162
HITs (human intelligence tasks), 2, 107, 238
HMMS (Hidden Markov Models), 13, 13, 22, 160

I

i2b2 NLP Shared Tasks, 43
IAA scores (inter-coder/inter-tagger agreement scores), 126
Imaginative topic area (Brown Corpus), 9
IMDb, 53, 71, 113
inductive learning, 164
information gain, 149
Information Retrieval (IR) tasks, 6
    precision and recall evaluations, 173
Informative topic area (Brown Corpus), 9
inline annotation, 94
    and Named Entities, 96
Institute of Electrical and Electronics Engineers (IEEE), 42
Inter-Annotator Agreement, 28
inter-coder agreement scores (IAA scores), 126
inter-tagger agreement scores (IAA scores), 126
ISI (Information Sciences Institute, 218
ISO (International Organization for Standardization), 80–83
    annotation specifications defined by, 82
    Data Category Registry (DCR), 81
    Linguistic Annotation Framework (LAF), 81
    and text encoding formats, 7
    TimeML, modifying to match ISO standards, 209–211
ISO-Space, 80, 264
ISO-TimeML, 209–211

J

joint probability distributions, 55–57
joint-features, 158
JU_CSE_TEMP, TempEval-2 system, 230

K

k-means, 22
K-nearest neighbor, 158
(κ) Kappa scores, 28
    Cohen's Kappa (κ), 127–128
    Fleiss's Kappa (κ), 128–131
Kernel Principle Component Analysis, 22
Key Word in Context index (KWIC), 6
    concordances, 10
Kucera, Henry, 8
Kuhn, Thomas, 7
KUL, TempEval-2 system, 230

L

LAF (Linguistic Annotation Framework), 81, 209
    development timeline, 82
Lancaster-Oslo-Bergen (LOB) Corpus, 6, 6
Laney, Doug, 241
language annotation, 1–2
    annotation, methods of, 105–135
    consuming tags, 27
    extent annotations, 119
    Human language technologies (HLTs), 2
    MATTER methodology, 23–24
    as metadata, 2
    nonconsuming tags, 27
    span of the tag, 27
Language Grid, 245
language models, 61, 63
    Markov assumption, 65
    maximum likelihood estimation (MLE), 65
Language Resources and Evaluation Conference (LREC), 42
LAPPs (Language Applications) Grid, 245
LDC (Linguistic Data Consortium), 41, 119
    and Google Ngram Corpus, 13
learning tasks, 142
Learning XML (Ray), 68
lemma, 58
lexical features, 146
lexical statistics, 58–63
    bigram probability, 62
    bigram profile, 62
    collocations, 62
    frequency spectrum, 60
    hapax legomena, 60
    n-grams, 61

specification, 27
testing/evaluation, 169–182
training/testing, 29
use of, in the TimeML and TimeBank, 195–215
maximum a posteriori (MAP) hypothesis, 152
Maximum Entropy classifiers (MaxEnt), 22, 157
Naïve Bayes vs., 157
Maximum Entropy Markov Models (MEMMs), 22, 161
Maximum Likelihood Estimation (see MLE (maximum likelihood estimation))
Message Understanding Conference (MUC), 119
Message Understanding Conferences (MUCs), 77
Metacritic.com, 90, 114
metadata, 2
metadata annotation, 88–93
multiple lables, 90
unique lables, 88
XML and, 91
micro-averaging, 159
Mining the Social Web (Russell), 46
Mitchell, Tom, 142
MLE (maximum likelihood estimation), 65, 153
model(s), 67–84
arity, 69
creating new vs. using existing, 75–80
creating, advantages/disadvantages of, 76–77
defined, 25, 67
existing, advantages/disadvantages of, 78–79
multimodel annotations, 74
Named Entities, adding to, 71
planning for the future with, 211–215
reporting on, 190
revising, 185
semantic roles and, 72
specifications, using without, 79
TimeML, defining and evolution of, 199–201
TimeML, results of MAMA cycle, 202–206
Model-Annotate-Model-Annotate (MAMA) cycle (see MAMA cycle)
Model-based sequence classification, 160
Movie Review Corpus (MRC), 113
MPQA Opinion Corpus, 156
Multidocument Adjudication Interface (see MAI (Multidocument Adjudication Interface))

multimodel annotation, 26, 74
Multipurpose Annotation Environment (see MAE (Multipurpose Annotation Environment))

N

n-grams
defined, 14
and lexical statistics, 61
Naïve Bayes learning, 22, 151–157
Classifier, 57
MaxEnt vs., 157
maximum a posteriori (MAP) hypothesis, 152
sentiment classification, 155
Named Entities (NEs), 24
as extent tags, 119
and inline tagging, 96
and models, 71
Simple Named Entity Guidelines V6.5, 120
Narrative Containers, 211–212
natural language processing (see NLP (natural language processing))
Natural Language Processing with Python (Bird, Klein, and Loper), 5, 45, 139
gender identification problem in, 147–150
NCSU, TempEval-2 system, 230
neg-content-term, 147
Netflix, 71, 116
New York Times, 199
NIST TREC Tracks, 43
NLP (natural language processing), 4–5
annotations and, 14–20
Cloud computing and, 244–246
corpus linguistics, 5–14
language annotation, 1–2
linguistic description, 3–4
machine learning, 20–22, 139–166
MATTER methodology, 23–24
multimodel annotation, 26
n-grams, 14
ontology, 19
POS tagsets and, 14–18
semantic value, 18
syntactic bracketing, 17
nonconsuming tags, 27

O

ontology, 19
overfit algorithms, 2, 180
overlapping clustering, 162

P

parsing, 143
part of speech (POS) tagsets, 14–18
Penn TreeBank corpus, 6, 8
    POS tagset, 14
    syntactic bracketing in, 17
"The Penn TreeBank: Annotating Predicate Argument Structure" (Marcus et al.), 95
percentage accuracy evaluation, 172
Phrase Detective (GWAP), 239
PMI (pointwise mutual information), 62
pointwise mutual information (PMI), 62
precision and recall evaluation, 173
probabilistic clustering, 162
probability, 54–58
    Bayes Rule, 57
    conditional probability, 56
    joint distributions, 55–57
    Naïve Bayes Classifier, 57
Probability for Linguists (Goldsmith), 54
Project Gutenberg library, 45
PropBank corpus, 199, 199
PubMedHealth, 234

Q

question answering systems (QAS), 4

R

Radev, Dragomir, 199
rank/frequency profile, 60
Receiver Operator Characteristic (ROC) curves, 177
relationship tags, 101
reporting, 187–192
    annotation, 190
    annotators, 190
    corpus, 189
    final test scores, 181
    ML Algorithm, 191
    model, 190
    on revisions, 192
    specification, 190

representation standards
    LAF (Linguistic Annotation Framework) standard, 102
    list of available, 266–267
    XML, 91
reproducibility, 117
Reuters, 199
Reuters-21578 text collection, 199
revising, 183–187
    annotation environments, 187
    annotation guidelines, 186
    and annotators, 186
    corpus, distributions/content of, 184
    model/specicication, 185
    reporting on, 192
    testing/training, 187
RottenTomatoes.com, 90, 114
rule-based systems, 143

S

S2T program (TTK), 226
scope (of annotation task), 36
semantic roles, 101
    and annotation guidelines, 120
    labels, 19
    and model definition, 72
semantic typing and ontology, 19
semantic value, 18
SemEval 2007 and 2010, 228
SemEval challenge (Association for Computational Linguistics), 42
semi-supervised learning (SSL) (see SSL (semi-supervised learning))
Sentiment Quiz (GWAP), 239
sequence classifiers, 160
sequence induction algorithms, 160–161
    Conditional Random Field (CRF) models, 161
    Hidden Markov Model (HMM), 160
    Maximum Entropy Markov Models (MEMMs), 161
    SSL (semi-supervised learning), 163–165
Setzer, Andrea, 197, 199
Simon, Herbert, 140
Simple Named Entity Guidelines V6.5, 120
Sinclair, John, 43
SLATE, 124
Slinket (SLINK Events in Text), 222
spec (see tag specification)

About the Authors

James Pustejovsky teaches and does research in Artificial Intelligence and computational linguistics in the Computer Science Department at Brandeis University. His main areas of interest include lexical meaning, computational semantics, temporal and spatial reasoning, and corpus linguistics. He is active in the development of standards for interoperability between language processing applications, and he led the creation of the recently adopted ISO standard for time annotation, ISO-TimeML. He is currently heading the development of a standard for annotating spatial information in language. More information on publications and research activities can be found at his web page, *http://pusto.com*.

Amber Stubbs recently completed her PhD in Computer Science at Brandeis University in the Laboratory for Linguistics and Computation. Her dissertation is focused on creating an annotation methodology to aid in extracting high-level information from natural language files, particularly biomedical texts. Information about her publications and other projects can be found on her website, *http://pages.cs.brandeis.edu/~astubbs/*.

Colophon

The animal on the cover of *Natural Language Annotation for Machine Learning* is the cockatiel (*Nymphicus hollandicus*). Their scientific name came about from European travelers who found the birds so beautiful, they named them for mythical nymphs. *Hollandicus* refers to "New Holland," an older name for Australia, the continent to which these birds are native. In the wild, cockatiels can be found in arid habitats like brushland or the outback, yet they remain close to water. They are usually seen in pairs, though flocks will congregate around a single body of water.

Until six to nine months after hatching, female and male cockatiels are indistinguishable, as both have horizontal yellow stripes on the surface of their tail feathers and a dull orange patch on each cheek. When molting begins, males lose some white or yellow feathers and gain brighter yellow feathers. In addition, the orange patches on the face become much more prominent. The lifespan of a cockatiel in captivity is typically 15–20 years, but they generally live between 10–30 years in the wild.

The cockatiel was considered either a parrot or a cockatoo for some time, as scientists and biologists hotly debated which bird it actually was. It is now classified as part of the cockatoo family because they both have the same biological features—namely, upright crests, gallbladders, and powder down (a special type of feather where the tips of barbules disintegrate, forming a fine dust among the feathers).

The cover image is from Johnson's *Natural History*. The cover font is Adobe ITC Garamond. The text font is Minion Pro by Robert Slimbach; the heading font is Myriad Pro by Robert Slimbach and Carol Twombly; and the code font is UbuntuMono by Dalton Maag.

Have it your way.

Get even more for your money.

Join the O'Reilly Community, and register the O'Reilly books you own. It's free, and you'll get:

- $4.99 ebook upgrade offer
- 40% upgrade offer on O'Reilly print books
- Membership discounts on books and events
- Free lifetime updates to ebooks and videos
- Multiple ebook formats, DRM FREE
- Participation in the O'Reilly community
- Newsletters
- Account management
- 100% Satisfaction Guarantee

Signing up is easy:

1. Go to: oreilly.com/go/register
2. Create an O'Reilly login.
3. Provide your address.
4. Register your books.

Note: English-language books only

To order books online:
oreilly.com/store

For questions about products or an order:
orders@oreilly.com

To sign up to get topic-specific email announcements and/or news about upcoming books, conferences, special offers, and new technologies:
elists@oreilly.com

For technical questions about book content:
booktech@oreilly.com

To submit new book proposals to our editors:
proposals@oreilly.com

O'Reilly books are available in multiple DRM-free ebook formats. For more information:
oreilly.com/ebooks

Spreading the knowledge of innovators   oreilly.com

Printed in the USA
CPSIA information can be obtained
at www.ICGtesting.com
JSHW052351050824
67593JS00010B/489